BILLIONAIRE BACKLASH

To Ella, Linus, Saralynn, Savannah,
Sebastian and Sophie

BILLIONAIRE BACKLASH

The Age of Corporate Scandal and How
It Could Save Democracy

PEPPER CULPEPPER
AND TAEKU LEE

BLOOMSBURY CONTINUUM
Bloomsbury Publishing Plc

50 Bedford Square
London
WC1B 3DP
UK

Bloomsbury Publishing Ireland Limited
29 Earlsfort Terrace
Dublin 2
D02 AY28
Ireland

BLOOMSBURY, BLOOMSBURY CONTINUUM and the
Diana logo are trademarks of Bloomsbury Publishing Plc

First published in Great Britain 2026

Copyright © Pepper Culpepper and Taeku Lee, 2026

Pepper Culpepper and Taeku Lee have asserted their right under the Copyright, Designs and
Patents Act, 1988, to be identified as Authors of this work

For legal purposes the Picture credits on pp. 271–2
constitute an extension of this copyright page

All rights reserved. No part of this publication may be: i) reproduced or transmitted
in any form, electronic or mechanical, including photocopying, recording or by means
of any information storage or retrieval system without prior permission in writing from the
publishers; or ii) used or reproduced in any way for the training, development or operation of
artificial intelligence (AI) technologies, including generative AI technologies. The rights holders
expressly reserve this publication from the text and data mining exception as per Article 4(3)
of the Digital Single Market Directive (EU) 2019/790

Bloomsbury Publishing Plc does not have any control over, or responsibility for,
any third-party websites referred to or in this book. All internet addresses given
in this book were correct at the time of going to press. The author and publisher
regret any inconvenience caused if addresses have changed or sites have ceased to exist,
but can accept no responsibility for any such changes

A catalogue record for this book is available from the British Library

Library of Congress Cataloguing-in-Publication data has been applied for

ISBN:	HB:	978-1-3994-2410-3
	EBOOK:	978-1-3994-2411-0
	EPDF:	978-1-3994-2412-7

2 4 6 8 10 9 7 5 3 1

Typeset by Lumina Datamatics Ltd

Printed and bound in Great Britain by Clays Ltd, Elcograf S.p.A

To find out more about our authors and books visit www.bloomsbury.com
and sign up for our newsletters

For product safety related questions contact productsafety@bloomsbury.com

Contents

	Preface	vi
	Introduction	1
	PART ONE CORPORATE SCANDALS AND DEMOCRACY	
1	Scandals and Public Opinion	11
2	From Watergate to Dieselgate	23
	PART TWO HOW SCANDALS WORK	
3	Goldman Sachs's Shitty Deal	43
4	Europe v Facebook	65
5	Cambridge Analytica and the Techlash	89
	PART THREE WHEN SCANDALS FAIL	
6	#ExxonKnew	113
7	FTX – Rashomon for the Crypto Era	137
8	Sasol and the Death of Mossville	153
	PART FOUR THE RENOVATION PROJECT	
9	The Fall of a Samsung Prince	179
10	Good Populism	203
	Acknowledgements	227
	Notes	230
	Picture credits and permissions	271
	Index	273

Preface

Corporate scandals bring people together in a powerful way. That is the simple argument of this book. It is also the story of our improbable collaboration.

We met as young academics in the late 1990s. But even our very first encounter was fraught. Political scientists, you see, tend to sort themselves into one of two camps. There are those who spend their time thinking about big structural forces, like the institutions and norms that shape our politics. Others focus on the individuals behind these institutions, and how their action or inaction determines our politics. The two of us sit on opposite sides of this intellectual divide.

Taeku keeps his eyes sharply trained on individual voters and the beliefs and values that guide their world views. He is in his intellectual happy place when a big new dataset drops on the most recent election. Pepper investigates the way organized groups influence policies, regarding elections as sideshows in the ongoing struggle for power that moneyed interests usually win, regardless of who the voters choose.

We are opposites not just in the way we understand politics, but in temperament and biography too. Pepper is a habitually over-caffeinated, fast-talking son of the American South who has spent much of his adult life living in Europe, whose politics he studies. Taeku, phlegmatic by comparison, is a Korean American who grew up by the beaches of Malaysia, moved to New York and now remains firmly rooted in the United States. Conversations between us are typically arguments, ricocheting between staccato outbursts and measured demurrals.

PREFACE

For a long time we stayed in our separate lanes of research. But one day Taeku read a draft of Pepper's book, *Quiet Politics and Business Power*, which argued that the only time big business ever loses is when an event catches the public's eye and concentrates public attention on the sausage-making process of modern politics. That's when politics becomes democratically responsive.

'Show me the evidence', said Taeku. These are fighting words between professors.

Then, like some *deus ex machina*, came the financial crisis of 2008, an event that transformed politics in rich democracies. In its aftermath, political leaders on both sides of the Atlantic found themselves whipsawed between public rage against the banks and bond market vigilantes who demanded austerity. The protest movement Occupy Wall Street seized media attention with its anti-corporate slogan, 'We are the 99 per cent', and previously pliable politicians suddenly tightened the screws on financial institutions.

Despite the upheaval on the streets, Taeku looked at the data and at first saw . . . nothing. Surveys showed little evidence that the American public wanted more regulation of business as a result of the financial crisis.

So it was game on. What followed was ten years of research, trying to understand what made people actually demand tougher rules from their leaders. We polled tens of thousands of voters across six countries and analysed thousands of media articles and social media posts. The war of words between us continued unabated. Pepper demanded that survey questions about policy ought to faithfully ask about actual proposals before legislatures. Taeku protested that the technical esoterica of policy language would be lost on most survey respondents. So went the hard yards of our collaboration over a decade of meetings, which stretched from Florence to Oxford to Berkeley to Boston.

Events like the financial crisis of 2008 don't come along every day. They are, thankfully, rare. Our eureka moment came when we discovered that more ordinary corporate scandals mobilize people in a way that looks a lot like what happened during the financial crisis. And unlike the crisis, these scandals are not at all in short supply. That insight gave us the leverage we needed to understand, across many democracies, why public opinion moves and when politicians respond to what the people want.

We began our journey as academics often do, setting our sights on convincing fellow political scientists of the importance of corporate scandals. This is a case we have made through a series of journal articles careful readers will find buried in the notes at the end of this book.

While that journey advanced, clouds of discontent gathered among voters around the globe. Scholars and pundits alike sounded the alarm of democracies under threat. It dawned on us then that we had a different story to tell. Established democracies are indeed facing a crisis of faith and legitimacy, but we could show that there were opportunities for democracy, as well as threats. Change might be inevitable, but a descent into oligarchic populism, in which billionaires and large corporations call the shots beneath a veneer of anti-elite pandering, is not.

At the heart of our story lies the biggest question facing our politics today. That question is, who makes the rules in modern democracies? Is it the few big corporations owned by billionaires who conspire to evade all governmental oversight? Or is it the many, the voters who consent to being represented by politicians they can hold accountable on election day?

We are an academic odd couple, prone to disagree on matters both trivial and significant. One of the few traits we share is that we are not optimists by nature. Our past research lays bare the weaknesses of modern political parties, the challenges of diverse societies and the structural advantages of big business in politics. Yet the result of our longest argument, and the mountain of data we have collected along the way, points us to the possibility of civic renewal through populism – a good kind of populism.

The current moment opens a window to use politics to channel a public pushback against the growth of corporate influence on our daily lives. There are enormous wellsprings of pent-up democratic pressure just looking for a way to get out. When scandals erupt, we see that force unleashed in politics.

We call it the billionaire backlash.

Introduction

In 1906, a young journalist named Upton Sinclair nearly destroyed America's meat industry by depicting the dire sanitary conditions in a meatpacking factory in Chicago. Americans reading his book, *The Jungle*, discovered that their sausages contained ground-up poisoned rats, and that chemical additives disguised the putrefaction of their canned meat. The floor of the packing house Sinclair described was covered in the tubercular phlegm of workers, who dragged carcasses across it that later found their way to American dinner tables.

The book sold out. Meat sales halved in a matter of weeks.

The Jungle contained passages so graphic that its first publisher, Macmillan, refused to print it. 'Gloom and horror unrelieved', was the verdict of the publisher's reader. 'As to the possibilities of a large sale, I should think them not very good.' Five other publishers rejected the manuscript on similar grounds. But when Doubleday finally published it, the book was not just a huge commercial success – it transformed food regulation in the United States.

The food safety concerns Sinclair so vividly exposed were not new. Many European countries had already banned imports of American pork because of the lack of hygiene regulations. Between 1879 and 1906, US legislators had introduced almost 200 food bills to Congress, but the political power of the big five meatpacking companies – known collectively as the 'Beef Trust' – prevented all but a handful from becoming law.

Disgusted by what they had learned about how the sausage got made, ordinary Americans finally demanded and got action from their lawmakers. *The Jungle* had only been in bookstores for six months when Congress passed two sweeping new laws that would enshrine federal oversight of food and drug safety, establishing the regulatory agency now known as the Food and Drug Administration.

Sinclair was a muckraker. He was one of a group of Progressive-era investigative journalists who focused on exposing the 'muck' of corporate corruption in America. Their number included Ida Tarbell, whose exposé of the unscrupulous business practices of John D. Rockefeller's Standard Oil – the largest monopoly in the United States – led the company to be broken up in 1911 into 34 separate corporations. This was no small feat. Rockefeller became the world's first billionaire in 1916. In comparison to the size of the American economy at the time, Rockefeller's fortune surpassed even that of Elon Musk today.

The muckrakers rose to prominence at a time when American businesses exercised unprecedented political power. The major conglomerates of the era – the railroad companies of Leland Stanford and Cornelius Vanderbilt, the financial empire of J. P. Morgan and Rockefeller's Standard Oil – defined the economy. Known as the 'robber barons', these corporate titans used their economic might to dominate American politics. David Graham Phillips, another muckraker, painted a picture of the corruption of the upper legislative chamber that nauseated American readers just as much as Sinclair's rotten meat. His series of articles in 1906, 'The Treason of the Senate', which detailed how prominent senators all got personally wealthy as they defended big corporations, also went viral.

These revelations about the scale of corporate wrongdoing in the Gilded Age fuelled the popular backlash that finally brought Rockefeller and his fellow titans to heel. Citizens had long been unhappy with the status quo, but until the muckrakers came along there were no obvious champions willing to lead political change. The waves of public anger unleashed by the muckrakers eventually forced politicians to pass significant reforms that asserted government oversight over the giant companies of the day.

Today our problems seem eerily similar to those of a century ago. The digital revolution has transformed the economic scale and political power of business around the world. Large banks, commanding gargantuan profits, are too big to fail. Oil companies show zero appetite for net zero. Like the railroads of yore, tech companies dominate multiple markets and have become essential utilities for the functioning of modern life. Huge companies like Facebook have shown they can 'move fast and break things', in the words of Mark Zuckerberg, but lumbering governments appear too slow or too beholden to corporate lobbyists to do anything about it. The single word that best describes the current political situation is 'blocked'.

Critics on the political left complain about how large corporations turn their economic might into lobbying power, short-circuiting democratic control of the economy. Those on the right lament the cultural influence of 'woke' corporations that use their domination of the economy to impose their values on workers and consumers. Both complain that monopolies destroy competition and degrade the situation of their employees. But across the globe, the same force that tamed Rockefeller once again threatens today's billionaires and the giant corporations they control.

Most people dislike the corporate domination of democratic politics, but it is not clear how they can stop it. Voters today, like voters in the Progressive Era, face what social scientists call a 'collective action problem'. Collective action problems arise when we would all like something that is mutually beneficial – such as a safe place for our kids to play, or a protest against a widely unpopular policy, or indeed a functioning democracy – but individuals, by themselves, have no incentive to bear the costs of organizing politically to make it happen. Across the wealthy democracies, the result is sclerotic politics and disillusioned voters. The more rigid and unresponsive the politics, the more disenchanted voters become, and the more vulnerable our governments are to having their economies tyrannized by huge corporations. So how can people overcome this collective action problem?

Corporate scandals are among the rare events that can jolt us out of our dysfunctional detachment. Scandals concentrate public attention, highlighting failings in politics and regulation that people may have long suspected but struggled to pinpoint, and give us all an opportunity for coordinated collective action. By doing so, they open a space for people we call policy entrepreneurs – activists inside and outside political institutions – to push through solutions that respond to public demands for change. The angry public creates the incentive for politicians to respond. The policy entrepreneur funnels that anger into a demand for a specific set of public policies.

These are people like Ralph Nader, the American consumer advocate whose 1960s campaign for car safety eventually led to the passage of laws requiring that manufacturers install seat belts. Or celebrity chef Jamie Oliver, whose healthy food campaign inspired the passage of a sugar tax in the UK in 2018 to reduce childhood obesity. Policy entrepreneurs translate seething public anger into policies that try to fix public problems.

The 2008 financial crisis almost incinerated the global economy and threatened to plunge the world into a depression. The iconic image of that event showed shell-shocked bankers streaming out of the headquarters of the defunct Lehman Brothers, a single cardboard box holding all that remained of their stint as masters of the universe. The crisis laid bare obvious shortcomings in financial regulation that had previously languished in the shadows. These failings had been hidden because big banks successfully thwarted efforts to regulate the seemingly incomprehensible alphabet soup of financial instruments that padded their profit margins – products with obscure names like CDO, RMBS, CDS and SIV. These instruments had allowed banks to make risky bets, which led to the calamity.

The financial crisis was a mega-scandal – a systemic act of malfeasance by many big banks at once. In one country after another, governments bailed out the banks that had made bad bets while ordinary people lost their homes and their livelihoods. That was the origin of the mass public outrage exemplified by the Occupy Wall Street movement. The eruption of anger meant that politicians suddenly became interested in tightening financial regulation.

Cynics will say financial reforms after the crisis happened too late. But we say, better late than never! Even if the most powerful banks are still too big to fail, the world's largest financial institutions are much safer now than they were before 2008. And that is a consequence of the political backlash that followed.

But just because a bunch of bankers crashed the economy, and just because the public was angry about it, reforms of financial regulation did not happen automatically. Significant reforms only happened when they were helped along by a policy entrepreneur: an obsessively committed individual who could focus inchoate public anger around a specific set of demands and drive through legal changes.

This book is shot through with tales of corporate villains. Policy entrepreneurs are the unlikely heroes of these stories.

Corporate scandals make it difficult for politicians to oppose regulatory change. They do so by drawing the attention of voters to the kinds of technical issues – like food and drug regulation or digital privacy – that most people don't know much about. Corporations keep a watchful eye on whether they might be regulated and spend a lot of money lobbying politicians to make any rules as lax as possible. So when voters don't think about these issues, politicians feel free to take the advice of lobbyists; they wind up being more responsive to the industry they regulate than to the people they supposedly serve. This is what scholars now call corporate capture, and what David Graham Phillips 120 years ago called 'the Treason of the Senate'.

Scandals shine a light on regulatory failings that result from corporate capture. Take the well-known scandal in 2001 at the energy firm Enron. At its peak, Enron was the seventh largest company in the United States, and it had been named the most innovative company in America for six years running. Yet Enron's growth rested not on energy market wizardry, but on a mirage of accounting deceit. Enron's accounting firm, Arthur Andersen, had looked the other way as bad deals were pushed under the carpet and dubious assets absurdly over-valued. The company's management had convinced financial markets that Enron knew something that no-one else did about how to make money.

In a similar way, today's venture capitalists are excited about the boundless prospects of artificial intelligence. Meanwhile, OpenAI – the maker of ChatGPT – is burning through record amounts of cash and has yet to make a profit. But people at least understand why the future possibilities of AI are exciting. No-one back in 2000 could figure out the value proposition behind Enron. Investors nevertheless didn't want to miss out on the potential gains. After he left the company, the former CEO of Enron's in-house oil company warned his friends about the risk of holding Enron stock: 'Nobody knows how they get their numbers, but as long as they make them, the market's going to accept it. But if they ever stumble, the stock'll fall twice as far as your worst bad dream.'

In April 2001, reporter Bethany McLean wrote an article in *Fortune* magazine noting Enron's apparent accounting irregularities. She dared to wonder in print if the company's stock was overpriced. Short-sellers – market participants who bet that a stock's price will decline – began to ask questions the firm couldn't answer, and investors deserted the company. It appeared the emperor had no clothes after all. The company's stock price went into free fall.

When Enron finally collapsed that December, it was the largest bankruptcy in American history. More than 20,000 employees lost their jobs. Those employees lost $2 billion in their retirement savings plans, which were heavily invested in the company's now worthless stock. Congress launched an investigation, and accounting heavyweight Arthur Andersen folded the following year. McLean followed her article with a book about the scandal entitled *The Smartest Guys in the Room*. Enron CEO Jeffrey Skilling would wind up being one of the smartest guys in the jail cell, after being convicted of 19 counts of fraud and spending 12 years in prison.

INTRODUCTION

Failures in disclosure and auditing allowed Enron to defraud investors, and after the scandal those failures suddenly attracted political scrutiny. Democratic lawmakers Paul Sarbanes and Michael Oxley proposed separate bills tightening up corporate governance rules in 2002. Republicans, who held majorities in both the House and the Senate, vigorously opposed the new legislation. Or rather, they opposed it until WorldCom, a telecom giant, also went bust after the revelation of its own fraudulent accounting practices, swiftly eclipsing Enron as the largest bankruptcy in American history. After this second scandal, Republican opposition vanished. Within a month, the Sarbanes-Oxley law passed the House 423–3 and the Senate 99–0. No politician wanted to be on the wrong side of voter anger.

The firestorm of public outrage set off by Enron and WorldCom illustrates the impact corporate scandals can have on voters. Scandals inform and enrage people, concentrating their anger on unblocking politics and activating previously dormant voices. In democracies, they can fuel real, meaningful reform.

Corporate scandals are one of the few moments when voters hold their leaders to account in contemporary democracies. That is why authoritarian leaders do everything in their power to keep them from breaking out. And it is why our current crop of billionaire owners should fear them.

In the pages that follow, we return to the scene of the crime of recent scandals that have roiled politics and changed policy in the United States, the United Kingdom, Europe and Asia. These scandals range from finance to technology to industrial conglomerates, with names that have entered popular lore, such as Cambridge Analytica and Dieselgate. We explain why some scandals have succeeded in moving public opinion while others have left little trace.

PART ONE

Corporate Scandals and Democracy

I
Scandals and Public Opinion

In 2008, in the run-up to the Beijing Olympic Games, infants in China began to fall ill. All the babies had one thing in common: they had consumed formula made by the dairy company Sanlu. Despite numerous complaints from the parents, the government failed to act for months. When Chinese journalists attempted to report on the complaints, they ran foul of censorship policies that prevented them from reporting on sensitive political topics in the period leading up to the Olympics.

After the Games, an investigation revealed that Sanlu had laced its watered-down baby formula with melamine, a by-product of the coal industry used to make plastics. Adding melamine to diluted milk products inflates their apparent protein content. That's because tests for protein do not measure protein directly; they measure nitrogen, which is indicative of protein. Melamine is very high in nitrogen, but it is also toxic to kidneys, and not just human kidneys. In a 2007 prequel to the Sanlu scandal, pet food containing melamine from a single company in China killed up to 8,500 cats and dogs in the United States. The animals apparently died of kidney failure.

In September 2008, Sanlu recalled more than 10,000 tons of its adulterated formula, but 300,000 babies became ill, at least 50,000 of whom were hospitalized for kidney problems. Six ultimately died from consuming the contaminated formula.

The three-year-old son of Zhao Lianhai, a former journalist, developed kidney stones after consuming Sanlu's formula. Zhao made his first blog post about the scandal two days after his child's diagnosis, urging families of affected children to mobilize to demand justice. On 25 September he founded a website called Kidney Stone Babies to serve as a clearing house for information for these families. Zhao became the face of the movement pressing for dairy firms to assist families with sick children – until he was arrested to prevent a planned news conference from going ahead.

Once released, Zhao continued his campaign to raise awareness of the hidden dangers of infant formula. In November 2009 the police again arrested him at his home in Beijing, impounding his computers and an address book. At his trial, the presiding judge denied his request to introduce video evidence of witnesses in his defence, saying the prosecution's case was solid. The same day Zhao was sentenced to prison, the Chinese government publicized a new initiative intended to reduce the spread of 'false news' that harmed public confidence in food safety.

Of course, it was too late for that. The scandal had already undermined public confidence in food safety. Chinese consumers, well aware that the government controls information, ignored the state's assurances and switched to formula manufactured outside the country. Hong Kong, Australia and New Zealand all restricted the sale of formula, after the sudden spike in demand from mainland Chinese shoppers led to shortages.

Meanwhile, general concerns about food safety continued to mount. One study found that only 12 per cent of people in China thought food safety was a problem in 2008, the year the scandal broke. By 2012, that number had jumped to 41 per cent. Today the Chinese public continues to distrust the ability of the government to safeguard its food supply.

The suppression of both media coverage and activism meant that the fundamental problem revealed by the scandal – a regulatory system that incentivizes companies to maximize profits without regard to the consequences for the public's health – did not change. The government fired officials, imprisoned company executives and even executed a dairy farmer and a formula salesman, but it did not allow itself to be held accountable for the failures revealed by the scandal.

After the sentences were announced, one parent protesting in front of the courthouse spoke about the two men sentenced to die: 'I feel sorry for them, but they are just scapegoats', he said. 'The ones who should take responsibility are the government.'

A second baby formula scandal, this one in France, unfolded very differently. In 2017, the French company Lactalis, which owns brands like Parmalat and Kraft, discovered salmonella bacteria at one of its milk plants in August, and again in November. In December, cases of salmonella infection tied to Lactalis began to spread across France. The company issued three recalls over the course of the month. Each time, the media accused the company of dragging its feet. The final recall removed from store shelves more than 7,000 tons of powdered milk products.

The total number of children affected by the Lactalis scandal is small compared to what happened in China. A total of 36 infants were sickened by salmonella, and none died. But the French didn't see a life-threatening, avoidable illness affecting children as a story to dismiss or bury. The French parliamentary committee investigating the scandal held 35 hearings to understand the sources of the failure. The government passed reforms requiring companies to report all adverse testing results to regulators, and in 2023, prosecutors opened criminal investigations of Lactalis for fraud and involuntary bodily harm.

That these investigations took place at all is thanks to Quentin Guillemain, whose three-month-old daughter consumed Lactalis products but did not fall ill. Guillemain began sharing his anger about the scandal on the internet. When he was contacted by other parents who felt the same way, Guillemain started a group which later became the Salmonella Contaminated Victims' Families Association. Under his leadership, the organization contested the low number of reported victims and condemned the government's failure to close the milk plant where the contamination originally took place.

The scandals in China and France both involved wrongdoing by companies who cut corners and put the health of babies at risk. In both cases, this led to public outrage. While the scale of the Sanlu scandal was much worse, only the Lactalis scandal led to regulatory change.

When defenceless children are put at risk – whether there are 36 of them or 300,000 – the public response is to ask, how did the government let this happen? And what is the government going to do to make sure this does not happen again? Corporate scandals generate a media frenzy until the problem they reveal is tackled.

That is why these scandals are so effective in generating a response in liberal democracies, where politicians must seek re-election. But in autocracies like China, leaders do not fear the voters' ire in the same way. Autocratic government can repress media coverage and clamp down on everyday citizens who dare to risk becoming activists. Quentin Guillemain's campaign, and the regulatory changes that followed, never would have happened if France were not a liberal democracy.

As we will see again and again, the political effect of scandals depends on activists like Guillemain. Even an angry public cannot necessarily solve its own collective action problems. Our outrage makes us want to act, but we often don't quite know how our action could be usefully channelled into creating the change in society we want to see happen.

Policy entrepreneurs like Guillemain do that work for us. They seize on the issues raised by scandals, and they organize demands for a political response. Without the anger that scandals generate, activists like Guillemain are unlikely to succeed. But without Guillemain, and people like him who put in the hard yards required to coordinate a response, corporate scandals do not change politics.

Autocracies, which arrest activists like Zhao Lianhai, suffer in contrast by not immediately addressing public concern. The Sanlu scandal has since metastasized into a much broader distrust of the health and safety of Chinese food. Lactalis lost market share after the French scandal, and it has never gained it back, but there has been no appreciable change in the extent to which the French trust the quality of the food they put on their tables every night.

Unlike China, France has a built-in check, unique to democracies, that allows it to maintain public confidence in the safety of its food. The result of the scandal might have been bad for Lactalis, but it was good for the safety of the food supply in France. China got no benefit from its scandal, because Chinese leaders feared the prospect of letting public anger get out of control. They executed scapegoats, but they didn't solve the problem the scandal revealed. Even now, years after the scandal, the Chinese people still don't trust the safety of their own food supply.

Corporate scandals draw their power from the fusion of three elements: emotions, information and existing public opinion. When these three come together under the hot glare of the public spotlight, they create politically consequential energy. We have already begun to discuss the activating role of the most important emotion for scandals, anger, which rouses people to action.

In the alchemy of scandal, public anger is connected to a second element: clear, comprehensible information. The details of regulation are often stiflingly dull and forbiddingly complex, even to those of us who study them for a living. Scandals clarify these thorny issues, thanks to their widespread coverage in the media. When journalists reveal that banks are selling complicated financial products to their clients while simultaneously betting against the value of those same securities, as Goldman Sachs did in the run-up to the financial crisis, people understand clearly that someone is being taken advantage of, even if they don't know the difference between a bond and a derivative.

The third and final element of a politically powerful scandal, alongside anger and information, is existing public opinion. There is always a reservoir of public sentiment about what corporations do that lurks beneath the surface of the 'public opinion' more regularly measured in surveys, such as approval ratings of the president. Scandals activate that lurking mass of public sentiment, which we call latent opinion.

American confidence in Wall Street was already declining dramatically when the financial crisis hit. It's true that after 2008 it plumbed new depths, but it's easier for people to get angry about a scandal when it confirms what they suspected all along. Similarly, the Chinese public only learned about the Sanlu scandal because the company got caught. But the revelation of that particular instance of criminal behaviour sat atop an enormous mass of pre-existing opinion that industrial food companies in China cannot be trusted.

The public may already suspect that companies are cutting corners to increase profit, putting consumer safety at risk. A scandal confirms – and hardens – their suspicions. The potential destructive force of this latent public opinion is activated by the scandal.

To further illustrate how latent public opinion works, consider the example of racialized police violence and the killing of George Floyd in May 2020. The American public knew, even if in incomplete and uncertain terms, that there had been numerous incidents of fellow citizens – mostly young Black men – dying at the hands of the police. There had already been flashes of outrage after the deaths of Michael Brown, Eric Garner and too many others.

The videotaped murder, showing a White officer pressing his knee on Floyd's neck for nearly ten minutes, served as a focusing event that sparked mass outrage. It propelled the Black Lives Matter movement into the largest outbreak of mass protest in American history, stirring millions to march in the streets demanding police reform.

Scandals, in other words, have an impact especially when they confirm what the public already believes to be true. These views are often vaguely articulated and do not necessarily form part of an individual's everyday politics. But they can, under certain conditions, become crystallized and politically activated, leading to a collective 'Aha!' moment.

To understand how and why public opinion can shapeshift from the anonymized and averaged polls we see on the nightly news to a menacing iceberg capable of sinking corporate titans, we need to introduce a twentieth-century giant of political science, Valdimer Orlando Key Jr.

Key challenged the prevailing scholarly view of public opinion. The classic books read by all graduate students of political behaviour defined public opinion as the 'pulse of democracy', yet simultaneously suggested that that pulse is easily manipulable and mainly shaped by elites in government. Other texts treated public opinion as synonymous with the results of polls, even though polls consistently showed public opinion to be ignorant, irrational and incoherent in its views on politics.

If ordinary citizens are indeed the bedrock of democracy, this prevailing view decreed that bedrock brittle and fickle. The conclusion that voters were the sheep and not the shepherds in a democracy is a grim one, at least for those committed to the ideal that the voice of ordinary people matters in democracies.

Enter V. O. Key: a wiry, bespectacled, aquiline-nosed Texan. Key proposed an alternative account of why it is that public opinion can seem ignorant, irrational and incoherent, but at other times strike real fear into governments. Key's first precept is simple: 'Voters are not fools'. He took seriously the reality that most of us, most of the time, are too busy with the daily exigencies of life to engage deeply with politics. A pollster who catches us off-guard while we're watching Champions League football or Little League baseball, or on a weekend evening while we're cooking dinner, should not be surprised if we give answers that seem uninformed or ill-considered.

For Key, there are three kinds of public opinion. There is 'mass opinion': the familiar stuff of polls asking ordinary citizens about which parties, candidates or policies they favour. 'Activated opinion' consists of the voices of activists, organizers and elites who are regularly engaged in civic and political affairs, and 'latent opinion' refers to people's fundamental beliefs and preferences about politics, which are not always discoverable through polling.

Key's insight was that, for governments, 'latent opinion is really about the only type of opinion that generates much anxiety'. Latent opinion is where the views of ordinary citizens ultimately end up if they have the time and motivation to become informed and engaged on an issue. Because this type of opinion is not yet activated, it represents a mystery that politicians and elites fear. In the words of the former American Defense Secretary, Donald Rumsfeld, mass opinion and activated opinion are the 'known knowns' of democratic societies, while latent opinion is the great 'known unknown'.

In short, latent opinion is an iceberg that always lurks beneath the surface of the more readily monitored 'mass opinion' waters of polling. Latent opinion can help us understand why some scandals can have a tremendous impact on politics, while others fail to have an impact, or even catch the public eye at all.

The recent Post Office scandal in Britain is a shocking example of corporate malfeasance that festered for years before it finally caught the public eye. Between 1999 and 2015, the Post Office and Crown Prosecution Service prosecuted 983 sub-postmasters on wrongful charges of theft and false accounting – that's more than one a week. Four of those people subsequently committed suicide, and many others' lives were ruined. More than 250 of the wrongfully accused have since died without receiving a penny of compensation.

The errors turned out not to be the result of theft, but of failures of the automated Horizon accounting system, developed for the Post Office by the Japanese corporation Fujitsu. The first media account of the story came out in 2009 in *Computer Weekly*, followed by one in 2011 in the satirical magazine *Private Eye*. Yet the UK's mainstream media almost completely ignored it. It was only when a dramatic television programme aired on ITV in January 2024 – *Mr Bates vs the Post Office* – that the scandal came to the attention of the broader public. Widespread public outrage ensued.

Why did the media largely ignore the British Post Office scandal prior to the broadcast of the ITV drama? Most importantly, the Post Office – a state-owned company – was for many years considered 'the nation's most trusted brand'. This reservoir of public good will meant there was not a clear public appetite for stories of Post Office wrongdoing, which would have factored into the decision of media outlets on whether to cover the story.

The presence or absence of an accumulation of negative popular sentiment towards corporations is important to our story of scandals, because what the public thinks beforehand affects the potential power of an event of wrongdoing to become a scandal in the first place and then to generate political change.

If we are to understand the impact of corporate scandals on politics, we therefore have to understand how people think about their relationship to big companies. Firms are the motors of innovation, growth and employment. For this reason, Americans used to say about their largest car manufacturer, General Motors (GM), that 'what's good for GM is good for the country'. That is, since big companies loom so large in thinking about the economy, the fates of a country and its corporate giants are likely to be tightly intertwined.

Where people view the fates of large companies and their country as one and the same, scandals are not likely to transform politics. Voters do not generally cut off their own nose to spite their face. It's true that scandals concentrate attention on the misdeeds of large companies. But it is only when people have begun to suspect, for some time, that those companies are no longer synonymous with their national interest that they are at risk from what we call the billionaire backlash.

Those looking to this book to foretell the destruction or bankruptcy of the large corporations that dominate the global economy will be disappointed. We do not foresee a revolution. That's not what the popular backlash generated by scandals actually looks like. Nor do we think, as do some of our more fervent scholarly colleagues, that between democracy and Amazon there can be only one survivor.

We do, however, believe that between the two there can only be one sovereign. Either Amazon and its titanic peers dictate the rules by which democratic markets function, or the popularly elected governments of those democracies do. The question for us is not whether these companies will be destroyed for their past sins. It is rather whether they are subject to democratically determined laws. For us, a situation where large company lobbyists effectively write the laws that are then rubber-stamped by the legislature is not a democracy worth the name.

Readers will approach this question with different convictions. Those concerned about economic innovation worry that states must protect the principle of fair competition to keep a few large companies from strangling the creative impulse of start-ups by acquiring their potential competition. Those concerned about the rights of workers will call for greater protections for labour unions and other forms of workplace organizing. Those concerned about the rights of consumers will demand greater regulatory oversight of markets. Different polities will choose different mixes of these solutions. But some combination of these claims represents the demands of a sizeable portion of the populace across the democratic world.

We have been here before. United States politics at the end of the nineteenth century was a plaything of the robber barons. America had the most dynamic economy in the world, but its politicians were controlled by mighty monopolies, which they called trusts. The American public had benefited from the economic growth

The Bosses of the Senate.

these monopoly trusts had unlocked but were agitated by the untrammelled political influence of the robber barons on politics. This unease was reflected in the resonant popular response to the publication of the 1889 cartoon, 'The Bosses of the Senate', which depicted the robber barons and their domination of Washington.

One year after the cartoon's publication, Congress passed the Sherman Antitrust Act, the first legislative move in the attempt to rein in corporate power in America. A series of scandals revealed by the muckrakers over the next quarter-century would generate a public outcry that enabled Progressive political entrepreneurs to pass the laws that would bring these large American companies back under the oversight of the elected government.

We are currently living through a period of disruptive economic change and disordered politics, this time not just in the United States. Giant corporations send rockets into space and lay the deep-sea cables that power the internet on which we all depend. The possibilities of artificial intelligence, which are racing ahead as this book is being written, lie almost entirely in the labs and boardrooms of large technology companies. These sorts of massive investments used to be the province of governments, and as such voters in democracies had some influence over them.

Today, governments stand on the sidelines as spectators passively watching the major advances of our time. Politicians of the right and the left, like Donald Trump and Keir Starmer, profess their desire to tame regulation in order to let innovation flourish. Yet what is flourishing in politics is incredibly cushy deals for political influence, as large companies and their controlling shareholders convert their market power into political protection to ensure they are not threatened by either pesky regulators or the next generation of start-up entrepreneurs. That doesn't seem a good recipe either for economic innovation or for solving the woes of contemporary democracies.

Are the conditions once again ripe for a public awakening around the balance between democracy and capitalism? In the early 1900s, the muckrakers ushered in a new, cross-party belief that governments had to make the rules for big companies, not the other way around. They did so by bringing to light what many people already suspected: that most politicians were looking out not for the public good, but for the interests of a few gigantic corporations.

Will revelations of corporate abuses finally bring our modern robber barons to heel? Are we entering a new age of corporate scandal? Over the last few years, we have surveyed more than 60,000 people in six advanced democracies to find out the answer to these questions. We have studied corporate scandals and their consequences on public opinion and public policy from Seoul to Sacramento to Sheffield.

This book tells the story of what we found.

2

From Watergate to Dieselgate

In 2014, American engineer John German uncovered the largest automotive scandal in history: the Volkswagen Dieselgate scandal. He came upon it by accident.

German worked for a think tank that produces research on automotive emissions. His original goal was to test diesel cars made by German companies for the American market, where emissions standards are stricter than in Europe. He was trying to demonstrate that European carmakers could affordably cut emissions in their home market, as they had supposedly done for the 'clean diesel' cars sold profitably in the United States.

He decided to forgo standard lab tests for emissions and instead enlisted a team from West Virginia University (WVU) to conduct road tests that simulated daily driving conditions. They assembled a portable emissions measurement gizmo that could be installed in the back of a car and hooked up to its tailpipe, somewhat resembling the mad scientist's time machine from the movie *Back to the Future*.

The researchers couldn't easily find diesel cars for rent in West Virginia. But they had done some previous work with the environmental regulator in California, the California Air Resources Board (CARB). CARB allowed them to use its testing facility just outside Los Angeles. There, the team rented two vehicles, a BMW X5 SUV and a VW Jetta, and were able to borrow a VW Passat. They then drove these cars all over Los Angeles, San Francisco and San Diego.

They even took the Passat on a road trip from Los Angeles to Seattle and back, a journey of several thousand miles.

'We were shocked and astounded when we saw the numbers', said German. 'We thought the vehicles would be clean. We didn't set out to show that VW was doing something wrong.' They had discovered that the Volkswagen diesel cars had been spewing up to 35 times more pollution into the air than was permitted by American law. At first the team wondered if their equipment was at fault, as there had been no reports of the 'clean diesel' cars failing their emissions tests in the US. But when the emissions numbers from the BMW X5 came back clean, they knew there was something wrong with VW diesel cars.

In 2014 German and the team shared their data and findings with CARB and the US Environmental Protection Agency (EPA). The regulators were intrigued. When they conducted their own tests, they found the same discrepancies that John German had seen between the measured emissions of Volkswagen diesel cars under the usual inspection conditions and their actual emissions when they were driven on the road.

German's team didn't know it yet, but the discrepancy was caused by a 'defeat device', which Volkswagen had specifically designed to get around legal emissions limits. German, who had previously worked for car companies Honda and Chrysler as well as the EPA, was immediately suspicious. He thought the evidence pointed to the existence of a defeat device. But he didn't reveal his suspicions, even to his team. 'It's not something you do unless you're sure', he said.

VW executives deliberated internally about what to do about the discovery of their defeat device. They knew they risked being caught, and they had even given the device a harmless-sounding codename for use within the firm – the 'acoustic function' – so they could discuss it without revealing its purpose. They eventually opted to double down on deception.

In December 2014, CARB and the EPA announced that VW would be recalling its cars to install a software fix for its emissions problems. VW assured the regulators that this software reinstall would be the end of the intrigue. Yet when the 'fixed' vehicles were tested again, they still had unusually high emissions levels. By September 2015, VW finally admitted that it had in fact installed a defeat device in its diesel cars that disabled the car's emissions controls, except when it sensed the car was taking an emissions test.

'This is actually the single most inexplicable thing about this whole business', German remarked. 'VW had a chance to fix the problem, and they continued to try and cheat and do what they had done. That's just amazing.'

News of VW's admission that it had cheated the system for years with a specially designed defeat device led to the full-blown scandal now known as Dieselgate. A media frenzy ensued, with headlines like CNN's 'Volkswagen Scandal: How the Company Cheated Emissions Tests' and 'Volkswagen Scandal: What Went Wrong?' from BBC News. Even in Germany, Deutsche Welle ran the headline, 'Lawsuit Tsunami Headed for Volkswagen'. Volkswagen shares immediately lost more than 20 per cent of their value, or $18 billion, when the scandal went public. The costs imposed on the company through fines and recalls today stand at more than $32 billion.

There were two big groups of victims from Dieselgate: those whose lives may have been cut short because of toxic VW emissions, and those consumers who had bought VW 'clean diesel' cars on the fraudulent basis that they were thereby reducing their impact on climate change. The health costs were especially severe in Europe, where diesel cars were widely used. A team of Harvard and MIT scientists in 2017 estimated the health cost for VW diesel cars sold in Germany between 2008 and 2015, by comparing the emissions enabled by the defeat device to those the VW diesel fleet would have released if they had instead followed the legally mandated European emission requirements. Their analysis found that the Dieselgate subterfuge led to 1,200 premature deaths, or 13,000 years of life lost.

These estimates are sobering. Yet numbers like these don't typically scare politicians into action. In part that's because voters are increasingly desensitized to statistics, and in part it's because corporations like VW can effectively argue that there is no smoking gun proof that their fraudulent emissions caused a particular individual life – someone's mother, someone's spouse – to end prematurely.

While statistics don't scare politicians, angry consumers do. That is because consumers are voters. And many car buyers were furious to learn about VW's defeat devices and the company's attempt to cover up what they had done: people like Chris Weldon, a video producer from San Francisco. Weldon bought his 'clean diesel' 2013 Volkswagen Jetta because it seemed to combine low emissions with high performance.

'Like everyone else, I feel basically ripped off', he said in a 2015 interview just after the revelations. 'I feel like I'm polluting the whole peninsula as I drive.' Having been deceived about the environmental costs of his car wasn't his only concern: in the wake of the revelations the Jetta's resale value had also plummeted.

For Volkswagen, Weldon's sentiments encapsulated the existential challenge the scandal would pose to Germany's largest carmaker. 'I don't want to drive a VW any more', he said. 'It comes down to a matter of trust.'

Dieselgate is a rare event in the modern media environment, because everyone heard the same story about it: VW had been caught cheating. Despite the proliferation of thousands of different sources of information in our digital age, the mass media is increasingly fragmented. This fragmentation makes it harder for citizens living in democracies to agree about the basic state of the world.

It also means that it is increasingly unusual for a shared story to cut through the welter of different interpretive slants to reach and inform the broader public. The closer the news comes to being politically relevant, the likelier it is to be covered through divergent partisan lenses. Our connections on social media, through which we share outrageous links with our like-minded friends, only compound the echo chamber effects of polarization.

People today lack common narratives around shared understandings of the world. Few stories capture the attention of the public and lead to a broad agreement across the political spectrum. Fewer stories still lead to clear diagnoses of what governments should do to solve the problem.

Corporate scandals like Dieselgate do both. The populist and the technocrat, the left and right, the climate activist and social traditionalist – all take away a similar message from the news about the biggest scandals at our biggest corporations. That is why scandals hold so much power in this fractured political moment.

This is not a feature of all scandals. It is especially a feature of *corporate scandals*, those involving the largest companies. In a world dominated by large companies, corporate scandals retain the power to shock and to outrage.

That shock resonates across political divides and different sources of news. Neither the right nor the left can defend egregious acts of corporate malfeasance to the public. This puts full-blown corporate scandals in that scarce class of terrible events – disasters and invasions being others – that can unite people belonging to different political tribes in the same country. Nearly uniquely in our contemporary media environment, corporate scandals can slice through the noise of our different media feeds and grab our undivided attention.

The tale of Dieselgate conveniently allows us to define the central concept of this book: the scandal. All scandals, corporate or otherwise, involve an initial transgression, the revelation of that transgression, and intensive public fascination with the transgression, typically in the key of moral disapproval.

The transgression at the heart of Dieselgate was the company's deployment of a device deliberately designed to evade legal emissions standards. Volkswagen was breaking the law, and the company's executives faced criminal charges. Even a child would understand this is clearly wrong.

Not all scandals involve law-breaking on the order of Dieselgate. Scandals simply require some form of transgression: the violation of a social norm. An action doesn't necessarily have to break the law to violate a shared social expectation about what is appropriate or fair. When such expectations are transgressed, the first criterion of a scandal is met.

For a transgression to become a scandal, it also must be revealed publicly. Here, the role of John German was fundamental. German first noted the discrepant performance of VW diesel cars on the road and in tests, and he passed that information to the American environmental regulators. After confirming the findings in September 2015, those regulators broke the scandal when they compelled Volkswagen to admit the existence of its defeat device to the public.

The existence of a transgression, and public knowledge of that transgression, are necessary but not sufficient ingredients for a scandal. For a scandal to truly take off requires a third component: public interest.

Scandals attract interest, much as do car crashes or sexual peccadilloes, because they appeal to our basest instincts. Someone of public renown has been caught in a transgression, and we just cannot look away. Even when the public is distracted by so many different sources of information, people pay attention to scandals and want to talk to one another about them.

The Irish playwright Oscar Wilde astutely took the measure of this social phenomenon. 'Scandal', he wrote, 'is gossip made tedious by morality.' Gossip-worthiness is the source of public fascination that keeps everyone talking about scandals after they happen. But the transgression at its root means that scandals have always been defined by the collective moral disapproval they inspire.

Many scholars believe that political scandals are more politically consequential than corporate scandals. From our vantage point in the polarized present, though, contemporary political scandals often lack shared moral outrage. Instead, political scandals are merely vessels for political partisans on one side to attack those on the other side, without convincing the broader public of a common narrative of wrongdoing revealed by the scandal.

This is a recent phenomenon. In years past, political scandals drew more of their power from the same sense of transgression that drives corporate scandals today. The Watergate scandal that brought down American President Richard Nixon in 1974, for instance, created cross-party consensus about the wrong that Nixon had committed. It has also provided the suffix to a variety of mini-me scandals ever since. Most of those -gate scandals are distinguished from their namesake by the conspicuous lack of bipartisan interpretation of the wrongdoing involved. Even when people agree about the facts of these scandals, they do not have a shared moral evaluation of what happened.

Take former Prime Minister Boris Johnson's so-called Partygate scandal. At the end of 2020, the prime minister was present at several social gatherings in his official residence of 10 Downing Street that contravened the lockdown rules in force at the time because of the COVID-19 pandemic.

When news of the parties broke, Conservative and Labour voters saw two starkly different realities. One side saw a government working in close quarters and having a few drinks after a hard day at the office, whereas the other side saw a set of elites blithely ignoring their own rules. Ordinary people followed these rules, which meant sometimes that families, heartbreakingly, left their loved ones to die alone.

This divergence in interpretation results from the tribalism of modern politics. Voting for a different political party doesn't just mean that you have different policy preferences than your neighbour who votes for a different party. It means that you listen to different news sources and belong to different social media networks. Even if you live next door to one another – which is unlikely given modern patterns of residential self-sorting according to political tribes – you and your neighbour occupy separate echo chambers.

We make assumptions about the motivations of those who come from different tribes, based on what we hear about 'the other side' in our own echo chambers. That these echo chambers often have little overlap with each other means we only rarely come to a shared reading of overtly political issues – like the drinks parties at Number 10.

The lack of a shared meaning across the political divide blunts the ability of modern political scandals to transform our shared understandings and teach us something.

To understand how the social impact of political scandals has changed, let's compare two political scandals separated by 25 years and the Atlantic Ocean. Both involve sex and a failed attempt to hide it.

In 1963, the British Secretary of War John Profumo was forced to resign after having an affair with a 19-year-old model named Christine Keeler. Keeler had been practising her own form of diplomacy by simultaneously having an affair with the Soviet naval attaché in London. All this carnality, involving important political figures in pre-sexual revolution Britain, landed the scandal on the front pages.

Having made all the papers, the Secretary of War foolishly tried to cover up his shenanigans. On 22 March, he rose from the packed government benches in the House of Commons and told the honourable members that 'there was no impropriety whatsoever in my acquaintanceship with Miss Keeler'.

The collective moral lesson of a scandal is often not to be found in the initial transgression that created the scandal, but in what sociologist John Thompson calls 'second-order transgressions', and what the rest of us would call 'cover-ups'. Volkswagen's defeat device was especially scandalous because the first time that John German's team discovered it, the carmaker tried to fool regulators with a software fix, rather than just admitting that VW had been cheating consumers for years. In other words, it's the attempted cover-up that sometimes causes the scandal, not just the initial wrongdoing.

Profumo's cover-up would force him to resign only weeks later, once a police investigation revealed that there had indeed been impropriety involved in his acquaintance with Miss Keeler. For a government minister to lie to the House is a resigning offence, and his resignation shook the government of Harold Macmillan, who himself resigned as prime minister in October of that year.

The difference between first- and second-order transgressions was so obvious it formed the heart of a popular limerick at the time.

> Oh, what have you done, cried Christine.
> You've wrecked the whole party machine!

> To lie in the nude
> May be terribly rude,
> But to lie in the House is obscene.

Private morality, in the form of adultery, was at the heart of the Profumo Affair. The coincident involvement of the Soviet naval attaché added Cold War intrigue. But the transgression that brought Profumo down was the fact that he had lied to the House of Commons. That is the importance, in British constitutional terms, of the House of Commons being able to hold the government to account. In that sense, the Profumo Affair reinforced a public morality about behaviour in the House of Commons that continues to define norms of acceptability in UK politics.

Like the Watergate scandal that would erupt a decade later, the Profumo scandal created shared moral understandings within public opinion that cut across party lines. Profumo's transgression of lying to Parliament reinforced the norm, in British constitutional terms, of the House of Commons being able to hold the government to account. It was the transgression of this public morality – Profumo's lie to the House – that brought him down.

Watergate and the Profumo Affair demonstrate the transatlantic ability of political scandals to create shared understandings in public opinion. Yet by 1998, when a sex scandal rocked the presidency of Bill Clinton, political scandals had lost that power, because the increasing polarization of Americans had even changed how they interpreted political news.

The cover-up at the heart of the Clinton scandal was that the American president had denied under oath that he had engaged in sexual relations with Monica Lewinsky, a White House intern. It later emerged that the president had indeed been involved with Monica Lewinsky in a way that fitted most definitions of sexual relations. The Republican-led House of Representatives voted for Clinton's impeachment because of the clumsy cover-up, but the Democrat-led Senate acquitted him of these charges.

As in the Profumo Affair, the Clinton scandal involved both alleged adultery and lies by the politician involved. But, in contrast to the Profumo case, Americans did not come to a shared moral judgement about the Lewinsky Affair. Republicans condemned the president for his behaviour and his lying, while Democrats said the behaviour was irrelevant to his job.

In other words, the scandal was less like Watergate and more like Partygate. Public opinion surveys suggest that most Americans greeted the media frenzy with a shrug. Clinton's party did not suffer in the mid-term elections of 1998, and in fact gained a few seats in the House of Representatives.

Clinton engaged in a cover-up, and the incident was a scandal, but it was a scandal without immediate political consequences. Those on the left and those on the right interpreted Clinton's transgressive act of lying under oath differently. Where you stood on the seriousness of the Clinton/Lewinsky scandal depended entirely on where you stood on the political spectrum. There was no shared moral outrage.

Corporate scandals are politically important today because they retain the capacity to create moral reactions that are widely shared across society – even across party lines. They present a rare instance when two polarized groups see the world the same way. But if a scandal is to create this kind of common understanding, the public has to learn about it, and it has to believe what it hears. So how did that happen in Dieselgate?

Corporate scandals combine interesting clickbait about clearly immoral actions – Volkswagen got caught cheating! – with information. The character of the information varies from one scandal to another, but it is generally about a subject that most of us know little about. These scandals reveal some kind of obscure but dirty truth about how big companies really make and deliver the products and services we use every day. This lack of pre-existing knowledge creates a possibility for collective learning on the part of the mass public.

When the Dieselgate story broke in 2015, most people knew nothing about how car companies comply with emissions regulations. Thus, the media had a big story about corporate cheating and a big job to explain what had happened. Explaining how cars control their emissions, and how engineers might vary that level of control depending on whether the car is undergoing a state-mandated test or not, is not rocket science. The concept, and therefore Volkswagen's transgression, is easy for people to understand, once the gist is explained clearly.

Diesel engines emit less carbon dioxide than do petrol (gasoline) engines, which is one reason European countries long promoted the use of diesel as a clean fuel. Where diesel engines are bad, in terms of pollutants, is in emitting more nitrogen oxide gases (NOx). It was these noxious emissions that Volkswagen had been deliberately hiding with its defeat device.

In 1991, the European Union had passed emission standards to limit pollution from cars, which was thought to be responsible for half the overall health costs resulting from ambient air pollution. Despite passing these rules, European policymakers had observed that air pollution did not decline after 1991 as much as expected. The revelation of Volkswagen's defeat device helped explain why: carmakers were deliberately subverting those standards by depressing emissions during testing.

Both of us are professors. When students come into our classrooms, they expect us to teach them things they do not know. That does not make our students uncritical. They often challenge us at every turn, whether about how interest group politics works or the gory details of how pollsters use small samples to tell us what the population thinks about a given political candidate. They come with their own experiences, which can include having been a lobbyist or having worked for a survey company as a summer job. But whatever their background, they enter our classroom to learn about something they do not fully understand from someone they think does: a teacher. Our students, in other words, arrive with a fundamental openness to listening to what we have to say.

Journalists do not always enjoy the same good faith that professors do when they are teaching a class. During corporate scandals, however, the public is more likely to extend this type of good faith to journalists. People do not understand what goes on in most large companies, and they expect the media to explain it to them. For that reason, scandals are collective learning moments. All of us are learning at the same time about how the world works. Journalists are our teachers.

To consider how unusual an educational moment the corporate scandal provides, contrast it with what we 'learn' during a political scandal. Political scandals typically do not deliver new information to voters, because politicians are already under media scrutiny all the time. Journalists follow them everywhere and are always looking for a story to write about them. By contrast, few journalists at the time were assigned to the emissions beat, and fewer still to Volkswagen. Yes, it is an important company, and its machinations interest financial analysts, but the public's interest in the day-to-day decisions of Volkswagen's engineers is limited, at best.

Meanwhile, politicians get a lot more media scrutiny than car companies, and that scrutiny is often from hostile sources. Political parties are always interested in suggesting to a media informant that their opponents are knee-deep in one scandal or another. Newspapers on the left are more likely to cover scandals of politicians on the right, and vice versa. In other words, political scandals are weaponized for partisan ends. Media consumers know this. Accordingly, they interpret political scandals through partisan lenses, as happened in the Clinton/Lewinsky Affair.

Journalists devoted many lines of newsprint to the most lurid details of Clinton's affair with Monica Lewinsky, but the American public learned nothing new. That Clinton could be involved in marital infidelity was not news to most voters. Clinton had, after all, already admitted under oath to an extramarital relationship with Gennifer Flowers. Over his years in the political limelight, numerous other women had publicly accused him of infidelity, harassment and even sexual violence. The scandal may have changed some Americans' views about Clinton's integrity, but it did not otherwise affect their knowledge of American politics.

Corporate scandals are not immune to this sort of partisan reasoning, if their protagonists come to be perceived from a politically partisan perspective. We will see this in action later when we discuss the case of the bankrupt cryptocurrency exchange FTX, whose disgraced founder was a large campaign donor to the Democratic Party. But on the whole, corporate scandals are less likely than political scandals to be interpreted through established partisan lenses. Most members of the public do not associate big companies with the left or of the right. After all, that would be bad for business. Because these companies lack a partisan identification, it is not clear how their wrongdoing serves partisan goals. In this way, CEOs of large companies are vastly different from political leaders, and more vulnerable to a reaction of shared moral outrage.

The learning that we all experience during corporate scandals thus creates common knowledge. The existence of common knowledge makes collective action easier, by ensuring that everyone sees the world the same way. In other words, when people share common knowledge, they are 'on the same page' in terms of their understanding of the facts at the heart of a scandal.

The fact that after corporate scandals everyone understands the world the same way makes it easier for the public to hold politicians accountable for punishing corporate wrongdoing. In the VW case, this meant that everyone understood that a major car company was deliberately cheating regulators. Everyone is starting from the same set of facts about the world, namely, that VW is polluting the air and deliberately hiding that fact.

When common knowledge has been established, everyone knows that *everyone else knows* about the facts of a scandal. A citizen knows her political representatives are aware of the facts of the scandal, and the political representative knows that the citizens are aware that a scandal has taken place. If political authorities do not act in response, citizens can both observe this failure and act accordingly. Citizens also know that their fellow citizens are aware of the issues, which makes it easier to rouse them to action.

Because it didn't teach them anything new about politics, the Lewinsky scandal did not create common knowledge among

Americans. It is true that everyone knew that everyone knew that Clinton had been involved in an intimate relationship with Monica Lewinsky. Given the relaxed attitudes in the United States about the relationship of infidelity to presidential fitness, that common knowledge was not relevant to politics. On the politically relevant questions – whether the cover-up of the Lewinsky affair represented a crime that was disqualifying for the presidency – there was no shared understanding between Republicans and Democrats.

The creation of common knowledge means that corporate scandals are also more likely than political scandals to lead to a collective interpretation of events. Big corporate scandals are interpreted collectively, not through a partisan lens. How you understood the Clinton–Lewinsky scandal depends on whether you were a voter of the left or the right. There is no such ambiguity about how voters on different sides of the political aisle viewed Dieselgate.

Volkswagen was cheating consumers by selling them cars that that had far higher emissions levels than the company claimed. And it was deceiving regulators by creating a sensor that allowed the car's computer to know when it was being tested and then – and only then – to engage the emissions control system. These cars were belching pollution into the air, which was resulting in increases in premature deaths in both Europe and the United States. There is not a bit of daylight between the way this story is understood by voters on the political left and those on the political right.

Markets understood the same message as voters. Volkswagen's share price suffered a steep decline following the scandal, and the company attracted vitriol on social media. These effects were not limited to VW. In the years following the crisis, other German carmakers, including Mercedes, were found to have used similar practices to cheat emissions testers, as had companies in several other countries. But it was *German* car manufacturers who especially suffered a loss of sales because of the scandal, through guilt by association, as did companies that were identified as suppliers to Volkswagen. That's what the business end of a collective understanding of scandal looks like. German car manufacturers are still recovering from Dieselgate.

Just as there are three definitional *features* of a scandal – transgression, revelation and public fascination – so too are there three characteristic *consequences* of corporate scandals that lend them the power to create political change. The first two consequences are learning and a shared collective narrative. Together, these two create the possibility for a third: the public demands a political response. When the scoundrels have clearly broken the law, that response might take the form of punishment. More often, politicians respond to public outrage by writing new laws to make sure such behaviour will not go unpunished in the future.

Punishment is the corrective response to the transgression involved in every scandal. The French sociologist Émile Durkheim observed that transgressions define the boundaries of what is morally acceptable within a given community, by highlighting shared outrage when miscreants cross those boundaries. Punishing the crime of assault reminds us that, however angry we may get, violent attacks are not socially acceptable.

At the level of society, corporate scandals do much the same thing. The shared disapproval that features so prominently during scandals reminds us, as a society, of the values we share, and how those values have been offended by the protagonist of the scandal. Our personal outrage is reinforced when others are similarly outraged – it binds us to a joint belief of what is, and is not, acceptable in modern capitalist society. That leads us to seek redress through our political institutions.

The legal system does not allow for punishing that which is not expressly illegal. Thus, corporate scandals may reveal a need for new rules by identifying a loophole exploited by transgressive but legal miscreants. These two responses – punishment and new rules – are ways that societies protect themselves from economic actions that violate collective norms of appropriate behaviour.

Dieselgate featured both types of protective response by political authorities. VW CEO Martin Winterkorn resigned within days of the revelation of the defeat device. At the time of writing, he is still being investigated by German authorities on criminal charges of fraud. In 2023, Rupert Stadler, the former head of Audi, became the first VW board member to be convicted of criminal negligence in the case, receiving a suspended jail sentence of 21 months.

Dieselgate also revealed some previously hidden legislative gaps. Germany is world-renowned for the quality of its engineering, and its car companies wield enormous political power in their home country. Indeed, in 2016 the German magazine *Der Spiegel* ran a story claiming that the European Commission had known since 2010, and the German federal government since 2012, of the possible use of defeat devices by diesel car manufacturers in Europe. Yet given the power of the German automotive lobby, neither acted on the information. It was left to the American regulator, the EPA, to bring the hammer down on VW's cheating. Which was not a terribly politically costly thing for the EPA to do, since American car companies have not promoted diesel models in the way European carmakers have.

In 2018 the European Commission devised new rules at the European level that would be difficult to pass in Berlin, given the hammerlock of German car manufacturers on German politicians. Brussels bundled together a set of consumer-protection measures called the New Deal for Consumers. These regulations, which empowered interest groups to litigate claims on behalf of consumers, offered a path to holding the mighty German automobile companies to political account. The New Deal moreover strengthened protections against consumer deception on environmental issues, including emissions. The new regulations responded to failings in European law that were only revealed through the Dieselgate scandal.

After Dieselgate, Volkswagen found itself facing an existential challenge: how to restore its battered reputation with the consumers it had cheated. Its answer, under new CEO Herbert Diess, was to stake out a radically new identity as a leading manufacturer of electric vehicles. Diess announced ambitious new targets for the company in 2019. By 2024, Volkswagen accounted for 8 per cent of the world's sales of electric vehicles, just behind electric-only manufacturers Tesla and the Chinese firm BYD.

In narrative terms, John German kicked off a scandal that revealed that VW was a villain. The pollution it was deliberately hiding from regulators was damaging public health. And its 'clean diesel' campaign was fraudulent, convincing customers they should pay more for a Volkswagen diesel because it was good for the environment. Despite the best efforts of the German car companies, that clear message managed to cut through today's cacophonous information environment. Governments around the world, and eventually Volkswagen itself, had no choice but to respond.

PART TWO

How Scandals Work

3
Goldman Sachs's Shitty Deal

Carl Levin was not a man who freely used profanity. The long-serving US senator from the state of Michigan was known for his rumpled suits and his sterling reputation, not for cursing like a sailor. But in 2010 he had a problem. As chair of the Senate's Permanent Sub-Committee on Investigations (PSI), he had to figure out how to use one of the world's more boring televised moments – a congressional hearing – to explain a pattern of complicated financial transactions in a way that American voters would understand. And he had just been scooped.

Levin had ordered senior executives and traders of the storied investment bank Goldman Sachs to testify before his committee at the end of April. He had selected the world's most famous investment bank as a case study to illustrate to the American people the causes of the financial crisis that had rocked the global economy two years earlier. He and his investigative staff had wanted to understand how Goldman had made a tidy profit during the crisis, when so many other banks had needed the government to bail them out.

One of the witnesses Levin had called was Goldman trader Fabrice Tourre. In 2007, Tourre had put together a financial security called Abacus. A security is simply a tradeable asset, like a stock or a bond, that represents ownership rights. Some securities derive their value from the price of other products, such as mortgages. These are called derivatives. The hedge fund Paulson & Co. had hired

Goldman to build a portfolio of derivatives based on the value of risky – or so-called subprime – mortgages, because Paulson wanted to bet against the subprime mortgage market. It was Tourre's job to sell Abacus to less sophisticated clients, who would without knowing it be on the other side of Paulson's bet.

Tourre, who called himself 'Fabulous Fab', embraced the mission with gusto. He bragged to his girlfriend that he 'sold some Abacus bonds to widows and orphans that I met at the airport', by which he presumably meant less knowledgeable investors. The widows and orphans did not do well: the three major long investors in Abacus soon lost more than $1 billion on their investment, while Paulson – the only investor on the short side of the bet – made over $1 billion. Goldman got a $15 million fee for the job.

That wasn't the only work-related email Tourre sent to his girlfriend, who like him was also employed at Goldman's London office. Another message, written in January 2007, suggested that he and the bank understood exactly where the market was going while he was developing these toxic securities:

> More and more leverage in the system, the whole building is about to collapse anytime now . . . Only potential survivor, the fabulous Fab . . . standing in the middle of all these complex, highly leveraged, exotic trades he created without necessarily understanding all of the implications of those monstrosities!!!

Levin had intended to use Tourre as his star witness to make the case that Goldman Sachs had systematically acted against the best interests of its own clients in order to turn its losses into gains as the subprime market soured. Yet unbeknown to the PSI, the American market regulator, the SEC, had filed a lawsuit against Goldman on 16 April, just days before Levin's planned hearing, charging the investment bank with defrauding investors through Abacus.

Goldman would eventually settle its civil suit with the SEC for $550 million, the largest fine ever imposed by the agency at that time. But in April, the SEC's suit meant that the facts about Tourre had been covered in the media, and thus would be old news, by the time of the PSI hearings.

Levin wasn't holding a trial in front of a judge. He was trying to convince a jury made up of the American public that investment banks like Goldman Sachs had cheated their customers routinely, and that this profiteering had contributed to the financial crisis of 2008.

Levin's team had to scramble to put together a new plan to make sure they dominated the news cycle when they held hearings. Their worry was that Goldman Sachs would once again wriggle off the hook, escaping accountability in the court of public opinion.

As head of the PSI, Levin was the only congressional chairman with the power to subpoena. That meant his summons had the force of law. Since taking over as head of the committee in 2001 he had been the scourge of corporate America. One prominent lawyer said that PSI stood for 'Pretty Scary Investigations'. *Politico* claimed that for corporate America, 'the scariest seat in Washington is the front row of a hearing room where Carl Levin holds the gavel'.

In Goldman Sachs Levin had chosen a worthy adversary. The dark prince of Wall Street, Goldman was the best bank for doing the biggest deals. While other bankers had shied away from publicity in the months after the financial crisis, Goldman CEO Lloyd Blankfein was defiant, claiming in 2009 that the bank was doing 'God's work'. God's work had proved lucrative, as Goldman routinely paid the biggest bonuses on Wall Street. That year, while the rest of the American economy was still seized up from the financial crisis, the bank posted a profit of $13 billion. After Goldman's bonus round that year, even President Barack Obama – whose 2008 campaign the firm had lavishly supported – had seen enough. 'I did not run for office to be helping out a bunch of fat cat bankers on Wall Street', he said.

Goldman had become the untouchable villain of the crisis, described by *Rolling Stone* in July 2009 as 'a great vampire squid wrapped around the face of humanity, relentlessly jamming its blood funnel into anything that smells like money'. Late-night host

David Letterman even included the bank in one of his famous Top 10 lists – Goldman's Top 10 Excuses – in which excuse number 5 was, 'Since when are financial institutions not allowed to screw their customers?'

By the time Letterman called out the investment bank, Levin had a pretty good idea how Goldman had done so well in the crisis. His staff had been investigating the question around the clock since 2008. Levin was a Democrat. Unlike most committees in Congress, the PSI under Levin worked in a bipartisan fashion, and he had selected his financial crisis case studies in close consultation with the ranking Republican on the committee, Tom Coburn. When it was eventually published, their final report would become the only bipartisan document that Congress produced about the financial crisis and its causes.

Levin and his staff had waded through the millions of pages of documents that Goldman had sent them. The investment bank tried to drown the congressional staff in paperwork, but the staffers managed to find the needle in the haystack. From this massive pile of memos and emails, the story they had pieced together was that bankers at Goldman had realized, earlier than many of their clients, that the subprime mortgage market was failing. They had packaged together complex securities based on these risky bets – like Abacus – and sold them to their clients.

These securities were called collateralized debt obligations, or CDOs. CDOs were one of the many arcane financial products that bankers developed prior to the financial crisis, often with the effect of bamboozling non-experts. This confusion was by design. The Goldman trading desk suggested staff use 'hard sell' tactics and that they prioritize clients with 'limited CDO familiarity'. In other words, the investment bank was aiming at selling to suckers, who may not have clearly understood what they were buying.

The bankers at Goldman did understand what was in the CDOs. They had bet that these securities – the ones they were selling to its clients – would fail. In other words, they had 'shorted' the same product they were selling. If the securities went down, the client would lose money and Goldman would win big, as their client Paulson had done with Abacus. When the market crashed, Goldman cashed in.

Abacus was not the only case of manifest conflict of interest the PSI had discovered. In 2006 Goldman created a CDO called Hudson Mezzanine. The 'Mezzanine' part of the name referred to the fact that the CDO contained securities with riskier credit ratings: those most likely to fail. Hudson was a $2 billion product, more than half of which was made up of junk securities already on Goldman's books, which the firm wanted to short, because it had understood the market for subprime securities was headed south.

Goldman hawked the Hudson security to its clients, claiming that its interests were aligned with those of investors in the security, because Goldman had taken a $6 million equity stake in it. What Goldman salespeople did *not* mention was that the bank had in fact shorted the entire $2 billion value of the security. It told buyers that it had the same interest they did, when in reality it was using Hudson to unload high-risk securities on its books and betting that the whole thing was going to lose value.

When the value of Hudson went down, Goldman made a cool $1.7 billion profit. The PSI report detailed several instances of securities like Hudson that successfully shifted risk from Goldman to its clients as a way to lessen its exposure and claw back its initial losses on the subprime market.

By late 2007, even Goldman employees were beginning to wonder if they were doing the right thing by sticking it to their clients. 'Real bad feeling across European sales about some of the trades we did with clients', wrote one salesperson in an email. 'The damage this has done to our franchise is significant. Aggregate loss for our clients on just . . . 5 trades alone is 1bln+ [more than $1 billion].'

For Carl Levin, that Goldman was selling securities to its clients that the bank itself wanted to fail was a clear conflict of interest. But he only knew that because he and his legendarily hard-working staff had spent months looking into it. Now that the SEC had already broken the story about the trades of 'Fabulous' Fabrice Tourre to widows and orphans, Levin was searching for a simple way to make that conflict of interest apparent to the American people, who were not going to read the committee's final 639-page report.

Levin found his answer in the trove of emails Goldman Sachs had turned over to the PSI staff. One of these discussed another security called Timberwolf, which was also made up of junk mortgages that were destined to fail when the subprime market crashed. In one email, a Goldman employee said, 'Boy, that Timberwolf was one shitty deal'. In another, a senior manager complimented two employees who 'worked their tails off to make lemonade from some big old lemons'.

It is exceedingly rare for American senators to use profane language in formal hearings. That, however, is exactly what Carl Levin did when he put Goldman on the stand. On 27 April, Levin led an 11-hour marathon public interrogation of several Goldman executives and traders, including CEO Lloyd Blankfein and the firm's chief financial officer, David Viniar.

'How much of that shitty deal did you sell to your clients?', he asked one Goldman trader. 'You didn't tell them you thought it was a shitty deal?' 'Should Goldman Sachs be trying to sell a shitty deal?' As the testimony dragged on, the pile of excrement-related questions grew. The phones in Levin's Senate office lit up, with outraged constituents complaining about his foul language.

When the time came for Viniar, the Goldman CFO, to take questions, he got the same treatment. Levin's glasses were perched on the end of his nose, like a puzzled professor trying to work out why an apparently smart student would turn in such a bad essay. He looked up from his notes and asked, 'When you heard that your employees, in these emails, said, "God, what a shitty deal", "God, what a piece of crap" – when you hear your own employees or read about those in the emails, do you feel anything?'

Viniar's response was vintage Goldman. 'I think that's very unfortunate to have on email.'

His answer brought the house down, with outraged laughter exploding in the spectator galleries behind him. Levin had used the pungent phrase 'shitty deal' to make the conflict of interest in Goldman's dealings apparent, and Viniar appeared only to regret that someone had put that down in an email. Very few people understood how the Timberwolf security was made, but after Levin's hearing, everyone in America knew what it was made of. Republicans, who up until that moment had been blocking American financial reform legislation, were quick to denounce Goldman Sachs. Everyone knew it was going to be the lead story on the evening news.

Scandals like the one that engulfed Goldman Sachs in April 2010 are especially likely to change minds around issues that people do not typically spend a lot of time thinking about. Financial regulation is not a topic that generally animates spirited talk among friends over drinks, except possibly at exclusive watering holes on Wall Street and in the City of London.

Those of us who study politics for a living distinguish between 'hard' and 'easy' issues. 'Easy' issues evoke clear symbolism and generate visceral reactions, while 'hard' issues require thinking through complexity and nuance. Ask an ardent Spanish soccer fan the question, 'Real Madrid or Barcelona?', and the response will not be long in coming. Ask that same person where they stand on digital trade, transatlantic data flows and antitrust thresholds, and you might want to go and get a coffee while waiting for an answer.

Politics is like that as well. Ask individual Americans what they think about abortion rights, and most will have a lot to say. Some will speak about how life begins at conception and equate abortion with murder. Others will stress the freedom of women to decide what happens to their bodies and champion reproductive rights. For most, these views are well-rehearsed and well established. They come from the gut, and that gut reaction guides their thinking. That makes abortion an 'easy' issue, in our terminology.

Hard issues, by contrast, are not visceral. Hard issues require cognitive work for voters to puzzle through conflicting considerations about how the choices before them relate to their own personal interests.

The easiness or hardness of an issue, as we use the terms, depends on what the public thinks and how it thinks about these issues.

When those views are easily accessible, tied to emotional symbolism and frequently mentioned in politics, they are easy. When they are more unfamiliar and have cross-cutting considerations, they are hard. Some issues that were once hard can become easy over time, if political parties argue about them frequently enough that their supporters automatically know what their leaders think. In recent years the issue of climate change, for example, has in some countries gone through this transformation from hard to easy issue.

Most types of economic regulation, including financial regulation, are hard issues in this sense. It is not obvious what a right-wing or left-wing position on financial stability is. Everyone, aside from extreme libertarians, thinks governments should provide some sort of framework for financial stability. Political parties may differ on the details of which regulatory scheme they prefer, but these differences are not immediately obvious to voters. People have to pay attention to the issue and think about it in order to reckon how such regulatory policy positions relate to their preferences. Most people's views on financial regulation do not flow from a gut reaction.

Some of our readers may say to themselves, 'But I understand finance pretty well'. If that's true of you, then you are unusual. We surveyed more than 27,000 people in six countries in 2020, asking them, 'How well do you understand the important issues about finance and banking' facing the country? The possible answers ranged from 'Not well at all' to 'Extremely well'. Nearly half the people – 48 per cent – said they didn't understand the issues of finance and banking at all, or that they only understood the issue a little bit. Very few, in any country, say they understand the issues around finance and banking extremely well.

Scandals that involve hard issues can be especially effective at changing people's views about what they want from government. These are the sorts of issues that people other than lawyers and lobbyists have not thought much about. When a scandal captures their attention and stimulates them to think about it, it does so in a context of larger malfeasance. The anger people feel in response to a scandal is visceral. In the case of a financial scandal, this anger transforms banking regulation from a hard to an easy issue, at least for a moment.

How well do you understand the important issues about finance and banking facing our country?

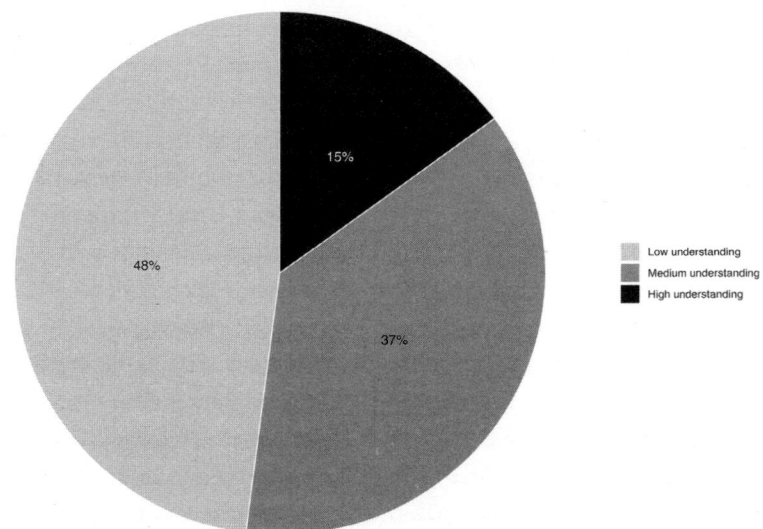

How well people in six countries say they understand the important issues about finance and banking.
Source: Culpepper, Jung, and Lee, 'Banklash', American Journal of Political Science, *2024*.

Carl Levin's problem was that financial regulation is a hard issue. His staff had pored over the email messages that Goldman Sachs had dumped on his committee. The staff members had educated themselves about complex financial instruments. They had spent more than a year becoming experts in the area. But a technical discussion between the committee members and Goldman bankers on what constitutes a conflict of interest was not going to set ordinary voters' hearts racing. And the SEC had stolen their thunder by bringing the lawsuit over the Abacus fund.

The challenge for Senator Levin was to make clear that the bank was acting against the interests of its own customers when it sold them CDOs like Hudson Mezzanine or Timberwolf. What Senator Levin understood, but the senior executives of Goldman Sachs did not, was that a bank betting against its own clients struck Americans as fundamentally unfair. And feelings about fairness come from the gut. If Levin could make Americans feel that sense of unfairness, he could change a hard issue into an easy one.

The public's reaction to Levin's revelation that Goldman had been cheating its customers was a microcosm of the anger that had been brewing since the worst of the financial crisis in 2008. During the crisis, the government had bailed out big banks on the verge of insolvency. Those same banks had generated bumper profits from their reckless practices in the years leading up to the crisis.

It was during the crisis that the phrase 'too big to fail' entered mainstream political conversation. Banks such as Citibank were tightly connected with other financial institutions. If Citibank failed, it would drag down other institutions with it, and then the world economy. For the government, it made more sense to use public money to keep Citibank from failing, as that would trigger a host of negative economic consequences.

The deal at the heart of this bargain, however, was one-sided. Large banks had been able to make risky deals because they knew the government would step in to protect them if they failed. And they were correct. This is what economists call moral hazard. And it's what the rest of us call unfairness.

The government saved the banks, but it would not step in to save the individual families who lost their homes and livelihoods as a result of the financial crisis. The bailouts worked, in macroeconomic terms. The government actually generated a profit on them. But they worked in favour of Wall Street and to the detriment of Main Street. That deal was not fair.

It was a shitty deal.

The American president understood this rage. At the end of 2009, the television programme *60 Minutes* interviewed Obama. The new president observed that bankers are 'puzzled, "Why is it that people are mad at the banks?"' After a pause, Obama continued. 'Well, let's see. You guys are drawing down ten-million-dollar, twenty-million-dollar bonuses after America went through the worst economic year that it's gone through in decades, and you guys caused the problem.'

What Carl Levin did in the US Capitol building on 27 April 2010 was to use the case of Goldman Sachs to explain to the American people, in terms they understood, the conflict of interest at the heart of investment banking practices. And he connected that particular case to the raw anger many people still felt about the bank bailouts.

His revelation, and the scandal it created around Goldman Sachs, would unblock the reform of American financial regulation. To understand how he did that, we first have to take a brief detour through modern political piracy.

If any single measure embodies the blocked politics of contemporary democracies, it is the American filibuster, which derives from the old Dutch word for pirate. The rule allows any senator to prevent a vote on a measure by talking for hours on end and refusing to yield the floor, so long as there are not 60 votes (out of 100) in favour of stopping debate. Given that the Senate overrepresents small and rural states, which have sparse populations, this means that 41 senators, representing a small minority of American voters, can block any measure from becoming law.

In April 2010, the draft bill on financial regulation, which is now universally known as Dodd-Frank, had fallen prey to political piracy: it failed multiple filibuster votes. The Republicans, who held only 41 seats, were using the filibuster to try to extract concessions from Democrats. But Levin's grilling of Goldman Sachs over their selling of a 'shitty deal' immediately put pressure on Republican senators – who had of course lined up at the hearing to lambast Goldman for its behaviour, because it was politically expedient to do so. Senator Susan Collins, Republican of Maine, sat next to Levin at the hearings. She accused Goldman executives of 'stonewalling' about their conflict of interest.

The day after the hearing, the Goldman story led the morning news television programmes in the United States. Carl Levin did a joint interview with Collins on NBC's morning news programme, the *Today* show. The show's host made Collins squirm, noting that Republicans, including Collins herself, had voted to block debate on the financial reform bill. 'How can you say in one room, "We have a major problem here", and how can Republicans say in another room, "But we don't want to debate it openly on the floor of the Senate right now"?'

Collins could only lamely reply, 'I'm sure there will be open debate on the Senate floor . . . We do need reform'. Given the media attention on Goldman Sachs following the hearing, Collins's Republican colleagues around the country felt the same pressure she did.

One Senate staffer pointed us to the Levin hearings as the moment that Republican opposition collapsed in the Senate:

> The drumbeat really hit its peak with the Goldman Sachs conflict-of-interest investigation. You know, 'It's a shitty deal', and you had Lloyd Blankfein there. Republicans who were on this committee, like Susan Collins, they couldn't defend that stuff . . . After that hearing the filibuster broke. So it was that level of centrepiece theatre, the centre of the national conversation – that made it so you couldn't hold it up.

By stopping the filibuster, Carl Levin had defeated the pirates, forcing the Republicans into allowing a vote on the financial reform bill. But he was not yet done. He joined with his colleague Jeff Merkley to sponsor the Volcker rule, a measure that would limit the banks' ability to engage in proprietary trading.

'Proprietary trading' is a complicated term that essentially refers to banks using customer deposits to engage in risky bets on securities. The rule itself was named after Paul Volcker, a former chairman of the Federal Reserve who had been crusading for tighter limits on banks' ability to play poker with the savings they held. Levin's amendment specifically precluded banks from investing in hedge funds and private equity, which are the riskiest class of bets involved in proprietary trading.

The Dodd-Frank Act was the biggest reform of American financial regulation since the 1930s, and the Volcker rule was a major reason why. Proprietary trading was estimated to account for 10 per cent of the revenue of Goldman Sachs before the crisis. Volcker's chief of staff, Anthony Dowd, was himself a former investment banker who had joined the crusade for reform. He clarified the connection between proprietary trading and the parts of the banking system that government has an obligation to defend. 'If we are going to put "too big to fail" back in the bottle, the first question is: Whom are we going to protect? The answer is: We are going to protect the banks.' Dowd continued: 'The second question is: What is a bank? The Volcker rule is a way of defining that, and it doesn't include speculative activities. Why should the government protect those?'

What the public hated about the bailouts was that their tax dollars were used to support reckless gambling by banks. That was a shitty deal. The Volcker rule's limit on proprietary trading responded directly to the outrage of American voters. Because of the Volcker rule, proprietary trading desks at big banks were shut down.

Big banks hated the Volcker rule, and they continue to hate it. The US still has very large banks, and the biggest ones are still too big to fail. But they are most certainly safer than before 2008, and the limitations imposed by Dodd-Frank are a major reason why.

What is interesting about the collapse of the filibuster in April 2010, and the subsequent passage of the Dodd-Frank law, is that no-one in Congress changed their minds on the substance of Dodd-Frank. The big banks were still ferociously lobbying to get their Republican allies to delay the bill, and Republican opposition to the content of the bill was unchanged.

What changed was the *political cost* to Republicans of opposing the bill. Carl Levin's exposure of the trading practices of Goldman Sachs had created a scandal that drew broad public attention to the goings-on in Washington DC. The day after the Levin hearing, the *New York Times* wrote that 'Republicans saw political peril in being depicted as impeding tougher rules for Wall Street'.

Barney Frank, the congressman who co-authored the financial reform bill, had the pithiest summary of what changed in April:

'Money is influential, but votes will kick money's ass any time they come up against each other. In the Senate, once public opinion got engaged, it blew away the lobbyists, the money, campaign contributions. Public opinion drove that bill.'

The intrusion of public opinion into the pitched partisan battle over a long and highly technical bill exemplifies the power of latent opinion. Americans in 2010 had not forgotten the financial crisis, even though many wished they could. But it had been pushed off the public agenda by other news, including debates over the health care legislation commonly known as Obamacare.

The PSI hearing on conflict of interest at Goldman Sachs created incendiary television – 'How much of that shitty deal did you sell to your client?' – in a way that rendered the stakes of financial reform clearly comprehensible. The little-understood issue of how investment banks dealt with their customers was suddenly on display for the American public, and the American public thought the deal stank.

Our own collaboration began with a study of the Levin hearings. Pepper studies interest groups and regulation. He knew that the only time elected governments pay any attention to public opinion is when the public cares intensely about something. Taeku, a scholar of public opinion, was interested in how the democratic public could possibly set the agenda, given its dismally low knowledge about public affairs and general disinterest in politics.

In 2016, six years after the Levin hearings, Pepper was shuttling between Washington and London, interviewing participants involved in the reform of the world's biggest financial markets. Through his conversations and contemporaneous reporting, he knew that the Levin hearings marked a watershed in American public opinion.

Taeku went to work investigating movements in public opinion surveys since 2008. At first, he could find little evidence that the public demand for regulating business had increased after the financial crisis. Whether on redistributive or regulatory policy, the cataclysm of the financial crisis appeared to have left no mark on the public's attitudes to these policies.

What had changed, however, was public confidence in big financial institutions. Every year, the Gallup organization asks the American public to say how much confidence they have in various institutions. In 2006, before the outbreak of the financial crisis, only 10 per cent of Americans said they had no confidence or very little confidence in banks. By 2011, that number had shot up to 36 per cent, meaning that more than a third of the public expressed little or no trust in banks.

Moreover, after the financial crisis, people's emotions towards big business executives turned colder. The drop in warmth towards the execs of big companies was much larger among those people who watched lots of television news. The more news you consumed per week, the more your evaluation of these execs plummeted between 2008 and 2009. This effect was even more pronounced among Republicans than among Democrats.

These findings suggested to us that we needed to understand how people were responding to the news they were getting from the media. After all, the Levin hearings had been televised live and replayed on countless evening news broadcasts. A story about the breaking of the filibuster and Levin's hearings appeared on the front pages of American newspapers the next day. To understand the political power of Levin's hearing, we needed to understand how people responded to media coverage of it.

Sadly, we had not had the foresight to survey people in 2010, at the moment the Levin hearings were taking place. It was now 2016. We therefore decided to use an online survey experiment, which was the next best thing.

Think of our survey experiment as being like a clinical trial for new drugs. In a drug trial, one group of patients gets the actual experimental drug. The other group gets a placebo, such as a sugar pill. The placebo is known to have no effect on the illness at which the experimental drug is aimed.

A survey experiment works in the same way. First, we take a representative sample of the population. Then we randomly assign people to different groups. Some groups get various forms of the treatment. And one group just gets the sugar pill. This allows us to compare the results of our treatment to the results among members of the placebo group to see if the treatment has any effect. Just as in a drug trial, participants do not know which group they are in.

But our treatment was not a drug. It was a media article. Receiving the 'treatment' meant reading one of several news articles about Goldman Sachs and its conflict-of-interest issues. In one of those articles, we used the exact language of the 'shitty deal' email, as had Carl Levin in his congressional hearing. To continue with the analogy of the drug trial, this group took the 'shitty deal' pill, while those in the placebo group took the sugar pill, which was to read no article at all.

The experiment would allow us to answer our big question: did consuming the 'shitty deal' pill – i.e. reading news about Goldman Sachs containing the 'shitty deal' reference – significantly change the views people expressed about politics?

Reading a single article in the context of our online survey is not the same as watching news stories as they happen on your network of choice, and then talking about them with your colleagues at work or your friends with whom you play football. But it does provide measurable purchase on whether the sort of news information reported after the Levin hearings changes political views.

Our experiment uncovered three striking effects on political attitudes: on emotions, on assigning responsibility for the financial crisis and on preferences for policy reform. Nearly half the people who took the shitty deal pill said they were 'very' or 'extremely' angry towards banks and bankers. Only one-third of those who took the sugar pill said the same thing. Moreover, that anger influenced their emotion towards specific actors.

People felt significantly colder towards Republicans after reading the shitty deal article. They similarly felt much colder towards big business and to Goldman Sachs itself. These results show why Republicans were worried about being tarred as the defenders of the banks in the wake of the Levin hearings, and why they were suddenly willing to let their filibuster of financial reform die.

We also asked, 'Which of the following groups do you think has the greatest responsibility for the financial crisis of 2008?' Possible responses included 'banks', 'government', the 'housing industry', and 'individual borrowers'. A majority of those who took the shitty deal pill assigned blame for the financial crisis to the banks. Only a minority of those in the placebo group did, with a striking difference of 10 percentage points between the two groups. In other words, the Levin hearings clarified people's shared understanding of the primary villain behind the 2008 financial crisis: the banks.

The Levin hearings made the horrendously complicated world of investment banking extremely simple. Maybe Goldman Sachs bankers were masters of the universe, but they also looked like fraudsters, selling their clients a product they then bet against. But when we ran our survey in 2016, the financial crisis of 2008 was already a distant memory. We wondered whether it could possibly change the way people thought about banking reform, eight years later, when most people don't think much about banking reform in their everyday lives.

We asked them a question that put the core issue of the Volcker rule to them, in the simplest possible terms: should investment banks be entirely separate from ordinary banks? We thought it was a long shot that people would have concrete views in response to this question, given the amount of time that had passed since this crisis. To our surprise, those who read the 'shitty deal' article declared themselves significantly more likely than those who took the sugar pill to want to separate investment and retail banks.

After the Dodd-Frank reform was signed into law, Goldman took decisive action. The bank banned employees from using profanity in emails and text messages! This led comedian Jon Stewart to opine that 'Goldman may still fuck you over, but from now on, they themselves will refer to it as making sweet love to you'.

In the years since the passage of the American financial reform law, Stewart's cynical view about the law's impact on the banks has become received wisdom among many Americans. That view goes something like this: American big banks are bigger than ever. They continue to make huge profits. Only a single banker went to jail as a result of the financial crisis, and he was not a senior executive like

Lloyd Blankfein. Meanwhile, sustained bank lobbying has steadily eroded the effect of the reform, most notably in President Donald Trump's 2018 law exempting smaller banks from the provisions of the law.

The cynical view exemplified by Stewart's quip is not wrong. But it is partial. It concentrates attention on punishment of banking executives – of which there was none – rather than on the passage of new rules and institutions that made the financial system safer post-crisis – of which there was plenty.

The Dodd-Frank law increased capital requirements for banks, which makes it less likely they will get into the over-leveraged situations that caused the crisis in the first place. Having capital on hand allows them to absorb losses without going to the government for a bailout. The Volcker rule placed severe limits on proprietary trading – or gambling with depositors' money – by big banks. The complex financial instruments known as derivatives, which the American public widely blamed for the financial crisis, were tightly regulated by the reform. Derivatives now had to be traded on exchanges, rather than over the counter, and cleared with central counterparties.

Each of these major changes is hideously complex. And we no longer have Carl Levin, who died in 2021, to explain complicated financial terms like 'central counterparties' to us. This is the dark side of the power of scandals to catalyse significant reforms. Sometimes, when the reforms happen, they are simply too complex for the broad public to absorb and recognize what has improved. Political leaders will remind us in their campaigns for re-election of what they have done to respond to the public demand for change. But a complicated political reform is never going to create the clarity, the strong emotion, and public fascination that corporate scandals like the one at Goldman Sachs did.

Carl Levin is not the only lawmaker to use a corporate scandal to explain complicated details of financial regulation to an angry but confused public. In the United Kingdom, the complicated term that would help change financial regulation was the unwieldy acronym LIBOR.

LIBOR, which stands for the London Interbank Offered Rate, was an international benchmark rate that served as the basis of trillions of dollars of mortgage and derivative markets. LIBOR was determined by the rates banks were charging each other for money, but it affected the mortgage rate consumers could get from the bank or the amount of interest people would pay on their credit card debt.

In June 2012, the British bank Barclays revealed that its traders had been manipulating its LIBOR submissions – in other words, lying about its interest rates – since 2005. Once again, there was an email trail that hit the newspapers and concentrated public attention on the gulf between the culture of the banking sector and everyone else. One trader at another bank begged his Barclays colleague to see about changing the LIBOR submission for that day, adding, 'if it comes in unchanged, I'm a dead man'. Later that same day, once the job was done, the ecstatic trader responded to his Barclays colleague, 'Dude, I owe you big time! Come over one day after work and I'm opening a bottle of Bollinger', referring to a pricey French champagne.

Tasting notes say that Bollinger champagne exhibits rich notes of peach and walnut. But to the British public, the LIBOR price-fixing story smelled like a shitty deal.

Barclays was immediately hit with $450 million in fines by British and American regulators, and its chairman and CEO both resigned.

In the wake of the Barclays revelations, a number of other banks revealed that they too had been manipulating their LIBOR submissions, including Deutsche Bank, Royal Bank of Scotland (RBS) and UBS. MIT Professor Andrew Lo said that LIBOR 'dwarfs by orders of magnitude any financial scam in the history of markets'.

David Cameron's coalition government announced that Andrew Tyrie, Conservative MP and head of the powerful Treasury Select Committee, would lead a Parliamentary Commission on Banking Standards (PCBS) to investigate banking culture in the UK. Tyrie's investigation would run alongside the parliamentary consideration of the Cameron government's financial reform law, which was the British equivalent of the Dodd-Frank law.

The headline feature of this British law, which had a similar intent to the Volcker rule, was to create a 'ring-fence' between retail and investment banks inside a single corporation. This proposal created big problems for three of the UK's four large banks – Barclays, HSBC and RBS. HSBC even threatened to move its headquarters out of London.

The ring-fence policy had been conceived by an independent commission of experts, led by noted economist John Vickers, the warden of All Souls College at Oxford. Given the anger of the British public against big banks after the crisis, all major political parties had quickly agreed to the recommendations of the Independent Commission on Banking (ICB). In 2012, the law implementing the ICB's recommendations was working its way through Parliament.

Tyrie used the LIBOR scandal to drive home to the British public the broader cultural failings of the banks. He insisted that the big banks had shown they could not be trusted to implement the ring-fence separation proposed by the ICB, and to explain to British voters the importance of the ring-fencing component of the law.

Tyrie proposed that, for the ring-fence to work, it needed to be 'electrified'. By that he meant that if banks failed to follow through on separating their retail banking from their investment banking divisions, regulators would have the power to forcibly separate the two – delivering the equivalent of a high-voltage shock to the banks. 'For the ring-fence to succeed, banks need to be discouraged from gaming the rules. All history tells us they will do this unless incentivized not to.'

For civil servants working on the new ring-fencing law, Tyrie's lack of precision on how to improve the policy was maddening. Pepper interviewed one who complained, 'on the detail they engaged frustratingly little. Instead, they put all their energy into the electrification'.

Yet as a political point, rather than a policy brief, electrification was a winner. The debate on ring-fence electrification was targeted at two groups Tyrie feared would undermine the law: big banks and their regulator, the Prudential Regulation Authority (PRA).

Representatives of the large banks later admitted that Tyrie's gamble was a political success. In 2015, one RBS banker Pepper spoke to told him that electrification 'was completely meaningless, but it caught the public imagination. In a sense, that's what we're now working on [as the law is being implemented]. What's the voltage and what's the height of the ring-fence?'

Another banker from Lloyds talked about how Tyrie's intervention affected regulators at the PRA. 'The only thing they're worried about – and they told us this – is having to sit before Andrew Tyrie defending what they've done. So . . . the only incentive they have is to be pretty hard-core on the degree of separation between the two entities.'

Just as the scariest seat for bankers in Washington was in front of Carl Levin, the scariest seat for regulators in London was in front of Andrew Tyrie.

Like Carl Levin, Andrew Tyrie understood that the politics of banking reform is about explaining complex policies in ways people can understand. The LIBOR scandal of 2012 gave him a bully pulpit from which to call bankers to testify before his committee, just as Levin had. And Tyrie managed to connect public anger to the details of policy reform in a way that made experts throw up their hands, but made bankers and their regulators pay attention.

The regulation of big banks since the financial crisis relied on scandals. At least temporarily, scandals can turn the hard issue of banking regulation into an easy one, one to which voters have a visceral response. And that visceral response runs in favour of more stringent regulation.

When legal reform efforts were stuck in the legislative doldrums, scandals unleashed the wind of a stormy public opinion to get them moving again. On the sea, the absence of wind is characteristic of a low-pressure system. In legislatures, that low-pressure system is a product of banking lobbyists' stranglehold on lawmakers, which often insulates them from the pressure of public opinion. Where we observe more rigorous post-crisis reforms – in supposedly neoliberal bastions of finance such as the United States and the United

Kingdom – it was scandals like the ones at Goldman Sachs and at Barclays that heaped public pressure on legislatures. These forced the lawmakers to respond to what voters wanted, helping laws sail through an armada of lobbying pirates, and addressing the worst excesses revealed by the financial crisis.

Without the fair wind of public opinion provided by a scandal, lawmakers find it extraordinarily difficult to break through the political power of big finance. In the European Union, efforts at banking reform were led by the Liikanen group, which took its name from its chairman, the head of the Finnish Central Bank, Erkki Liikanen. Liikanen's proposals to reform banking in the EU drew from both the American and British reform laws. In 2014, the European Commission proposed a draft regulation to enact these recommendations. The draft proposed a ring-fence between retail and investment banks, and it included a ban on proprietary trading by the largest banks.

European banks dismissed the Liikanen proposal as overregulation, and threw their lobbying into overdrive to defeat it. There was an active debate of the proposal in the European Parliament, and the civil society group Finance Watch led a coalition of pro-regulation groups supporting the measure. But there was no 'European' scandal to concentrate public interest around this apparently esoteric debate. And no European policymaker emerged to play the role of Carl Levin, explaining the complex issues involved in ways that citizens could easily understand.

The Liikanen reform remained stuck in the legislative doldrums in Brussels. In 2017, it finally came to a gruesome end at the hands of European banking lobbyists. It's scandalous how often the pirates win battles like these.

4
Europe v Facebook

On 6 June 2013, the *Guardian* and the *Washington Post* published front-page stories divulging the details of a highly classified operation that allowed an American spy agency to gather data directly from the major American technology companies. Their source was a trove of 1.7 million documents that had been leaked to them by a contractor working for the National Security Agency (NSA), the super-secret communications intelligence bureau of the United States. The leaked documents allowed the journalists to describe in forensic detail a programme called PRISM.

PRISM gave the NSA almost unfettered access to the servers of Microsoft, Google, Facebook and Apple, among others. The NSA could view email messages, chats, photos and videos held on these companies' servers. The main target of PRISM was the 'metadata' in those messages: who had contacted whom, and when. But the access given to them by the tech companies meant that government agents could see pretty much whatever they wanted.

Microsoft had been the first of the big companies to join PRISM, back in 2007. At the time of the PRISM revelations, Microsoft was running advertisements assuring the public that 'Your privacy is our priority'.

The man responsible for the leak was Edward Snowden, a computer intelligence analyst with Booz Allen Hamilton, a consulting firm that did contract work for the NSA. Snowden was a self-taught high school dropout with an aptitude for technology.

In the course of his work for the NSA, he was horrified by the extent to which the agency was snooping on its own citizens, using the tech companies as a conduit for mass surveillance. In May 2013 he took a medical leave of absence from the agency. He travelled to Hong Kong and, while there, met with the journalists Glenn Greenwald and Ewen MacAskill and filmmaker Laura Poitras.

The information he shared with the journalists showed that GCHQ, the British counterpart of the NSA, also got in on the act. Through a programme called Tempora, GCHQ installed interceptors on the fibre optic cables that transmitted internet data under the Atlantic, often with the cooperation of the companies that laid the cables. Tempora arguably gave the UK more access to metadata than available directly to the US, though the UK shared that data freely with the Americans. 'It's not just a US problem. The UK has a huge dog in this fight', said Snowden in a *Guardian* interview. 'They [GCHQ] are worse than the US.'

Over the following months the leaks kept coming. In September came the revelation that technology companies had worked with the NSA to get around encryption on their own platforms. In October, people around the world learned that the American government had even been wiretapping the mobile phone of the German prime minister, Angela Merkel.

Snowden considered himself a whistleblower. The United States government considered him a traitor, eventually cancelling his passport when he was in Russia en route to Latin America, where he planned to seek asylum. A dozen years later, he remains in Russia.

Writing in the *New Yorker*, George Packer succinctly captured how the information revealed by the Snowden scandal had transformed global public opinion: the 'story has fundamentally changed the public's picture of Silicon Valley and its relation to the state ... The biggest companies in the computer business – Microsoft, Yahoo, Google, Facebook and Apple, among others – have been giving vast amounts of user data to the government's chief surveillance agency, in some cases for years.'

Corporate scandals have a direct effect on public opinion. That then leads the public to demand change from policymakers.

This is the demand side of scandal politics, which generates the power to create political change.

Yet there is also a supply side of scandal politics: solutions waiting for policy problems to solve. These solutions are often driven by the people political scientist John Kingdon has called policy entrepreneurs. Policy entrepreneurs connect a policy solution to a public perception of a problem. In the case of American financial reform, Carl Levin used the Goldman Sachs scandal in 2010 to identify a public problem: investment banks were behaving like gamblers. He then championed a pre-existing policy proposal – the Volcker rule, which eliminated most forms of proprietary trading – to address the problem he had identified.

Carl Levin was a policy entrepreneur on the inside of the political system. But not all policy entrepreneurs are powerful insiders in the mould of Levin. Some operate outside the political system. Outside entrepreneurs hold no public office or obvious source of political influence. They are often simply dogged fighters, enraged by what they see as corporate abuses.

Policy entrepreneurs on the outside can find allies on the inside. Often, an entrepreneur on the inside will work in tandem with one on the outside to push their preferred policy solution through the political system. The insider brings knowledge of political institutions and players: whose vote you need to win, and how to wage guerrilla warfare against powerful interest groups using parliamentary procedure. Outsiders are devoted advocates to policy solutions – they bring expertise and the citizen viewpoint. And, crucially, they advocate for their solution with terrier-like zeal.

Potential policy entrepreneurs often start out at the margins of politics, viewed as harmless cranks. But whether they are existing policy experts or outsiders who have seized on a policy problem with what they view as an obvious solution, they need to be seriously obsessive people in order to push for their solutions against long odds.

Don Quixote tilted at windmills because he thought they were giants. His jousts gave us the word quixotic, meaning exceptionally, even foolishly, idealistic. Many insiders view policy entrepreneurs as quixotic – that is, until the moment the political mood changes, and the policy entrepreneurs transform into visionaries.

Corporate scandals open a window of opportunity for policy entrepreneurs. They draw public attention to a problem for which policy entrepreneurs have a ready-made solution. Sometimes the entrepreneurs have been banging on about an issue for years, like Don Quixote. Suddenly, a scandal convinces other people that their quest may not have been so unrealistic after all. What if the windmills, which seem to have rendered our lives so easy by centralizing the milling process, really are giants who are out to get us?

The Don Quixote of European privacy regulation was a young Austrian named Max Schrems. His tilt at Big Tech began with a term paper assignment. In the spring of 2011, Schrems was a 24-year-old law student who was spending a semester abroad at Santa Clara University, in the heart of Silicon Valley. While there, he took a seminar on privacy law taught by Dorothy Glancy, an expert on privacy and state surveillance. Prior to becoming a legal scholar, Glancy had served as counsel to the US Senate Judiciary Subcommittee on Constitutional Rights during the Watergate scandal.

One day, the class had a special guest lecturer: Ed Palmieri, a lawyer from Facebook who spoke to the seminar about privacy. Palmieri's cavalier ignorance of European privacy laws startled Schrems. 'He was basically saying: "Fuck it, we do whatever we want to and there's no consequence".' The law offered few incentives for companies to comply, as the maximum penalty for a violation was only €20,000. Intrigued that Facebook's privacy lawyer seemed to neither understand nor care about European privacy law, Schrems decided to write a paper on it as a class assignment.

Once Schrems was back on European soil, he filed a formal request for Facebook to turn over all the data it held on him. European Union law empowers its residents to request such personal data and requires that companies comply within 40 days. Six weeks later, after 23 emails, Schrems received a CD in the mail. The collection contained 1,222 pages of information. That included every message he had ever sent or received, every picture he'd uploaded, and every post he'd ever liked. It also included the information of anyone else who had signed into Facebook using his computer and the IP address of every computer he'd ever used, as well as email addresses he had not provided, but that had been harvested from the contact lists of his friends.

To his surprise, the CD even had information that Schrems had previously deleted from his account. The most alarming passages revealed messages Schrems had exchanged with a friend of his who had spent time in the locked ward of a psychiatric hospital in Vienna. In her messages, 'she kind of explained a lot of the reasons she has psychological issues, and the only way she could communicate at that point was Facebook'. He had deleted her messages from his phone to preserve her confidentiality, but there they were on the CD and on Facebook's servers.

Outraged, Schrems filed 22 separate complaints with the European regulator responsible for overseeing Facebook. One complaint included Facebook's use of facial recognition technology to automatically 'tag' users without their permission. Tagging a user identifies them and creates a link to their profile. Another complaint noted the surreptitious way the company employed the seemingly harmless 'like' button to track users. On Facebook, someone can express their appreciation for a post by giving it the thumbs-up. Schrems observed that the company was using the thumbs-up to hitch a ride with users, unbeknown to them, as they surfed across various sites on the web. A third complaint objected to the company's sharing of private data with third-party software developers.

At the time, Schrems seemed to many like an eccentric European idealist, the sort of person who wears Birkenstocks with socks to class. His challenges to Facebook, however, would ultimately inspire European policymakers to pass the world's most stringent privacy law.

Schrems sent his complaint about Facebook to the Irish Data Protection Commission (DPC). The DPC is located in Portarlington, a small town southwest of Dublin. Many of the

American technology giants, including Facebook and Apple, had established their European headquarters in Ireland for one reason: to avoid billions of dollars in taxes. An unintended consequence of Ireland's company-friendly corporate tax environment was that the Irish DPC was responsible for regulating most questions of data protection in Europe.

That meant that Portarlington – population 7,788 – became the de facto capital of EU privacy regulation. At the time Max Schrems lodged his complaints, the regulator's office was located above a convenience store. Its 26 employees enforced European privacy law on tech companies across the continent, just steps away from the Bulmers Irish cider on sale downstairs.

The DPC refused to engage with Schrems, who kept asking follow-up questions. 'At a certain point I just said, "I'm just going to call you every hour now", and after a couple of hours I got a text message from them saying they're not available to speak to me any more.'

The Irish regulator did, however, request that Facebook make some voluntary changes, such as turning off facial recognition for EU users. Facebook was happy to comply, if turning off facial recognition would get the DPC off its back.

Schrems remained unsatisfied, claiming that the regulator had ignored 90 per cent of his complaints. He wanted to see the company's evidence for its supposed privacy protections.

At the same time, Schrems wanted to avoid the impression that his campaign was the idiosyncratic concern of a single law student with too much time on his hands. After returning from California to Vienna in the summer of 2011, he had founded an activist group called Europe v Facebook (EVF). He redacted his personal information from the file that Facebook had sent him and posted it on the group's website. The word spread about how much information Facebook had gathered about Max Schrems.

A German newspaper used the information from Schrems' file to create a network graph of his friends from the data, which included the GPS coordinates of every picture posted. 'That's basic FBI stuff', Schrems told the *Washington Post*. 'Thirty years ago you [would] put up a pin and look for the connections. Now you know in a click.'

By February of 2012, 40,000 people had followed Schrems's example and contacted Facebook in Ireland to request their personal information. Given the sudden influx of requests, Facebook could not respond to each of them within the legally mandated 40 days.

Schrems had become a minor media sensation, popping up in interviews with the *New York Times* and *Bild*, the largest German tabloid. He was a regular feature on the German evening news. Facebook was getting nervous. The company was just about to go public – in other words, to sell its stock to outside investors. It didn't want a public fight that would put it in a bad light.

The social media giant dispatched Richard Allan, a former British MP who had become Facebook's European director of policy, to Austria to talk with Schrems. He was accompanied by a Facebook privacy lawyer. On 6 February 2012, the three of them met at the upscale NH Vienna Airport Hotel, immediately across from the airport arrivals hall. The meeting lasted for almost seven hours, but it left Schrems dissatisfied.

'The main purpose for me was to narrow down the issues in some way', Schrems said in an interview with the American public television network PBS. But, he continued,

> on most points, their pants were down, like they simply didn't have an answer. However, they knew that the Irish are not going to enforce this, and the problem is that if the Irish regulator doesn't enforce something, you as the person that's concerned can sue the regulator, but that's going to cost a couple of million euros. An average guy is done if the regulator doesn't do its job.

He posted a summary of the arguments Facebook had made in their meeting on the website of Europe v Facebook, saying this was to make 'the negotiations more transparent than most other proceedings around Facebook'. His campaign continued. Most observers viewed the young Austrian's quest for privacy as an implausible attempt to battle the dazzling technological innovations of Silicon Valley.

In 2012, 28-year-old Facebook CEO Mark Zuckerberg was so famous that a critically acclaimed movie had already been made about his founding of the company. Like Facebook itself, the movie *The Social Network* was a huge commercial success. Facebook's Silicon Valley neighbour Apple had overtaken ExxonMobil the previous year as the largest American corporation by market capitalization. Tech companies were the next big thing, and Facebook was the darling of the moment.

For its initial public offering, the company did not need to convince anyone of its market prospects, allowing Zuckerberg to wax messianic in his formal letter to potential investors: 'Facebook was not originally created to be a company. It was built to accomplish a social mission – to make the world more open and connected.' Zuckerberg and his valuable company would get so rich in the process that in 2014 they could easily afford to gobble up messaging competitor WhatsApp for $19 billion worth of Facebook stock. Even before the IPO, Facebook had already bought Instagram in 2012 for the bargain basement price of $1 billion.

By 2010, the year *The Social Network* premiered, Zuckerberg had already decided that privacy was no longer something people cared about. This was not the case when he had started the website as a student at Harvard. Then, privacy had been a paramount concern. His first attempt at a networking site, FaceMash, had landed him in front of a disciplinary hearing after two student groups and Harvard's computer services office complained. To build his network, he needed people to be willing to put their information online. He needed them to trust him with their data.

To address this concern, Facebook told users that their information, such as who they followed, would only be visible to their Facebook 'friends'; that is, to people they had explicitly selected. In other words, it was a closed network. As late as 2008, Zuckerberg still publicly proclaimed that privacy 'is the vector around which Facebook operates'.

Market domination, however, was the real vector around which Facebook operated. And in 2009, a new social media network was rapidly gaining traction: Twitter. Unlike Facebook, Twitter was an open network. Anyone could follow anyone. Faced with what he perceived as the imperative to keep up with the buzz around Twitter, Zuckerberg decided to open the Facebook network, which meant making people's data public. To do so, he unilaterally imposed a new privacy policy on all of Facebook's users.

Zuckerberg justified the change not in terms of business strategy, but in terms of changing social norms around privacy, arguing 'that social norm is just something that has evolved over time'. Putting himself and his company at the forefront of innovation, he then declared that 'Doing a privacy change for 350 million users is not the kind of thing that a lot of companies would do. But ... we decided that these would be the social norms now and we just went for it.'

Zuckerberg and Facebook faced some complaints from privacy advocates at this volte-face. But they could afford to ignore them. At the time, the public had an extremely favourable view of Facebook and its Big Tech brethren. Facebook's user numbers increased from 400 million at the start of 2010 to one billion by September 2012. Large tech companies, which had often started in university dorm rooms or garages, had delivered incredible new capabilities to users. From Google's search engine to Apple's iPhone to Facebook's social network, these companies had revolutionized the world of possibility in little more than a decade. By opposing them, Max Schrems seemed to be standing in the way of technological progress itself.

When in 2010 Zuckerberg talked about privacy as a social norm, he spoke as a CEO unencumbered by legal constraints in his home country. No federal privacy laws had been passed in the United States since the 1990s, when the internet was in its infancy. The laws that did exist imposed no serious checks on the American tech giants. In effect, the only thing regulating the actions of companies like Facebook in the United States, at least when it came to privacy, were social norms – what people would accept.

Europe was a different story. The EU had an existing privacy law, the 1995 Data Protection Directive, upon which Schrems had founded his initial complaints to Facebook. That law required all member states of the EU to adopt comprehensive privacy rules and empower independent regulators, such as the Irish Data Protection Commission, to safeguard those rules. Given the advances in technology since 1995, the European Union was already in the process of updating its privacy law when the conflict between Schrems and Facebook broke out.

Viviane Reding, the vice president of the European Commission, led the reform of European privacy law. The Commission is essentially the executive branch of the European Union – it proposes laws, which are then debated and amended through the European Parliament and the European Council.

Reding came into the position with a no-nonsense reputation as a fighter for consumers. The words 'pugnacious' and 'tough' were frequently used to describe her. In 2006, the association of UK internet service providers voted Reding their 'internet villain of the year' award because of the rules she imposed for registering internet domain names.

Reding had famously initiated the Commission's decade-long crusade to abolish mobile phone roaming charges in the European Union, beginning in 2006. Our American readers may have had the unwelcome experience of discovering, upon return from a fabulous few days in Paris, that they had been incurring sky-high roaming charges when they used their smartphones abroad. Europeans no longer pay these punitive costs when they visit other countries in the European Union because of a law Reding initiated when she was European Commissioner for Information Society and Media. Reding was accustomed to taking on quixotic battles against giant companies on behalf of European consumers.

Reding was the insider counterpart to Schrems. She once observed in an interview that 'most of the decision-makers in the Commission don't know the Parliament and don't know the manoeuvring power it can have if you know how to use it.' But Reding did know parliament, and she knew how to work it. That knowledge would come in handy as she tried to fend off the lobbying offensive of the tech giants against her new privacy bill.

When Reding was appointed as European Commissioner for Justice, she put data protection at the top of her list of legislative priorities. Reding, the insider, drew explicitly on the example of Schrems, the outsider, when she presented her draft bill to the European Parliament in January 2012.

Max Schrems had drawn the attention of the European public to a problem it did not know existed. Viviane Reding had written a law that tackled the problem that Schrems now personified. Now all she had to do was get it through the European Parliament and the European Council, where national governments are directly represented in the EU.

Reding called her bill the General Data Protection Regulation, or GDPR for short. You've probably felt the effects of the regulation she eventually passed if you've ever received a notification from your web browser asking you to allow cookies from a website you are visiting.

That banner is a product of the GDPR, which is now considered the most stringent law of privacy protection in the world. The law requires user consent for collection of any of your personal data, beyond what is technically necessary to access the website. Those notorious cookies, for example, track your moves online to generate targeted advertisements for products suggested by your browsing history, which you may or may not want websites to know about.

The GDPR makes that data about the sites you visit personal to you. It requires that you expressly allow technology companies to use the data before internet companies can harvest it. More fundamentally, it also enshrines in law the general principle that personal data collection requires explicit prior consent.

Back in 2012, when the Big Tech companies learned of the provision in the draft law that required explicit prior consent, they went bananas. Facebook said the measure would create 'a disrupted or disjointed internet experience' for consumers. Google complained that the measure would create 'uncertainty and significant burdens for organizations', presumably including organizations such as Google itself. Amazon and Facebook likewise bridled at these 'formalistic and rigid requirements', and both companies proposed amendments to eliminate the principle of explicit consent.

The tech bro CEOs also objected to the toughening of financial penalties that appeared in the draft GDPR. The measure called for steeper fines for companies violating the dictates of national data protection authorities (DPAs). Depending on the nature of the violation, the fine could range from 0.5 to 2 per cent of a company's global revenue. To put that in perspective, Microsoft's global revenue for 2012 was nearly $74 billion. Two per cent of that revenue would equal $1.5 billion, a number that might be enough to make even Bill Gates want to have a stiff drink.

The Big Tech companies launched a lobbying onslaught the likes of which Brussels had never known. Viviane Reding, who had faced down the mighty telecom companies on roaming charges, complained that she had never 'seen such a heavy lobbying operation'. An Austrian MEP supporting the legislation echoed her lament: 'we are bombarded with emails and meeting requests by companies who want to water down the proposal. I had never experienced such lobbying in my life.'

The lobbyists working for the tech companies tried to defang the law with amendments. The American Chamber of Commerce in Europe – called AmCham for short – served as the lead lobbying organization for watering down the bill. AmCham asked to cap the possible financial penalties for violations of the law at figures so small as to be effectively invisible to the naked eye of the billionaire tech CEOs.

Over the course of 2012 and into 2013, AmCham hosted several conferences with like-minded members of the European Parliament to warn them of the dangers for business implicit in the new GDPR. Sweden, the UK and Germany all came out strongly against the GDPR within the European Council.

As the days got longer in the spring of 2013, the lobbying was having its intended effect: the GDPR bill was bleeding to death.

One senior official observed that there were more Google lobbyists working on the GDPR than there were officials from the European Commission.

Jan Philipp Albrecht was Reding's field general on the floor of the EU Parliament. In an interview with the French newspaper *Le Monde* on 2 June – four days before the publication of the first stories about the PRISM programme – Albrecht despaired of the chances of passing the bill in its current form. He lamented that the GDPR had received more than 3,000 amendments, and '80 per cent of those amendment proposals are arriving from abroad, from companies, primarily from Silicon Valley giants', turning many parliamentarians against the bill.

This was the moment the scandal unleashed by Edward Snowden changed the course of privacy regulation in Europe.

Scandals are moments of intense public attention that create public learning. Both in the United States and the United Kingdom, the PRISM leak was a near-death experience for the intelligence agencies involved. Spymasters at the NSA and GCHQ, used to operating in the shadows, suddenly had to deal with political anxieties created by the unfamiliar glare of the public spotlight on their activities.

What the European public had learned in the PRISM scandal was that Zuckerberg and his counterparts in Big Tech were not just connecting the world, but also connecting their data to government spy agencies. They were no longer the cinematic heroes of *The Social Network* but the enablers of the sort of surveillance associated with George Orwell's *1984*. It was not a good look.

Snowden's revelations drew the angry glare of the European public immediately to the labyrinthine halls of the European Parliament, where the GDPR bill lay dying.

We can call the period before June 2013 BS: Before Snowden. During this time, the public was not paying attention to tedious debates about privacy in the European Parliament. The American technology companies used their place in the shadows to maximum effect, lobbying lawmakers while the public's attention was directed elsewhere – such as towards the election of a new pope, Francis, in March of that year.

In the period we should call AS – After Snowden – the spotlight turned its remorseless glare on the grubby legislative deals going down in Brussels. The media published stories about members of the European Parliament submitting amendments copy-pasted from the briefing papers of the tech companies. In the words of Max Schrems, 'Snowden was the Chernobyl of data protection. It was for me the major change. Suddenly it became a much more mainstream debate than it was before.'

Like the failed Soviet nuclear power plant, which rained radioactive dust over most of Europe in 1986, the Snowden leak became *the* subject of European political conversation in 2013. European media mentions of data privacy shot up after the Snowden revelations, and they stayed higher than they had been pre-Snowden for the next two years.

The publicity changed the way Europeans thought about large technology companies. Google was transformed from the company whose motto was 'Don't be evil' to one that was funnelling information about private citizens to a spy agency of the American government, which sounds kind of evil. Every major technology company that participated in the lobbying campaign against the GDPR had experienced the same reversal of fortune. Having long been lauded as pioneers of radical technological innovation, these corporations were suddenly the bad guys.

The scandal caused by the Snowden leaks permanently blighted the reputation of Big Tech in Europe. That reputational damage also fuelled public demand for regulation. Public opinion polling in 2015 – two years after the revelation of the PRISM programme – showed that, across the European Union, those who knew about the Snowden leaks had lower trust in tech companies than those who did not know about the leaks. Moreover, those who knew about the leaks were also more likely to favour the explicit consent measure of the GDPR than those who didn't.

The PRISM scandal immediately transformed the state of play on the GDPR in Brussels. Prior to the leaks, many of the proposed amendments to the GDPR legislation either deleted the entire section on fines or raised the burden of proof for malicious intent on the part of the company. After the leaks, the amendments moved in the opposite direction – increasing the proposed fines to 5 per cent of global revenue or up to €25 million. As the public attention continued to escalate, so did the proposed cap on fines. The highest proposal capped fines at €100 million, a 200-fold increase over the figure of €500,000 AmCham had promoted, with a straight face, only months earlier.

The mood in the European Parliament had clearly changed, but so had the mood in the European Council, where national ministers vote. Viviane Reding struck while the iron was hot. At a meeting of national justice ministers in the European Council on 19 July, six weeks after the Snowden leaks, Reding told the ministers that the world had changed: 'PRISM has been a wake-up call. The data protection reform is Europe's answer.' Germany, in particular, moved decisively out of the camp of those opposing the GDPR into the coalition of countries in favour.

Reding used her knowledge of the workings of the European Parliament to good effect. Conservative political groups in the Parliament, which had been leaning against voting for the GDPR, changed their position on the law and even demanded the inclusion of an anti-NSA surveillance clause. Further attempts to water down the law were rejected, and the bill passed in March 2014 by a vote of 621–10, with 22 abstentions. The European Council would take longer to approve the bill, and demand some compromises, but approved its own version in June 2015. Reding had routed the American tech giants.

Scandals not only help pass laws. They also create a window of opportunity for outside policy entrepreneurs to revitalize their campaigns. Max Schrems got the memo. In response to the initial Snowden revelations in 2013, his organization Europe v Facebook immediately filed a new complaint against Facebook with the Irish Data Protection Commission. The complaint observed that the company's assent to 'mass transfers' of personal data to a foreign intelligence agency, the American NSA, violated European privacy law.

The Irish Data Protection Commissioner, Billy Hawkes, dismissed the Schrems complaint on the grounds that it was 'frivolous and vexatious'. Vexed, Schrems appealed this ruling directly to the High Court of Ireland. The Irish judge in turn referred the case to the highest court in the EU, the European Court of Justice (ECJ).

The case had to go to the ECJ because, back in the year 2000, the EU had recognized a 'Safe Harbour Framework' to resolve inconsistencies between data privacy governance in the United States and the EU. The Safe Harbour framework had itself been a response to a previous EU Privacy Directive in 1995, which the American government had worried could undermine transatlantic online commerce. Safe Harbour was 'an industry-developed solution to privacy problems' intended to ensure that American companies could collect European data without running afoul of European privacy law.

Safe Harbour was also a government euphemism of the sort George Orwell warned readers about. 'Safe Harbour' would be a good name for a retirement community or country getaway, given that it connotes solid protection from the vicissitudes of nature. But the safety in 'Safe Harbour' does not refer to the safety of citizens' data.

Instead, safe harbour provisions are legal devices that protect companies from regulatory liability if those companies meet certain conditions. As long as American Big Tech companies met the provisions of the Safe Harbour framework, they were free to collect the data of European citizens without having to meet onerous European privacy provisions. In other words, its architects designed the harbour with some very big American ships in mind. The framework would protect them from any storms of regulatory enforcement.

The PRISM scandal had revealed information about what these companies were doing with the data of EU citizens that the European Court of Justice could not ignore. The lawsuit brought by Max Schrems forced the court to acknowledge the change in the weather.

In October 2015, Europe's highest court struck down Safe Harbour, to the consternation of the more than 4,000 American tech companies covered by the agreement. The court's findings held that the fundamental privacy rights of European citizens trump any agreement aimed at shielding big companies from legal challenge.

The day the court handed down its ruling, Edward Snowden tweeted from exile in Russia: 'Congratulations, @MaxSchrems. You've changed the world for the better.'

Facebook and the other giant American tech companies previously protected by Safe Harbour were not so happy. The ruling immediately put all their data transfers from Europe at risk of legal challenge. Eric Schmidt, the chair of Google's parent company, said that the ruling threatened to undermine 'one of the greatest achievements of humanity'. Not to be outdone in the art of overreaction, Microsoft's president warned of the return to the 'digital dark ages'.

The American government and the European Commission quickly set to work to cobble together an alternative to Safe Harbour in a post-Snowden, post-GDPR environment. The fundamental new fact of that environment was that previously latent opinion in Europe about the right to individual privacy had hardened into a substantial iceberg.

This was a dramatic change from the conditions under which European and American representatives had negotiated Safe Harbour. As scholars Henry Farrell and Abraham Newman observed, the combination of a febrile public and the ECJ ruling had altered the balance of power on the European side of the negotiating table, empowering privacy activists and regulators. Even so, when negotiators finally reached a new agreement in 2016, Privacy Shield, the deal still offered more safety to Big Tech than to European consumers. Like Safe Harbour, this was another Orwellian linguistic sleight of hand – the shield protected companies, not citizens.

Max Schrems immediately got to work. He lodged yet another complaint against Facebook with the Irish Data Protection Commission. This time, the DPC knew better than to dismiss a complaint from Schrems as frivolous and vexatious. Instead, the commissioner referred several questions to the Irish High Court, which again referred the issue to the ECJ.

In a landmark decision in 2020, the ECJ again ruled in favour of Schrems, invalidating Privacy Shield on similar grounds to those on which it had struck down Safe Harbour. The problem was one of proportionality: American law enforcement had unfettered access to the personal data of EU citizens once it had been transferred to the US. European citizens had no judicial recourse to prevent such access. This was still a violation of fundamental European rights. The score was Max Schrems 2–Big Tech 0.

Henceforth, according to the 2020 decision, companies would have to rely on their standard contractual clauses to protect citizen data. This decision hurts companies because it shifts the burden of data protection in a foreign jurisdiction from an intergovernmental agreement like Privacy Shield on to individual firms.

Companies would have to be proactive in ensuring that personal data would be protected when it was transferred outside the EU. Meta – the parent company of Facebook and Instagram – warned that it might have to withdraw its services from Europe, though it backed down quickly from that threat. In subsequent years, the internet giants have moved closer to localizing the data of Europeans in Europe. In effect, they have bent the knee before the assertion of European privacy law over their market interests.

For European policy entrepreneurs looking to seize on the growing iceberg of public hostility towards Big Tech, privacy wasn't the only game in town. Among the European policy elite, attention was turning to the broader issues involved in antitrust and online disinformation.

In 2019, a new European Commission came into office, with an explicit priority to build a 'Europe fit for the digital age'. The woman leading this campaign was a Dane named Margrethe Vestager. Media reports regularly described Vestager as the regulator Silicon Valley feared the most.

Vestager had already turned herself into the undisputed rock star of the European Commission by taking on Google and Apple over issues of antitrust. She brought stardust from her previous position in the Danish government, where she had inspired the character of prime minister in the hit TV series *Borgen*. A centrist politician with a strict Lutheran upbringing, Vestager had a reputation for being incorruptible and funny – qualities in somewhat short supply in the capital of the EU – and she had brought that reputation with her to Brussels in 2014. But she also came into her job with scars from political fights at home. She keeps in her office a sculpture of a raised middle finger, a gift from irate Danish trade unions during her time as deputy prime minister.

Back in 2015, Vestager had indicted Google, saying 'dominant companies can't abuse their position to create advantage in related markets'. For good measure, she added a second charge: that Google's Android operating system favoured its eponymous search engine and the Chrome web browser, also owned by the company.

In 2017, the European Commission ruled on the first charge that Google had indeed favoured its own services over those of competitors. The Commission hit the search giant with a penalty of $2.5 billion, which more than doubled the previously highest penalty for violating European antitrust rules. At the time the ruling was announced, Vestager suggested it could serve as a framework for other investigations.

But the cool Dane was just getting started. In 2018, on the second charge, the Commission decreed that Google had indeed used the dominance of the Android operating system to promote its own search engine and other Google apps. The fine this time was $4.5 billion, which at the time of writing still stands as the largest antitrust fine ever levied in Europe. Silicon Valley was on notice that there was a new sheriff in Brussels, and she did not do deals.

By the beginning of 2018, however, it was also clear to the European Commission that it needed more than tough regulators. If it was going to take on Silicon Valley, it needed tougher laws.

In 2024, Pepper met with Margrethe Vestager in Oxford to talk about why the Commission decided to go for tougher laws. She responded that court cases were simply too slow. 'One of the things that has been painful for me in these ten years is that it takes so long.' She explained why. 'First we have to prove that you're dominant. If we open an Amazon case, for instance, and say, "Well, you're dominant in an e-commerce", they say, "No, no, we're just one per cent of global retail, how can you think of us as dominant?"'

The second problem Vestager and her colleagues ran into was the failure of enforcement against one company to deter other tech companies. The tech companies were better at asking for forgiveness than permission. She needed to speed things up.

Vestager's battle had two fronts, one involving competition, the other online disinformation. The proposed law for competition, the Digital Markets Act (DMA), imposed onerous requirements on the most dominant tech firms. The DMA designated the six largest companies as 'gatekeepers'. Among other things, the DMA requires that these companies make their services interoperable – meaning that Facebook's Messenger App has to be able to communicate with other, non-Meta chat services, like Apple's iMessage.

The other proposed law, the Digital Services Act (DSA), aimed to combat illegal content and disinformation. The DSA would require companies to release information about their algorithms and would explicitly ban targeted advertising. Companies designated as very large online platforms (VLOPs), such as Facebook or YouTube (which is owned by Google), would become responsible for policing illegal content and impact on election processes, with steep fines for lack of compliance. Facebook and Google would be subject to annual audits on disinformation.

Just as they had in their battle against the GDPR, the large tech companies ferociously lobbied against the DMA and the DSA. In the first six months of 2020 alone, the five large American tech companies spent €19 million on lobbying. Margarida Silva of the Corporate Europe Observatory, which studies EU lobbying, was aghast: 'We've never seen this kind of money being spent by companies directly.' Between October 2020 and September 2021, Apple nearly doubled its own spending on lobbying. Meta had become the largest single lobbying spender in the EU by 2023, spending €8 million, up from the €5.8 million it had spent in 2021.

Google was especially active in lobbying against the DMA and the DSA. In a dossier that leaked to the French newspaper *Le Point*, the search giant laid out the details of its strategy. Paid lobbyists would aim to reframe the discussion around how consumers would be hurt by the laws, using apparently independent third parties such as think tanks to reinforce their message. The American government would be called on to argue against the law on behalf of its tech giants. The company even detailed its plan to play off departments and individual European commissioners against each other, so as to undermine proponents favourable to breaking up the company. Google CEO Sundar Pichai had to apologize publicly for the document, but it was clear that his corporation was really only sorry to have been caught.

The lobbying playbook looked eerily similar to the campaigns against the GDPR in 2013, with companies warning about the economic costs of the new laws. Nick Clegg, former deputy prime minister of the UK, was Meta's president of global affairs at the time. Speaking on behalf of his new paymaster, not the voters he used to work for, Clegg warned that the DMA could 'fossilize' innovation in the digital economy.

For all their dark mutterings and splashing out of cash, the tech lords lost the battle. The activated public sentiment against Big Tech in Europe had made it too costly for individual legislators to be picked off one-by-one. German MEP Andreas Schwab guided the legislation on the floor of the chamber. He faced strong lobbying both from the Biden White House and the Big Tech companies, who kept trying to arrange meetings with him even as the legislation was about to come up for a vote, but he consistently waved them off. 'I tell big companies to not even bother sending me anything', was Schwab's message. 'It's over.'

The EU Parliament adopted both the DSA and the DMA in July 2022 with huge majorities, and in September the EU Council followed suit.

Together with the GDPR, the DMA and DSA have turned the EU into the world regulatory leader for technology policy. The ultimate effectiveness of the DMA and DSA remains to be seen. As of this writing, the American tech giants continue to lobby for the weakening of both laws, and they have enlisted the second Trump administration as an ally in that fight. What is already clear is that on the major dimensions of public concern about technology companies – privacy, fair competition and misinformation online – the EU now has a tough set of measures on the books. The PRISM scandal has crystallized a large iceberg in European public opinion, and American tech giants must reckon with it any time they leave their safe harbour to cross the Atlantic. In Europe, those companies are no longer playing by their own rules, but by laws passed by democratic institutions.

We know more about the outcome of the GDPR, which has been on the books since 2018. And what we know is that the law is cumbersome. Giving people the right to control their own data has created headaches for every organization that collects information about people, from Facebook to local churches and football teams.

The law moreover depends on enforcement by data protection authorities located in the member states. As we have seen, many American tech companies are headquartered in Ireland. This makes the Irish Data Protection Commission the regulatory bottleneck of Europe. The DPC has theoretical power to levy huge fines, but the number of companies it supervises – and the complexity of assessing appropriate punishments – have led some observers to assert that the DPCs, especially the Irish one, are captured by the companies they are supposed to oversee.

In 2017, Max Schrems established an NGO dedicated to seeking enforcement of European privacy rights. The organization is called NOYB, which stands for None of Your Business. On the day the GDPR went into effect – 25 May 2018 – NOYB simultaneously filed lawsuits against Facebook and Google in Austria, Belgium, France and Germany. The NOYB suits sought fines totalling $8.8 billion. The organization has since kept at it, having filed more than 800 lawsuits based on the GDPR.

One person who has a balanced view of the GDPR is Schrems himself. 'At a global level, it's the least stupid privacy law we have so far', he says. Still, he gives the GDPR a failing grade on the enforcement part of GDPR, which still relies on DPCs. In 2023, on the five-year anniversary of the GDPR's coming into force, he blasted the obstacles to enforcing privacy rights in Europe. 'It often feels like there is more energy spent in undermining the GDPR than in complying with it', posted Schrems on the NOYB website. 'While companies know that Ireland is the "go to" jurisdiction for non-enforcement, there is hardly a "go to" jurisdiction for citizens, as there are enforcement issues in basically all Member States.'

Policy entrepreneurs learn from one another. Margrethe Vestager, for one, learned from the shortcomings of the GDPR, and she therefore sought centralized enforcement of the DSA and DMA. As she related in our Oxford interview, 'one of the reasons why we have the . . . commission enforcement of the DMA and the DSA comes from the distrust of the Irish doing the privacy enforcement'.

By itself, the GDPR represents a massive recognition of an individual right to control one's own personal data. This is often inconvenient in practice, and many people simply click through consent screens so they get to the latest cute cat pictures online. But like the cute cats, the law itself has claws, which advocates like Schrems have used to lacerate the tech giants.

Between 2018 and 2024, European data protection regulators imposed more than $5.9 billion in fines on tech companies. The largest single data protection fine levied so far is for $1.3 billion, against Meta, Facebook's parent company. Of the five largest fines, Meta has received three of them, with the others charged to Amazon and TikTok.

Scholars often describe the European Union as a 'regulatory superpower'. The phrase suggests that Europe's market of nearly 450 million people is so valuable that companies around the world automatically choose to follow its rules in such areas as chemical regulation, antitrust rules and airline emissions, even when those rules are stricter than in their home markets.

Prior to the passage of the GDPR, Europe was not able to compel the big technology companies to follow its rules on data privacy. In June 2013 those same American companies were well on their way to gutting the GDPR. Then the PRISM scandal broke out. The scandal fundamentally altered the public perception of the companies whose products had revolutionized the world economy in the first decade of the twenty-first century.

That change created a window of opportunity. Insider Viviane Reding pushed the GDPR through that open window. Outsider Max Schrems used the information revealed to the public by the scandal to challenge the Safe Harbour and Privacy Shield agreements in Europe's highest court. Insider Margrethe Vestager built on the momentum against Big Tech to put sweeping new laws about competition and online safety into force.

The scandal unleashed by Snowden transformed public opinion in Europe. That changed the terrain for the policy entrepreneurs Schrems, Reding and Vestager. As is the case with many policy entrepreneurs, Reding's solution to the problem of protecting the privacy of European consumers existed before the scandal ever came to light. She would have tried to pass her law whether or not the scandal had broken out. But until the PRISM scandal broke, the tech giants were skewering her bill with amendments in the European Parliament.

Max Schrems was to law enforcement what Viviane Reding was to law writing. Schrems was the policy entrepreneur who repeatedly challenged government agencies to enforce European law. When they did not, he took them to court, over and over again.

Reding, Schrems and Vestager remind us that scandals require policy entrepreneurs to convert public outrage into legal change. Without the action of these insider and outsider policy entrepreneurs, it is unlikely that European laws around privacy, antitrust and online safety would have changed so drastically.

Max Schrems never finished the term paper on Facebook he started in 2011. He still has an incomplete grade for the course he took at Santa Clara University. He has been busy with other things, still out there fighting today, trying to turn those rights into a reality.

5
Cambridge Analytica and the Techlash

Alastair Mactaggart was in the shower when he decided to take on the lobbying might of Big Tech. Mactaggart is possibly the last person you would expect to invest years of his life in a long-shot bid to regulate big companies. With a full head of hair and chiselled good looks in his late fifties, Mactaggart is the sort of person you might see talking reassuringly on CNN about stock market fluctuations. Or possibly stepping off the ski slopes in Lake Tahoe to grab a mug of hot chocolate.

Running a family real estate firm in northern California had made Mactaggart a wealthy man. As he told a Berkeley professor whose expertise he was seeking, 'I don't want to kill businesses – I'm a businessman'. Yet the problem of data privacy had begun to bother him. Seeing what the Europeans had done with the GDPR had been an epiphany for Mactaggart.

'I'm like Paul on the road to Damascus', was how he described it to Pepper in a 2024 Zoom interview he joined one morning after dropping off his kids at school in northern California. 'I originally thought, "What's the big deal? Who cares?" And then at one point it occurred to me, "Isn't it interesting that I have more rights over my own information with respect to what governments know about it, than with respect to the corporations?"'

That seemed wrong to Mactaggart, and he decided to do something about it, at least in California.

The state of California is unlike any other sub-national region in the world. If California were a sovereign country, it would possess the world's fourth largest economy. California also has an initiative process – similar to a referendum – that allows citizens to put a law directly to the voters, rather than having it pass through the legislature.

For Mactaggart, the idea of doing something about privacy regulation in California came at just the right time. 'I was at a stage in my life where I'd had cancer, and I was past that. My kids were little and I thought, "Do I really just want to keep on being in business the rest of my life?"'

He continued: 'I had the sense of something lacking in my life. And I thought, "The smartest people are authors, are people who come up with ideas that kind of change the world." I'm not an author . . . so how else could I make a change?'

That's when the idea came to him. 'And then that day in the shower, it hit me: "You know, I should do it. I could do an initiative."'

The California initiative process was, like the muckrakers, a product of the Progressive Era. When Governor Hiram Johnson introduced it back in 1911, he hoped it would allow the people of California to use their voice to counterbalance the stranglehold of the state's industrial magnates on the legislature. At that time, Leland Stanford's Southern Pacific Railroad dominated the state through a political machine known as the Octopus, whose tentacles wrapped firmly around the state's political institutions. The initiative process allowed activists to ask voters directly about an issue, bypassing corporate lobbyists in the legislature.

Alastair Mactaggart's initiative had the same goal. He wanted to do an end-run around the legislative influence of the modern monopoly giants Google and Facebook.

Privacy struck Mactaggart as a winning issue at the ballot box. 'Every time I talked to anybody, people were like, "They're listening to me, they know everything about me, I don't like it." And so I thought to myself, "This could be susceptible to a voter intervention. And there might be a way to spin it where almost no matter what [the tech companies] spent, the voters would still approve it."'

Together with his friend and neighbour Rick Arney, Mactaggart waded into the complicated policy thicket of internet privacy. Mactaggart put together a small team to try to get expert advice on what to include in the ballot initiative. As he told us, 'It was much more difficult than I had imagined to get familiar with the dynamic, to try to find the battle lines, and try to find where leverage would best be applied. You know, I kept on expecting to find a door that was just locked, and I kept on being surprised I was able to open them.'

Mactaggart settled on a proposal that would allow any consumer in California to require large companies to disclose what private information they had collected from them. If consumers were not happy with what the companies held on them, they could opt out, which would prevent the company from selling that data to third parties.

In November 2017, he submitted his proposal to the Attorney General's office in Sacramento, the state capital. A month later, the title and summary of the initiative approved, Mactaggart and Arney were free to start collecting the several hundred thousand signatures they would need from fellow Californians to put the measure on the ballot.

Mactaggart admitted that he kept waiting for the other shoe to drop. 'I was like, "There's no way some random business guy could be able to put something like this together. It doesn't make any sense. Why isn't everybody doing it?" And again, little did I know there was a reason why: I was seeing just the tip of the iceberg in terms of what's required to get an initiative passed in California.'

When Mactaggart talked about an iceberg, he meant something quite different from the iceberg of latent opinion we have discussed throughout this book. He meant almost exactly the opposite: that the hard work in an initiative campaign only started once the lobbying machine of the giant tech corporations roared into life. And he didn't have to wait long to discover what that opposition looked like.

Big Tech mobilized to defeat the initiative soon after Mactaggart registered it in Sacramento. The California Chamber of Commerce established a group purpose-built to defeat the initiative: the Committee to Protect California jobs. Facebook and Google immediately contributed $200,000 each to the group; Amazon and Microsoft each donated $195,000. The group would amass a war chest of over $2 million by the summer, driven almost entirely by donations from a handful of large tech and telecommunications companies.

The anti-initiative lobbying group issued a press release calling the measure unworkable, and warning California voters it would wind up 'limiting our choices, hurting our businesses and cutting our connection to the global economy'. The battle was on, and Big Tech intended to win it.

For Alastair Mactaggart, the lobbying onslaught from the tech industry offered a crash course in the facts of political life. 'What I was starting to realize was actually, truth didn't matter. My unsophisticated, quixotic idea of "the truth will out and will prevail" – that's just not the case when you are up against unlimited money … I did the math and the market cap of all the companies opposing me – who had actually contributed money to the committee opposing me – was over six trillion dollars. And that was back before there were really any trillion-dollar companies. And so I was like, "I'm going to get smoked here".'

Part of the reason the politics of modern democracies seems blocked is the power and influence of giant corporations. Those companies and their owners pour money into political campaigns. A revolving door between government agencies and the industries they supervise means that regulators in charge of policing companies may think twice before imposing stiff penalties on their potential future employers. And, as large companies never cease reminding politicians, companies are innovators and job creators. Rules that restrain companies may also encourage those companies to invest somewhere else, depriving an economy of jobs and economic growth.

For many years, the companies that now dominate the technology sector claimed they did not need to invest in lobbying. Indeed, many of their leaders professed a libertarian ethos that disdains government generally. That disdain, and the desire to 'move fast and break things', sometimes tipped over into an approach to politics that actively sought to undermine government.

In 2014, for instance, the ride-hailing app Uber designed a programme called Greyball, which deliberately misled regulators in jurisdictions where Uber was operating illegally. Uber deployed the programme in American cities and in Europe, but also in Australia and South Korea. When the app detected a ride request from a likely regulator or cop – for example, users who spent a lot of time looking at the app at police stations – it played for them a phantom Uber experience, where they kept booking rides with Uber drivers who appeared on their screen and then suddenly cancelled.

Uber's strategy, like many of its tech brethren, was to dominate markets before regulators could crack down on it. The name of the game was to make yourself indispensable to consumers, who could then serve as a valuable political constituency, once they had become dependent on the convenience of ride sharing. Uber successfully deployed this political strategy against New York Mayor Bill de Blasio in 2015, when the mayor first tried to impose a cap on for-hire cars.

Uber enlisted its users in its lobbying campaign against De Blasio's new regulations. When people opened the app, they encountered a pop-up screen offering them a way to send a complaint against De Blasio's proposal directly to city hall. In political science terms, Uber figured out how to overcome the collective action problem of mobilizing those who wanted to act on its behalf, while lowering the cost of political protest almost to zero, by making the letter-writing process work easily through the app.

For many years, Big Tech companies counted on the tacit support of consumers, whose lives they had made much easier. With co-author Kathleen Thelen, Pepper has coined a term for this tacit support: platform power. And as the example of Uber shows, the alliance with consumers proved politically potent.

At least at first, platform power allowed tech companies to wield their influence on the cheap. In 2008, Facebook spent nothing on lobbying. But as the companies have become more politically controversial, and as the scale of their data collection became better known, the largest tech companies began to pour money into more traditional lobbying. We have already seen how much the tech companies spent on lobbying in Europe. They did not ignore their home country. By 2021, the lobbying expenditure of Facebook's parent Meta in the United States had reached $20 million per year.

Armed with both platform power and conventional lobbying muscle, Big Tech has successfully strangled repeated attempts at privacy regulation at the federal level in the United States. It's also worth mentioning that corporate lobbyists hold an unusual amount of power in the US, compared to other rich democracies, because of the lack of restrictions on spending for political campaigns. One recent estimate puts American campaign contributions at 50 times the size of European political contributions.

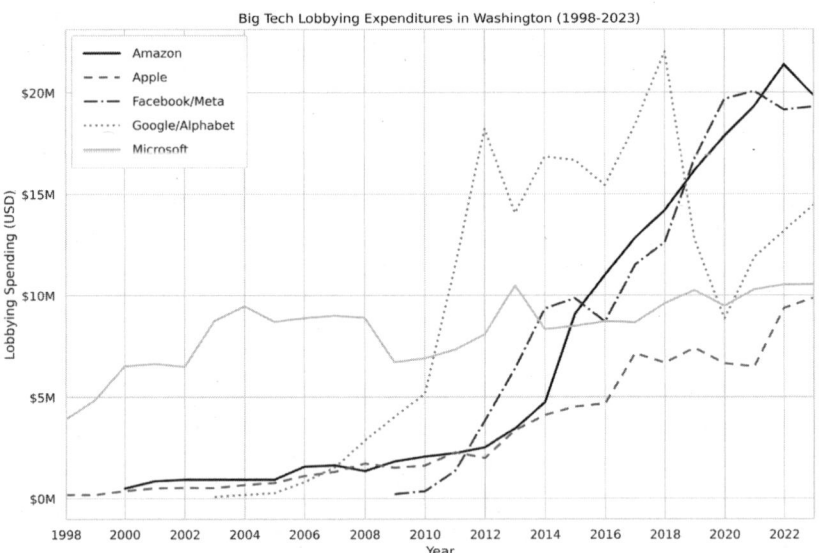

Big Tech lobbying expenditures for the US federal government over time. Source: OpenSecrets.

There is, however, a possible workaround for policy entrepreneurs stymied by political blockage and corporate influence in the United States. In the American federal system, each state has its own regulatory process. The existence of multiple points of regulatory authority in the American federal system multiplies the possibilities for activists like Alastair Mactaggart to get around the death grip that corporate lobbyists have on Washington DC.

Mactaggart had begun his campaign in California because the United States has no federal law on data protection. While the public outrage provoked by the PRISM scandal fuelled the passage of a strong privacy law in Europe, in the United States the effect was different. It turbocharged distrust between the Obama administration – on whose behalf the NSA had collected all the data that Edward Snowden leaked – and the Big Tech companies the scandal had painted as NSA stooges.

In Europe, citizens united with their political leaders in fury that a foreign government agency had been spying on them. On the other side of the Atlantic, the scandal deprived Obama's data privacy advocates of moral authority. The Snowden leaks showed that the American government had been collecting data from tech companies with one hand, while trying to write privacy regulations to bind tech companies with the other. The administration was torn between its supporters' calls for reform of privacy law and maintaining its relationship with Big Tech.

The relationship with Big Tech won. Rather than cracking down on technology companies after PRISM, the US government went on a charm offensive. Commerce Secretary Penny Pritzker led the charge. In 2012 Pritzker, the heiress to the Hyatt Hotel fortune, had served as the co-chair of Obama's re-election campaign. She toured Silicon Valley and reassured the American tech giants, from one billionaire to another, that the government had their backs.

And she delivered on that promise. When the administration wanted to release a draft consumer privacy bill of rights in tandem with a high-profile presidential address at the Federal Trade

Commission in January 2015, Pritzker demanded a delay for wide consultation with the tech industry and its lobbyists.

'Delay for wide consultation' is a synonym for 'weakening to satisfy industry'. The result of Pritzker's delay was a thorough defanging of the bill. By the time Obama sent the privacy bill to Congress in 2015, lobbyists had succeeded in reducing penalties and increasing exceptions across the board. The bill did not impose regulations on companies, but rather invited them to come up with their own rules and have those self-made rules approved by the Federal Trade Commission.

The compromise draft succeeded in uniting both privacy activists and Big Tech firms against it. One prominent privacy advocate railed that 'the President allowed the process to be hijacked by the Commerce Department which is more aligned with the data lobby than the American people.' Meanwhile, the lobbyists who had urged Pritzker to water the bill down thought it was still too drastic, warning of the threat to economic innovation in the United States. The bill was a guaranteed loser from the moment it was published, and it disappeared from public view without a trace.

That was the end of the American discussion over privacy regulation until 2018. Even in the sympathetic Obama White House, the lobbying muscle and economic heft of Big Tech was simply too much to overcome, at least in Washington.

On 17 March 2018, the *New York Times* and the London *Observer* broke the story that the British political consulting company Cambridge Analytica had harvested the data of tens of millions of Facebook users without their knowledge or consent.

How did it happen? In 2014, Cambridge University psychologist Aleksandr Kogan had created a personality test fielded in the form of a Facebook app, called This is Your Digital Life. Only 305,000 people had downloaded the app but, once installed, it hoovered up reams of information about people's Facebook friends. Even people who had never downloaded the app were not safe. If they had a Facebook friend with the app, their data went straight to Kogan.

Thanks to the network effects of Facebook friendship, Kogan's app captured the personal data of almost 90 million users.

The leak revealed the magic behind otherwise mediocre apps like Kogan's personality quiz. Facebook had been collecting jaw-dropping amounts of data on its users, and the company made that data available to app developers like Kogan. This information was of enormous value to anyone in advertising who wanted to target their message precisely.

Targeted advertising enables advertisers to deliver their messages straight to the people who will be most receptive, or vulnerable to, the pitch. Big pharma companies marketing weight-loss drugs might target those who have searched for diets online and who have a credit card history of ordering ice cream sundaes, for example. It's effective, but creepy.

Ian Bogost is a professor and video game designer who also writes for the *Atlantic* magazine. In 2010, Bogost developed a popular Facebook app called Cow Clicker. When the Cambridge Analytica scandal broke in 2018, he observed that 'if you played Cow Clicker, even just once, I got enough of your personal data that, for years, I could have assembled a reasonably sophisticated profile of your interests and behaviour.'

Political campaigns and the companies that work for them covet this sort of detailed knowledge of people's data. It was why Cambridge Analytica acquired Kogan's data. Cambridge Analytica boasted that it could use the information gleaned from Facebook to allow political campaigns to manipulate the behaviour of voters. Company executives claimed to have been behind Donald Trump's 'Defeat crooked Hillary' campaign message in 2016. A senior company executive was caught on tape saying, 'We just put information into the bloodstream of the internet and then watch it grow ... And so this stuff infiltrates the online community, but with no branding, so it's unattributable, untrackable.'

CEO Alexander Nix was a better salesman than he was a political campaigner, and there is no evidence his company affected any election outcomes. But Trump's election victory in 2016 nevertheless gave the Cambridge Analytica story an overtly political angle. Many people don't care about the privacy of their data in the abstract. But the 2018 revelations linked Facebook's reckless disregard for consumer privacy directly to a company specializing in the dark arts of micro-targeting voters in close elections. It created a scandal that ricocheted around the world's democracies, many of whose citizens' data had been leaked in the affair. But in no country was the effect more explosive than in the United States, home to both Facebook and the largest number of people affected by the data leak.

Public trust in Facebook collapsed after the Cambridge Analytica scandal broke. In June 2018 – three months after the outbreak of the scandal – Georgetown University commissioned the American Institutional Confidence Poll to measure the state of American public opinion. The poll asked 5,400 Americans about their confidence in 20 major institutions, including the technology companies Amazon, Google and Facebook. Amazon and Google were near the top of the list, meaning many people trusted them. The only institution that outscored them in the trust of the American public was the military.

Facebook sat third from bottom – meaning most people distrusted it. It was less trusted than banks and organized labour. In the court of public opinion only political parties and Congress fared worse. By the time the poll was repeated in 2021, Facebook had fallen below even those two reviled institutions. A separate survey that month reported that Americans believed that technology companies should be regulated more heavily.

It is tempting to attribute the public's disapproval of Facebook directly to the Cambridge Analytica scandal. But as political scientists, we know that correlation is not causation. Just because confidence in Facebook fell far below that of Amazon and Google, and then below even that of Congress, does not mean the Cambridge Analytica scandal caused that drop-off. Furthermore, low confidence is not the same as demand to regulate the excesses of tech companies.

To test that connection between scandal and regulatory politics, we returned to a survey experiment. In Chapter 3, if you remember, we showed how survey experiments work in the same way as a medical drug trial. We start by inviting a representative sample of the population. We then randomly assign those who accept to two groups, each asked to read one of two different news articles. One reads an article with no content related to a tech scandal. This is the placebo group. The second reads an article about the Cambridge Analytica scandal. Any difference between the groups in their appetite to regulate technology companies can be attributed to reading about the scandal.

In 2023, five years after the scandal broke out, we conducted a large survey experiment to see whether media coverage of it would affect public opinion. We blended coverage from the *New York Times* and the *Observer/Guardian* – the two newspapers that broke the original Cambridge Analytica story – into a summary article about Facebook's role in the scandal and the subsequent legal challenges. We compared their views with those of the second group, whose members had read an unrelated article about Office Depot, a well-known but innocuous company.

What we found was that reading a single news article about the Cambridge Analytica scandal – five years after the scandal actually became known to the public – increased the demand of Americans for stricter regulation of tech companies. It also increased their perception of the importance of regulating technology. Social science and common sense thus converge on the finding that the Cambridge Analytica scandal made people want tighter regulation of the tech sector.

Alastair Mactaggart and his neighbour Rick Arney didn't need our survey experiment to understand the effect of the Cambridge Analytica scandal on public opinion. When we left them earlier in this chapter, they had just discovered that the largest tech companies were pouring money into an advertising campaign to defeat their ballot initiative on privacy.

Mactaggart was funding the campaign on his own, having little success raising outside money. Meanwhile, he needed to pay canvassers to go out and collect signatures to secure enough signatures to get his measure on the ballot. Mactaggart is a multimillionaire, so he had the resources to hire people to help him collect signatures. But even multimillionaires wince at the amount of money it takes to run an activist campaign without deep-pocketed financial backers. 'I am writing hundreds of thousand-dollar checks, every two weeks', said Mactaggart, for whom the prospect of failure was ever-present. 'Still to this day, I'll never forget the stupid hold music on Wells Fargo, where you had to type in your PIN. And you had to repeat that phrase, "My voice gives me access to proceed." I almost felt like throwing up every time I dialled in to send the money, because it was just terrible. I was terrified.'

Then the Cambridge Analytica scandal hit.

'Hey, I caught a break here – ray of hope', Mactaggart reflected. 'Smart people thought, "Oh, there's an issue here now." And it helped in the legislature because people started paying attention to it.'

For Arney, who was still trying to secure enough signatures to get the initiative on the ballot, the scandal presented an unanticipated gift. Canvassers no longer had to explain why a long-shot initiative measure on privacy was worth supporting. In Arney's words, 'after the Cambridge Analytica scandal, all we had to do was say "data privacy".'

Ultimately the group collected 629,000 signatures – far more than it needed – which meant the measure would be put to a vote of all Californians in the autumn of 2018. Only Mactaggart could withdraw it. With the popular wind in his sails, he had become a kingmaker. California lawmakers scurried to cut a deal with him.

At about the time the Cambridge Analytica scandal broke, Mactaggart had met Bob Hertzberg, a state senator who had previously been a speaker of the California Assembly. Mactaggart was not overwhelmed at first. 'I thought all of his proposals were just hot air, because he kept on being like, "We'll take this off the ballot. You can get your signatures. There's a provision where you can negotiate with us. We'll pass the law."' Battle-hardened by several months of campaigning, Mactaggart was sceptical about the prospects of the captured California legislature passing a privacy law with teeth. But he also doubted he had the resources to win a campaign against the deep pockets of Google and Facebook. 'At the time, I still thought it was like, a no per cent chance that we're going to get this thing done with the legislature. If I could avoid the fight, that would be great. And by this point, I was pretty sure I was going to lose, just because I'm having zero success raising money.'

With both sides worried they might lose, the haggling began. Mactaggart gave the legislature a deadline of 28 June, the last possible day on which he could withdraw his initiative from the ballot for November, to pass its law.

During the bargaining, Mactaggart got most of what he wanted from the lawmakers in the California State Assembly. But he did concede one important point from his initiative to the tech lobbyists. Consumers would not be able to take companies to court directly for breaches of their privacy. This ability to sue was called the private right of action. Big Tech hated it, and now it was gone.

Mactaggart the businessman thought that was a deal worth making. 'We went back and forth. In the course of that, it transpired that they were willing to give me "See your actual data" and "Delete your data". And in return for that they wanted [me] to give up the private right of action. So I was like, "That is a pretty good trade, frankly."' Mactaggart had only included the private right of action on the suggestion of his attorney, who helped him draft the initiative. 'I really didn't think about it very much. I'm really not a lawsuit guy. I'm a business guy. So viscerally I didn't love it. But then I thought, "Hey, these are big companies. And the average person is not going to have the money to sue them. So, sure, throw one in."'

That decision had given him a valuable bargaining chip with the tech companies, who conceded on other privacy issues to get rid of a sweeping private right of action. With that important change, the bill – the California Consumer Privacy Act (CCPA) – passed the legislature unanimously on 28 June, Mactaggart's deadline. California immediately became the national leader in privacy regulation in the US.

The story did not end there, however. In the heated negotiations over the final bill, the lobbyists for the Big Tech companies had inserted a little-remarked amendment to the law. They exempted 'service providers' from the restrictions on using individual data. Once the law passed, Facebook and the other large tech companies immediately claimed that the 'service' they were providing their paying customers was microtargeted advertisements. They were therefore not constrained by the law.

'I caught a bunch of the things they were trying to do, but I didn't catch that one', conceded Mactaggart. The tech companies similarly took advantage of the law's prohibition on the 'sale' of personal data by saying that websites people visited in a Google search were simply 'sharing' the data with Google, not 'selling' the data to them.

Moreover, because the measure passed as a law and not an initiative, it could be changed by amendment. That was another thing that Alastair Mactaggart had not seen coming. 'Oh, now I understand why they let me do this', he recalled, speaking of the tech companies and the politicians that did their bidding in the California Assembly. 'Because they introduced like 37 amendments that would have just crushed the thing. And I'm sitting there fighting, fighting, fighting, fighting. I spent so much time in Sacramento, so much time in committees.'

Bob Hertzberg was now the majority leader of the state Senate, so Mactaggart had powerful allies. But the tech companies were wearing Mactaggart down. 'I was able to stop a bunch of bad laws in 2019, but it became really apparent to me: "I am screwed. I can't do this. I can't keep this pace up".'

Most of the time, when big company lobbyists render a law toothless by inserting loopholes and amendments, they win. The legislature and the public shift their attention to other subjects, and corporations easily bypass the restrictions in the watered-down law. This is why big companies pay big bucks for lobbying.

That indeed was Mactaggart's view of how he got his law passed in 2018. 'My ex-post view of things is that in 2018, Big Tech looked at this [CCPA] and thought, "OK, we're getting rid of the private right of action. We don't have to spend a hundred million dollars, we don't have the reputational hit of spending against privacy post-Cambridge Analytica. And you know what? We'll clean this up next year, because we own Sacramento.'"

But Facebook and Google and their allies had misjudged the depth of the public's anger after the Cambridge Analytica scandal. And they had underestimated the determination of Alastair Mactaggart. More than half a million people had signed the petition for Mactaggart's original ballot initiative, and many of them were still mad.

Mactaggart sat down and wrote a new ballot measure – this one was 52 pages long – to overcome the shortcomings of the CCPA. The new ballot measure was known as Proposition 24, the California Privacy Rights Act (CPRA). It went to the voters in November 2020.

The CPRA fixed three weaknesses of the previous law: loopholes, enforcement and vulnerability to being diluted by subsequent lobbying. It closed the two loopholes on sales and service providers, clarifying that the ban on selling data applied to the 'sharing' of data between companies, and that 'service providers' were subject to the law's strictures on treatment of personal data. It also expanded the limited right of private action of the CCPA.

In addition, the 2020 measure created a new regulatory body charged with enforcing the law, the California Privacy Protection Agency (CPPA). And finally, in a move intended to send shivers down the spines of lobbyists everywhere, the CPRA included a measure that the initiative could not be weakened by amendment. Its measures to secure digital privacy could only be strengthened.

Proposition 24 passed easily on 3 November 2020, with 56 per cent of Californians voting in favour. The CPRA took effect at the beginning of 2023, giving consumers in California levels of protection roughly equivalent to those afforded by the GDPR in Europe.

The Cambridge Analytica scandal had resulted in a sustained collapse of public confidence in big technology companies in the US. The titanic tech companies thought they would simply crush the initiative of Mactaggart and his band of activists. But they ran straight into the iceberg of a distrustful public, enabling Mactaggart to get the CCPA passed in 2018. When he realized his law would be amended to death, he went back to the people of California with another measure in 2020. And he won a convincing victory against the billionaires of Silicon Valley.

The story of Alastair Mactaggart and Big Tech in California is a privacy geek's version of *Star Wars – A New Hope*, with Mactaggart in the role of Luke Skywalker. Plucky businessman takes on the assembled ranks of the Big Tech empire. Fighting with only a motley bunch of friends and no big money supporters beyond himself – though Mactaggart spent at least $9 million of his own money – he gets a law passed that imposes real limits on the Big Tech companies. The story is not as exciting as *Star Wars*, but it's way more consequential.

Mactaggart has Jedi-like confidence in the example that California sets for the rest of the country. 'Probably the most important theory I've been operating on, which has luckily come true: if I could get something done in California, it would probably spread to the rest of the country. That would be the thin edge of the wedge and would hopefully start a movement. And that has totally happened.'

Readers will recall that the next episode of the *Star Wars* saga is *The Empire Strikes Back*. And that is more or less what happened when other states tried to follow the example of California and adopt their own privacy laws. Big Tech was aware of the danger of laws diffusing from California to other states and becoming a de facto national standard. Just like the galactic empire of George Lucas, the tech companies and their lobbyists went on the offensive. Their goal: to keep California from becoming a model for other states.

Every time legislators from other states wanted to adopt significant new privacy legislation, storm troopers funded by the tech sector came in and killed the bill. Those same storm troopers – by which we mean lobbyists – proposed weaker texts, broadly supported by the industry, that posed few real constraints for large tech companies.

After the defeat in California, the tech companies decided that if they were going to have rules, they wanted to write those rules themselves. They chose Virginia – right across the Potomac River from the nation's capital – as the next battleground. In March 2021,

Virginia would become the second state to adopt privacy legislation. Amazon, which has established a second headquarters in Virginia, actually drafted the Virginia bill, as acknowledged by state senator David Marsden, who introduced the legislation. Both Microsoft and Amazon testified publicly in favour of the bill. The tech firms had deliberately chosen Virginia as an alternative model to California. The bill contained no right to private action, no universal opt-out possibility and weak enforcement measures.

Ashkan Soltani worked with Alastair Mactaggart on the California measures. He was the first executive director of the regulatory agency the law created in California, the CPPA. As Virginia was passing its bill, Soltani made his view clear: 'The effort to push through weaker bills is to demonstrate to businesses and to Congress that there are weaker options', he said in a 2021 interview. 'Nobody saw Virginia coming. That was very much an industry-led effort by Microsoft and Amazon.'

The tech companies have since continued to push the adoption of the 'business-friendly' Virginia model as states around the country deliberate about privacy. They have also tried to kill harsher bills modelled on California's law, including in North Dakota and Florida. In Connecticut, the Senate majority leader introduced a strong bill in 2020, which included a private right of action. At the bill's public hearing, he saw that the room was 'literally filled with every single lobbyist I've ever known in Hartford [the state capital], hired by companies to defeat the bill.' That bill died, as did its successor the following year. When Connecticut finally adopted a privacy bill in 2023, it was explicitly modelled on the weak Virginia law, though it had been somewhat strengthened.

That story would repeat itself in one state after another. Jennifer Lee, the technology policy lead for the American Civil Liberties Union in the state of Washington, underlined how outside California privacy advocates have been thoroughly outgunned. 'It's been this coordinated national push to advance really weak privacy bills. We've definitely felt outnumbered. They have tremendous resources and time to really influence the conversations happening in the legislature.' California has a significant new online privacy law, and some states like Colorado have adopted laws with tough enforcement measures. But at least at the time of writing, the second round of the state legislation fight has gone in favour of Big Tech.

The big prize for the tech companies would be federal legislation that pre-empts Mactaggart's law, effectively prohibiting California from imposing stricter measures on the tech firms. Such a law was proposed in 2022, but scuttled by fierce opposition from California lawmakers, including then-Speaker of the House Nancy Pelosi. A 2024 bill never made it out of committee. For now, the California law has escaped the threat of federal pre-emption.

Ironically, privacy advocates once wanted to pass a federal law, and the tech companies blocked them. Now, many of those advocates fear a federal law will be used as a 'wolf in sheep's clothing' to invalidate the law that California has adopted.

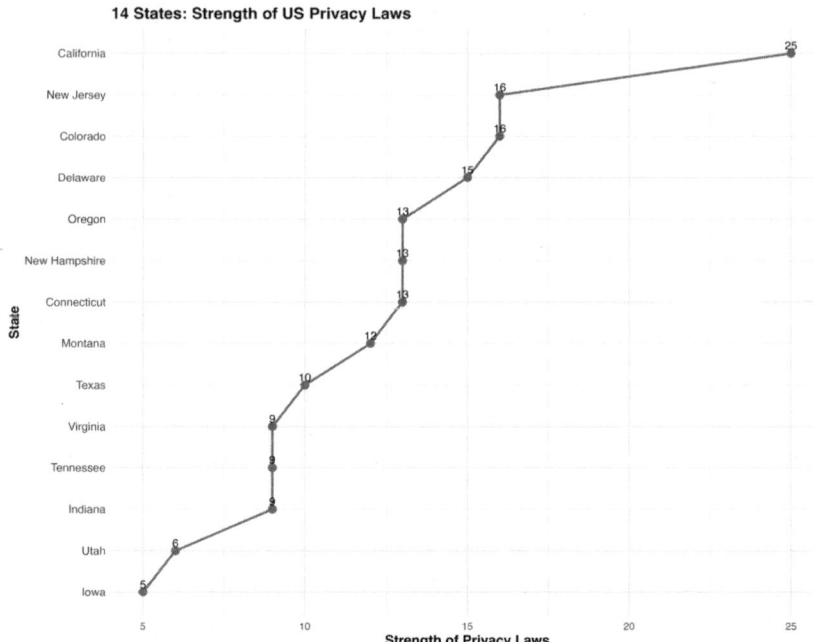

State privacy laws compared by their inclusion of various stringent features, such as private right of action and limits on data collection by companies, as of 2024. Source: Electronic Privacy Information Center.

Federal pre-emption sits at the top of Alastair Mactaggart's list of concerns about the future of privacy regulation – 'that somehow Big Tech is able to do an end-around and go to DC and get them to sign something that looks like a sheep, but is actually a wolf'. Yet, having seen how the original *Star Wars* trilogy finishes, Mactaggart remains upbeat, despite seeing the tech firms having success in so many other states. 'Other states passing laws that are also [wolves in sheep's clothing], that's not great. But I do think that long-term, that turns around. I think California is so big, it's one in eight Americans. I think . . . there's a gravitational pull towards the most restrictive laws, because do you really want to have a bunch of different standards? So my hope is that businesses will probably just [say], "If I could just meet California's requirements, I know I'm good."'

All the companies people mean when they say 'Big Tech' have their global headquarters in the United States. And in their home country those corporations have been able to use their economic power and lobbying dollars to minimize rules they oppose. But while Big Tech still commands enormous power in Washington, in the aftermath of the Cambridge Analytica scandal American public opinion has hardened against it. The political sentiment against large technology companies resonates on both the left and the right, despite the deep polarization that currently besets American politics. And outside the den of dysfunction known as the US Congress, that bipartisan disapproval of Big Tech has created consequences.

When Democratic President Joe Biden's administration came to office in 2021, it used the existing tools of competition and antitrust law to push back against Big Tech. Biden issued an executive order that broadened the terms under which regulators could pursue antitrust actions. The executive order observed that 'excessive market concentration threatens basic economic liberties, democratic accountability and the welfare of workers, farmers, small businesses, start-ups and consumers'. This order set the stage for the Federal Trade Commission (FTC) and the Department of

Justice (DoJ) to challenge the abuses of market power by the largest tech companies.

After years of going soft on its tech firms, the United States in 2021 appointed creative and aggressive enforcers of existing antitrust law. Lina Khan, Biden's head of the FTC, has been an activist on tech concentration since her days as a student at Yale Law School. While still a law student, she published an influential article that took American antitrust law to task for its woeful inadequacies in dealing with a retailer like Amazon. The argument was that law enforcement ignored Amazon's market power as long as it was good for consumers.

At the FTC, Khan pushed through a culture change that reoriented the agency to focus on problems of economic power, and not merely consumer benefit. Several of her decisions led to court challenges from tech companies, but she successfully prevented AI-chipmaker Nvidia from taking over the chip designer ARM for $40 billion.

Khan's counterpart at the Department of Justice was Jonathan Kanter, the assistant attorney general responsible for antitrust. Kanter came into the office with a long record as a critic of Big Tech. He brought memorable taglines to his initiatives at the department, calling his plan to investigate corporate executives the 'Billionaire Accountability Project'.

Working closely with Khan's FTC, Kanter invigorated the DoJ's enforcement of antitrust policy. In August 2024, Kanter won a landmark case against Google. The 268-page decision ruled that Google was a monopolist that had used side deals with Apple and other companies to protect its search engine dominance. In 2022, for example, Google had paid Apple $20 billion to ensure its search engine was the default on the iPhone's Safari web browser.

In April 2025, the DoJ won a second antitrust case against Google, as the court ruled that the search giant 'wilfully engaged in a series of anticompetitive acts to acquire and maintain monopoly power' in parts of the digital advertising market. The Justice Department is also suing Apple, accusing the company of designing an ecosystem for its iPhone that violates antitrust law. The FTC, meanwhile, has separately sued Meta and Khan's old nemesis Amazon. As Jonathan Kanter said in a 2024 interview, 'the current movement about corporate power and antitrust, it's not coming from us. It's coming from the people, right? And so we are being responsive to the demands of the people.'

With the election of Donald Trump in November 2024, Kanter and Khan were both out of a job. Khan's successor as FTC chair, Andrew Ferguson, came into office saying he would 'end Lina Khan's politically motivated investigations', while at the same time promising to keep up the pressure on monopolies in Big Tech. Gail Slater, who succeeded Kanter at DoJ, has a record of supporting antitrust measures against the biggest tech companies. However, the heads of the largest tech companies publicly allied themselves with President Trump. When he was inaugurated as president in 2025 they sat immediately behind him.

That fealty has this far bought them little. The cleavage over supporting Big Tech cuts straight through the Trump administration, and both the FTC and Justice Department continue to challenge Big Tech. Despite intense lobbying of the new president by Mark Zuckerberg himself, the new FTC chair Ferguson brought to trial the antitrust suit begun by Khan against Meta. The bipartisan popular pushback against the monopoly power of Silicon Valley appears to have survived the transition to President Trump.

We may be academics, but we are not naïve. Pepper has spent his entire academic career studying how business exercises influence in politics. He has challenged political scientists who engage in mystical thinking to try to show that the desire of politicians to attract the median voter in electorates will somehow overwhelm the money and economic power of the largest companies. Business, both collectively and individually, wins in politics far more than it loses. Politicians have many reasons, even beyond campaign contributions, to favour economic powerhouses that create innovation and jobs. As long as the public doesn't care about issues of economic regulation, those rules will reflect the interests of dominant companies. That is how democracies work.

But when the public does start to care about such issues, the world can change. That is why corporate scandals can have such a convulsive effect on politics. They draw public attention to an issue and accentuate shifts in public opinion that may have been ongoing for some time. They are one of the few forces capable of upsetting the comfortable capture of government by large corporations. This corporate capture is the fat that blocks the arteries of legislatures in most contemporary democracies.

After the Cambridge Analytica scandal, the public demanded that governments do something about Big Tech. Facebook and Google and their tech bros spent big on lobbying to try to ride out the storm, hoping some other issue would displace them from the headlines. That did not happen, on either side of the Atlantic. In fact, the scandal even gave birth to a new word. In 2018, 'techlash' – a portmanteau of technology and backlash – was shortlisted as word of the year.

Even so, in Washington money talks, and a paralysed Congress has played to the advantage of the tech companies that at first wanted to avoid federal privacy regulation. It was at state level that Alastair Mactaggart and his ragtag band of reformers found a way to convert the Techlash into the toughest privacy legislation in the United States.

As we wrapped up our interview with Mactaggart, we asked him what he had learned from his experience in California about the process of regulation. His answer was sobering. 'Money is even more powerful than I thought it was. And I'm a guy who's a real estate developer. Trust me, I understood how important it was to raise money. What I hadn't really realized is just the unlimited potential for regulatory capture at every stage of the way, in the normal course of business in a democracy.'

PART THREE
When Scandals Fail

6

#ExxonKnew

In September and October 2015, *Inside Climate News* (ICN) published a six-part exposé on ExxonMobil and climate science. The series of reports used internal company documents and interviews with former employees to show that Exxon had developed sophisticated models of climate change as early as the 1970s. Those models confirmed the scientific consensus around human-generated climate change and in 1977 communicated that message to senior management. One year later – in 1978 – a senior Exxon scientist told the company that 'present thinking holds that man has a time window of five to ten years before the need for hard decisions regarding changes in energy strategies might become critical.'

However, despite the warnings from its own scientists, from the 1980s Exxon had deliberately sown doubt about the certainty of climate science. The uncertainty campaign reached its climax in 2001, when Exxon's lobbying helped persuade the new administration of the former Texas oilman, President George W. Bush, to withdraw the United States from the Kyoto Protocol, the international treaty committing countries to fight global warming.

Inside Climate News is a small non-profit news organization based in New York. Its story scooped the much larger *Los Angeles Times*, which ran its own story on Exxon's deliberate obfuscation of climate science on 9 October 2015. ICN's story was a Pulitzer Prize finalist. Together, the two publications provided detailed and

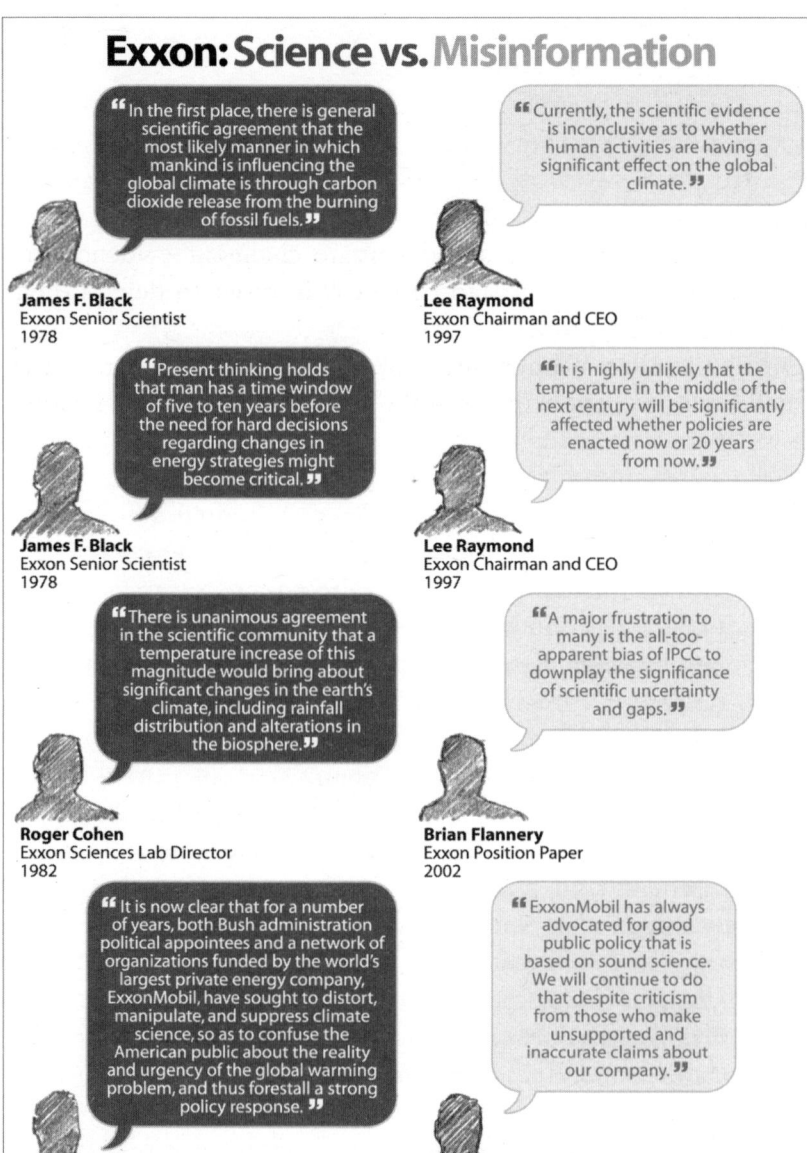

Picture from the Inside Climate News *story on the Exxon strategy of challenging climate science.*

credible evidence of the cover-up that critics had been alleging about the oil giant for years.

For Sheldon Whitehouse, a US senator from Rhode Island, this was the smoking gun he'd long been searching for. The reports supported the claims that Whitehouse had been making for years, that ExxonMobil and the other big oil companies had been undermining scientific evidence about climate change – evidence the companies themselves knew to be true – in order to defend their ability to make big profits.

On 27 October, Whitehouse took to the Senate floor to rouse his colleagues to action in the wake of the revelations of Exxon's deceit. 'There is a moment in combat', said Whitehouse, quoting Napoleon,

> when the slightest manoeuvre is decisive and gives superiority; it is the drop of water that starts the overflow. Is the tide turning, Mr President? Despite documented warnings from their own scientists dating from the 1970s, ExxonMobil pursued a strategy of deceit, denial and delay. They may soon have to face the consequences.

A decade on from those revelations, Senator Whitehouse is still waiting for those consequences to move American public opinion. The scandal, which trended on Twitter under the hashtag #ExxonKnew, sank without leaving a visible trace on American climate policy.

Senator Whitehouse was used to taking on thuggish opponents. He had made his name as a prosecutor for the federal government. Rhode Island's capital city, Providence, is famous for its history of organized crime connections to the Patriarca family, as chronicled in the first season of the hit podcast *Crimetown*. Whitehouse's first criminal conviction was of Gerard Ouimette, one of the longtime lieutenants of the Patriarca family. He also initiated the investigation that led to the conviction of six-term Providence Mayor Vincent 'Buddy' Cianci for racketeering.

By the time Whitehouse was elected to the Senate in 2006, his focus had shifted from cleaning up Providence to cleaning up the planet. The issue of climate change had come to his attention when his wife, Sandra, was a doctoral student in marine biology at the University of Rhode Island in the 1980s.

'I remember one of the first wake-up calls I got was talking to one of her professors', Whitehouse said in a 2013 interview.

> He was talking about the warming of Narragansett Bay, and it was just a few degrees. So I scoffed and I said, 'You know, I can't tell the difference between sixty-three and sixty-five degrees [Fahrenheit] when I jump in. That doesn't sound like it's a very big deal.' And he said, 'Well, that's because you don't live in those waters . . . This is an ecosystem shift happening.'

Sandra was working on the life cycle of winter flounder in the Narragansett Bay. 'That was important research', Whitehouse continued, 'because the winter flounder was such an important cash crop for fishermen trawling in the bay. When my wife was doing her research, it was one of the most important fisheries [in Rhode Island]. And now it's virtually gone – it's down I think nearly ninety per cent.'

Right from the start, Whitehouse understood that the risks of climate change were economic as well as existential. In his first year in the Senate he sponsored three major climate bills. At the time, Whitehouse was a voice in the wilderness, as Congress repeatedly ducked climate bills. Whitehouse thought he knew why: the oil companies were peddling fake science to both lawmakers and the American people.

For the next eight years, there was a recurrent pattern in the US Senate. Sheldon Whitehouse would speak in favour of acting on climate change. Bills would look like they might pass. Then, after a lobbying blitz, nothing would happen.

Whitehouse accused his Democratic colleagues of being intimidated from even talking about climate change. In 2012, he began

Senator Sheldon Whitehouse making one of his 'Time to Wake Up' speeches in the Senate.

a series of regular speeches to the Senate called 'Time to Wake Up'. He often gave these talks to an empty chamber, with just the CSPAN television cameras for company. 'I just decided, look, we're not going to stop talking about climate change in this place.'

In mobilizing public opinion against the oil companies, Sheldon Whitehouse faced a more difficult problem than his Senate colleague Carl Levin, whom we met in Chapter 3. Levin was dealing with financial regulation, which is a 'hard issue' – that is, an issue voters have to puzzle through before knowing where they stand. Levin was trying to get the American people to understand that Goldman Sachs was betting against its own clients. Democrats and Republicans both learned something in that episode, and they were both outraged. Levin translated a hard issue into an easy one.

Climate policy is as technically complex as financial regulation. But it is not what political scientists call a 'hard issue', at least not in the United States. The issue has long been on the political agenda, and Republicans and Democrats have clear and strongly divergent views about it. In 2024, 83 per cent of Americans said they understand global warming 'very' or 'fairly' well. Only half of people gave equivalent answers for financial regulation, as we saw in Chapter 3.

When people say they understand climate change 'very' or 'fairly' well, they are not taking a science test. They are responding to a public opinion survey. When they answer this question, their 'knowledge' is really their certainty in what they know. Climate change is a fact. But there are people who do not accept the current scientific consensus on climate change, and yet are nevertheless confident that their own understanding is the correct one.

Americans are unusual in this respect. We know, because in 2023 we conducted our own survey of climate change attitudes. It was a very large survey of 36,000 people, and we didn't survey only Americans. We also surveyed British, French and German voters. Our survey showed two particularly interesting things about American attitudes towards climate change.

First, on average, Americans are not that different from voters in other countries in what they want from climate change policies. They want a little more such regulation than do German voters, and a little bit less than British voters. More Americans strongly oppose *any* climate change measures than do residents of any of the other three countries, but the average American wants about the same amount of climate change regulation as the average French person.

We also asked people in our survey how certain they were that they knew enough about the issue of environmental regulation to state an opinion. On this question, Americans scored far higher than voters from any other country we surveyed.

That is our second important finding. Americans are not exceptional in what they *think* about climate change and the environment. But they are exceptional in how *certain* they are that they understand the issue well enough to have an opinion about it.

This is the sense in which climate change is an 'easy' issue for most American voters. They know what they think, and they do not need more information to come to a view about it.

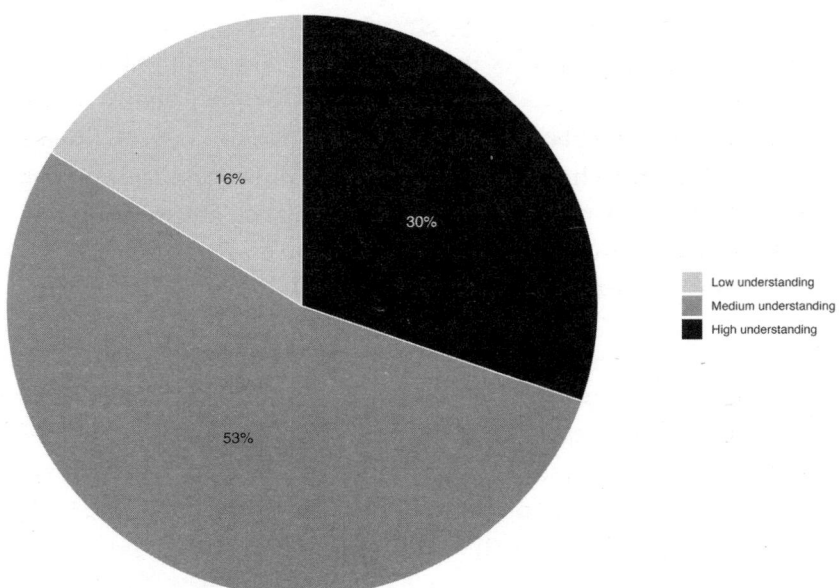

*How well Americans say they understand the issue of climate change.
Source: Gallup.*

Sheldon Whitehouse therefore had a different problem from Carl Levin's. Instead of trying to teach Americans something they didn't know, he was trying to convince them that what he thought about Big Oil was what they should think about Big Oil. He wanted to persuade the American people that fossil fuel companies were bullying Republicans into opposing climate change measures that those Republicans secretly favoured. 'The dirty secret is that climate change is not really a partisan issue in Congress', he would write in the *Washington Post*.

Like most Americans, Whitehouse was certain about his views on climate change. He was also certain that the American public and his Republican colleagues agreed with him about the urgency of legislative action to fight climate change. He was convinced, as are many Americans who want to adopt more aggressive policies to reduce carbon emissions, that the big oil companies were the only thing standing in the way.

Senator Whitehouse was wrong about that. It is certainly true, as Whitehouse says, that fossil fuel companies exert strong sway over politicians. But oil company influence is not the only reason Republicans and Democrats in Congress disagree about climate change. Democratic and Republican *politicians* disagree at least in part because their *voters* disagree, both about the risk posed by climate change and the policies that should be adopted to deal with it.

It was not always this way. As late as 1992, Republican and Democratic voters had indistinguishable views about climate change. Voters for the two parties were equally worried about the effects of climate change and equally likely to believe that the effects of global warming had already begun. At that time, climate change was still a 'hard' issue for Americans. Only half of voters in 1992 said they understood the issue of global warming, as it was then called, 'very' or 'fairly' well.

Since the 1990s, however, public opinion has followed the consistently partisan messages that politicians have been sending. Compared with Democratic voters, Republican voters have become much more sceptical of climate science and less favourable towards federal spending on climate change policies. The environment went from being among the least polarized issues in 1992 to the most polarized by 2015.

When a corporate scandal involves a 'hard' issue, whether regulating banks or technology companies, it has a good chance of activating widespread public anger and, ultimately, forcing policy change. As Sheldon Whitehouse was about to find out, a corporate scandal involving an 'easy' issue is a much harder sell.

In May 2015, Whitehouse landed on a new strategy for fighting the fossil fuel companies. In an opinion article published in the *Washington Post*, he proposed that the government use the same racketeering statute – RICO – that had sent Providence Mayor Buddy Cianci to jail, to go after fossil fuel companies for their conspiracy to mislead American regulators and citizens.

There was even precedent for using the RICO law against big companies accused of coordinated deception. In 2006, the major American tobacco companies had been convicted of a massive fraud against the public. The lawsuit had revealed the extent of the companies' decades-long, coordinated campaign to 'spread doubt about the real science' of how smoking affects human health. The big cigarette companies were found guilty of running a deception racket.

Whitehouse bears all the hallmarks of the policy entrepreneurs we have seen throughout this book, who seize on a scandal to push through game-changing new rules. He was willing to expend serious energy pushing his cause single-mindedly, against the objection and eye-rolling of many of his Senate colleagues. He knew the importance of continuing to talk about the issue until the public paid attention. He even had a set of legal remedies ready to pursue. He was just waiting for the right scandal to strike.

For a very short while after the #ExxonKnew scandal first came to light, it appeared that Whitehouse was winning. 'Sheldon Whitehouse got his man' was the first line of a *Wall Street Journal* opinion article in November 2015 about the legal investigations opened by New York attorney general Eric Schneiderman in response to the revelations.

The opinion page of the *Wall Street Journal* is considered to be on the political right. The article expressed a worry of many on the American right when it denounced the use of lawsuits to 'stamp out disagreement' on the science and policy of climate change.

Though there would be more of them, the lawsuits would go nowhere. The United States public did not rise up and demand accountability from Exxon for the duplicity of its climate science uncertainty campaign; neither, thus far, has the American judicial system. Indeed, the oil giant continued to rake in monster profits every year since the revelations, except the pandemic year of 2020. And climate change policies continued to stall in the United States Congress.

Some people were scandalized by the #ExxonKnew revelations. But these were predominantly from the political left. Sheldon Whitehouse thought that once the climate deception of Exxon was revealed to the American people, the grip of oil companies on the system would break down. But he had misdiagnosed the problem.

The problem was not that Republican voters and lawmakers did not *know* what Exxon was doing. The problem was that they did not *care*, because they hold starkly different beliefs than Democrats about the desirability of stronger policies to fight climate change.

That, in a nutshell, is why it is so much harder for corporate scandals to change public opinion on 'easy' issues than on 'hard' issues.

In 2015, against this background of polarized American opinion, the #ExxonKnew scandal failed to create a story about Exxon that was shared by voters across the partisan divide. For Sheldon Whitehouse and some of his Democratic allies, the scandal showed that Exxon had been at least duplicitous, and at worst fraudulent. The oil giant had generated scientific research that modelled global warming accurately while emphasizing to the public that the science about climate change was uncertain.

For Republicans, however, the scandal was no scandal at all. It was an attack on big companies and free speech. Former Florida Senator Marco Rubio, who was running for president in the 2016 Republican primaries, met a young university student when campaigning in New Hampshire in January. She asked him if he supported an investigation of Exxon by the Department of Justice in the wake of the revelations of the scandal.

'No, I don't. That's nothing but a left-wing effort to demonize industries in America', Rubio replied. Before moving on to the next voter, he added, 'We're not going to prosecute people who don't believe in climate change.'

At a New Hampshire Town Hall meeting back in October 2015 the presumptive Democratic candidate, Hillary Clinton, had answered a similar question very differently. When asked whether Exxon should be investigated, she responded, 'Yes, yes, they should. There's a lot of evidence they misled people.'

In the midst of a fraught election year, Loretta Lynch, the attorney general for the Obama administration, faced the delicate question of whether to open a legal investigation of ExxonMobil, as Senator Whitehouse and some of his Democratic colleagues in Congress had demanded. Predictably, Republicans bridled at reports that Lynch was even considering an investigation. In March, a group of five senators, including Ted Cruz from Texas, wrote to her to insist that she desist immediately from any investigations into whether oil and gas companies had lied about the risks of climate change, either to the public or to their shareholders. For Republicans, the issue had become one of freedom of speech, not fraud.

Attorney General Lynch parked her investigation. However, some state attorneys general – all from reliably Democratic-voting states – did take cases against ExxonMobil to court. New York, Massachusetts and California have all sued ExxonMobil for fraud and deception about the risks posed by climate change. Several of these cases will be ongoing for years, but none has yet succeeded, at least so far. In court, as in the court of public opinion, the #ExxonKnew scandal has not yet resulted in the censuring of Exxon.

Protestors in front of the New York Supreme Court in 2019. The court ruled in favour of Exxon.

That was only the beginning of the disappointment for Sheldon Whitehouse. Just over a year after the scandal came to light, Donald Trump was elected president of the United States for the first time. The Trump administration opposed climate change legislation and in June 2017 withdrew the United States from the Paris climate agreement. For the next four years the climate change agenda languished in the US Congress.

For Whitehouse and the other Democratic critics of #ExxonKnew, Trump's appointment of Rex Tillerson as Secretary of State added insult to injury. To accept the position, Tillerson had to resign from his previous job: CEO of ExxonMobil.

After four years of shouting into the void, the arrival of Joe Biden in the White House in 2021 gave the Rhode Island senator renewed reason to hope. In January, the United States rejoined the Paris agreement within hours of Biden taking office. In the 2020 elections, Democrats had retaken both the House and the Senate, though only by the smallest of margins. The Senate was tied 50–50, giving the tie-breaking vote to Democratic Vice President Kamala Harris. This slim majority control meant that the Republicans would no longer be able to block climate bills from being voted on in the Senate.

One week after Biden's inauguration Whitehouse gave his 279th 'Time to Wake Up' speech on the floor of the Senate, announcing that it would be his final speech on the subject. 'A new dawn is breaking, and there's no need for my little candle against the darkness – my little pilot light can now go out.' And he theatrically punctuated his final speech with a mic drop.

The moral of this story is: don't drop your mic before your carbon is taxed.

Economists typically propose two approaches to decarbonization, through negative or positive incentives. The first entails pricing carbon through either taxes or an emissions trading system, in which polluters buy and sell emissions permits. The second creates economic incentives for companies to invest in renewable energy sources.

Whitehouse, along with many advocates for strong action on climate change, believes that carbon pricing is the most effective way to bring down carbon emissions. Carbon pricing imposes costs directly on polluters, such that those polluters have to pay for the damage their emissions cause to the environment. In 2021, Whitehouse introduced the Save our Future Act, which would have introduced carbon pricing on a wide scale in the United States.

Big emitters of carbon, like the oil industry, typically oppose carbon pricing. The policy would cost them a lot of money. When they have supported such measures, research suggests this is a strategic move to shape legislation they oppose just in case it passes. For these companies, Whitehouse's Save our Future Act was a non-starter.

In their goal of blocking the Whitehouse proposal, fossil fuel companies were helped by Congressional mathematics. Every Republican was going to vote against the bill. The balance of power therefore lay with two Democratic senators, both with close ties to the fossil fuel industry: Joe Manchin of West Virginia and Kyrsten Sinema of Arizona. Manchin had received more political donations from energy firms than any other senator. With Manchin dead set against carbon taxes, the bill had no chance of passage.

The fossil fuel industry found a little more to like in a new environmental law proposed by the Biden administration in 2022, which included incentives for renewable energy. The law, which was eventually named the Inflation Reduction Act (IRA) in August 2022, passed only after Manchin and Sinema ensured it included significantly more carrots than sticks. The IRA added sweeteners that favoured big fossil fuel companies, such as requiring increased leasing of federal land for oil and gas before making offshore wind leases available.

While the IRA is the most significant single piece of climate legislation ever passed in the United States, its most ambitious targets, which included penalties for non-compliant energy companies, were dramatically scaled back. The IRA's achievements are not insubstantial, but it fell well short of achieving the decisive change in US climate policy that Sheldon Whitehouse, and many Democratic voters, were hoping for.

Whitehouse resumed his 'Time to Wake Up' speeches.

In January 2023, five months after the IRA passed, the #ExxonKnew scandal got a second wind. Harvard researcher Geoffrey Supran and two colleagues published an article in *Science*, one of the world's premier journals of general scientific inquiry, that dug down into the technicalities of Exxon's own models for climate change. They showed that those models were some of the best around. They were as good as most governmental and independent academic assessments of the rate of climate change, precisely predicting the increases of 0.2 degrees Celsius per decade that have in fact taken place. The researchers also found documents showing that Exxon scientists had conclusively rejected the claim that the warming of the earth was not a product of human emissions.

You don't get an article published in *Science* on the basis of hearsay. This was hard evidence that Exxon's models were excellent – bang on the money in their predictions – and that they had been excellent for a long time. Supran understood what they had shown: 'We now have airtight, unimpeachable evidence that ExxonMobil accurately predicted global warming years before it turned around and publicly attacked climate science and scientists.'

For Sheldon Whitehouse, the second life of the #ExxonKnew scandal came too late. Republicans had retaken the House of Representatives in the November 2022 mid-term elections. No legislation on climate change was going to pass Congress.

For us, the timing of the new Exxon scandal was a gift. It gave us a fresh scandal that was front page news around the world. We could examine what difference it made in public opinion, and whether that effect looked different in the United States compared to other countries, where climate change policy is not such an 'easy' issue.

Our climate opinion experiment was identical in structure to the one we performed with Cambridge Analytica, discussed in Chapter 5: the survey equivalent of a drug trial with two groups of people. Both groups were randomly chosen and aimed to be representative of the adult population. The drug we were testing, so to speak, was news and opinion coverage of the #ExxonKnew scandal. That is what the treatment group read. We created the article by blending coverage from actual news articles about the breaking story of the *Science* publication with historical information about #ExxonKnew. The other group read a placebo article about Office Depot.

We constructed similar articles about the Exxon scandal based on national media coverage in France, Germany and the United Kingdom. These articles also linked the #ExxonKnew scandal to similar charges against companies headquartered in those countries, as happened with the British oil company Shell and the French oil company Total. We included links to the scandals of domestic companies to ensure that the response of readers to the articles was not driven by the fact that Exxon is an American company.

When the British or the French or the Germans read an article about the #ExxonKnew scandal, two things happened. First, they wanted stricter climate change policies than those who read the placebo article. And secondly, they rated climate as a significantly more important political issue than those who got the placebo. These effects are the same across all three European countries.

In the United States, reading the article had, on average, zero effect on people. It did not lead a politically representative sample of Americans to demand more stringent climate change policies, nor did it lead them to think the issue is more politically important.

Our readers will know, however, that averages sometimes hide important variation. As professors, our day job partly involves marking tests. In a course with 20 students, an average exam score of 60 could tell you two very different stories. One possibility is that almost every student scored between 55 and 65. In this story, the students all understood the issues about the same amount.

Sometimes, though, the results suggest you are really teaching to two different groups. An average score of 60 could mean that half the people scored a 90 and half the people scored a 30. Half the people understood the material well enough to teach the class, and the other half didn't understand anything.

This latter situation, it turns out, is relevant to what's going on in our American survey. How people responded to reading the article about #ExxonKnew depends almost entirely on whether or not those people are Republicans.

In our survey, 37 per cent of the respondents in our survey described themselves as being very close or somewhat close to the Republican Party. When we re-ran our analysis, but excluded these Republicans, guess what? The article changed the climate change opinions of independent and Democratic-leaning Americans just as much as it did for the British, French and German respondents. The failure of the #ExxonKnew scandal to have any effect on public opinion is entirely driven by the responses of Republicans, who on average want *less* climate change policy after reading the article.

We are not the only ones to discover that Republicans react differently to real world events related to the environment than do other Americans. Two academics from the University of California, Chad Hazlett and Matto Mildenberger, studied the effect of wildfires on voting behaviour in later California ballot initiatives related to climate change policies. If you live in an area that is within three miles of a large wildfire – an increasingly common event in California – you are 5 to 6 percentage points more likely to vote for those ballot initiatives, compared with people who live 22–25 miles away.

However, like us, Hazlett and Mildenberger found that these effects are concentrated among those who live in Democratic-voting areas. Those who live in highly Republican-voting areas show an effect close to zero. In the polarized United States, close proximity to a rapidly moving wall of flame is not enough to shift deeply partisan beliefs about climate change.

The two of us are not experts on climate change, but we do consider it an existential challenge. Taeku lived for more than two decades in northern California, and he has seen haze descend on the Bay Area for days on end from the increase in wildfire activities.

Pepper's family is from Louisiana and North Carolina, and he has seen up close the destructive force of increasingly violent hurricanes, which store up energy from a warmer ocean before striking the coastline. These experiences are anecdotal, but they conform to an overwhelming scientific record suggesting that severe events like hurricanes and wildfires are increasing in severity due to anthropogenic climate change.

We are, however, experts in politics and public opinion. And our reading of the evidence suggests that the laggardly climate change record of the United States is not only a problem of fossil fuel companies like Exxon buying political influence to block swifter action on climate change. That inaction is also a product of a divided American public opinion.

We were hopeful, when we first undertook this project, that even the most intractable political issues could be unblocked by the breaking of a corporate scandal. We have seen this effect in action in many other areas, from finance to technology to auto emissions.

But the #ExxonKnew scandal is a fair test of our theory of scandal-driven policy change. It is a scandal that directly links a long-standing campaign to undermine climate science with a lobbying campaign to stop the United States from joining international efforts to combat climate change.

What's more, if we had hired a casting director to come up with a corporate villain likely to excite outrage across the body politic, they might well have sent us a company that looked like ExxonMobil. Exxon is the inheritor of John D. Rockefeller's Standard Oil. As recently as 2013 it was the most valuable company on earth. And in the #ExxonKnew scandal, the evidence made the company look so bad that even John D. Rockefeller's great-great grandson publicly denounced the source of his own fortune.

Our lesson throughout this book has been that scandals only have cataclysmic effects when they can draw on a large iceberg of latent opinion hostile to companies. When it comes to big fossil fuel companies, that iceberg does not currently exist in American public opinion. American public opinion is fractured on this issue, and a fractured iceberg is just a bunch of big ice chunks. Ice chunks won't sink a titanic company like Exxon. The #ExxonKnew scandal essentially broke twice – in 2015, and again in 2023. Both times, the scandal failed to resonate across the political spectrum.

When corporate scandals run head-on into 'easy' political issues on which there is deep disagreement between voters from different parties, those scandals risk becoming nothing but temporary blips in the news cycle.

The #ExxonKnew scandal was not enough to unite the American public around the issue of climate change. Yet history suggests that any breakthrough in the partisan deadlock we have just described will come from a dramatic focusing event that transforms public opinion, whether it is a corporate scandal or an environmental disaster.

The last time the United States broke through blocked politics around environmental policy was at the end of the tumultuous 1960s. The first movement in the awakening of public opinion came in 1962, when Rachel Carson published *Silent Spring*. Her book was an immediate blockbuster, sitting atop the *New York Times* bestseller list for 31 weeks. The book denounced the hidden consequences of the pesticide DDT. Rachel Carson would die of breast cancer at age 56, only two years after the publication of her clarion call about the insidious effects of chemical poisoning of the environment.

Carson castigated the big chemical companies and their stranglehold on the politics of the day. The chemical companies fought back. They threatened her and her publisher with lawsuits, attacking the book as disinformation. Politicians dismissed Carson herself as a childless spinster who surrounded herself with cats. DDT-manufacturer Monsanto, which also produced the herbicide Agent Orange for use in the Vietnam War, railed against the book and lobbied hard against the adoption of any new regulations on pesticides.

The popular success of *Silent Spring* began to raise American awareness around the use of pesticides and the environment. In the words of environmentalist Kirkpatrick Sale, Carson's book 'galvanized a constituency that no-one realized was there, energizing the somewhat sluggish traditional conservation groups as well as many who had never given a thought to the natural world before.'

The first national poll measuring American opinions about air and water pollution came out in 1965, fielded by the Opinion Research Corporation. At that time, 28 per cent of people thought air pollution was a serious problem, and 35 per cent thought water pollution was a serious problem. By 1970, these numbers would balloon to 69 per cent and 74 per cent, respectively. In our language, an iceberg was forming. That's what the awakening of latent opinion looks like.

Icebergs need events to transform their latent power into political change. Scholars credit two focusing events in 1969 with the breaking of the logjam on American environmental policy: the Santa Barbara oil spill in January, and the burning of the Cuyahoga River in June.

The oil spill, which littered the California coast around Santa Barbara with dead seals and seabirds bathed in viscous oil, transfixed the country. The vision of devastation on the prosperous coast of California, home state of Republican President Richard Nixon, seized the public imagination. Part of the political impact of Santa Barbara was a product of the people it mainly affected: Republican voters. 'Not only was Santa Barbara geographically far from northern industrial cities, its residents were largely rich, white, and Republican.'

Denis Hayes, who would organize the wildly successful first Earth Day the following year, credits the Santa Barbara spill for the event's success. 'There was something about Santa Barbara that I think no-one could explain, except that I think the time was ripe.'

Cleveland lies more than 2,000 miles away from Santa Barbara, in the heart of the American Rust Belt. No-one has ever called Cleveland picturesque. But a picture of the city would soon come to dominate the national conversation in 1969, when the Cuyahoga River burst into flames.

Cuyahoga is a Native American name, meaning 'crooked river'. The crooked river had become both the sewer and the toxic waste dump for the industry of Cleveland, the city it passes through before emptying into Lake Erie.

The 1969 burning of the Cuyahoga, which began when a railroad spark ignited an oil slick on the river, was not big news in Cleveland. The river had caught fire at least a dozen times before, and this fire was small in comparison with some of the others. The fire was contained in relatively short order, meaning there was not even time to take a picture.

When the national news magazine *Time* ran a story on the burning of the Cuyahoga at the beginning of August, that meant it didn't have a picture of the blaze. Instead the editors used a much more dramatic picture from a 1952 fire on the river. The accompanying article described the Cuyahoga as a river that 'oozes rather than flows'. It quoted a government report that the river had 'no visible signs of life, not even low forms such as leeches and sludge worms that usually thrive on wastes'. The story chronicled similar failings in the nation's other major rivers, lamenting that 'The trouble is that pollution rarely gets a high priority until profits are affected or people are killed.'

The Cuyahoga burning.

Time had manufactured a media event by running with a 17-year-old picture, but that dramatic picture caught fire in the public imagination. In 1969 the American Environmental Protection Agency (EPA) did not yet exist. Carol Browner, who would later become head of the EPA in the 1990s, was then 14 years old. Her searing recollection of the photo is shared by many: 'I will never forget a photograph of flames, fire, shooting right out of the water in downtown Cleveland. It was the summer of 1969 and the Cuyahoga River was burning.'

The burning of the river in a de-industrializing heartland, coming on top of the oil spill on the well-to-do California coast, broke through the corporate capture of the political system that had stymied American environmental policy up to that moment. That breakthrough would lead to the creation of the EPA, the agency later to be led by Carol Browner.

President Richard Nixon privately dismissed the environmental movement as 'crap for clowns'. But he knew a vote-winner when he saw one. In December 1969 the National Environmental Protection Act, which would lead to the creation of the EPA, passed the Senate by a unanimous vote. Nixon signed the Act into law on the first day of 1970. In his state of the union address later that month, he claimed environmental restoration was the defining challenge of the new decade.

What followed was a string of legislative achievements. Congress adopted amendments giving teeth to the Clean Air Act in 1970 and the Clean Water Act in 1972. In 1972 it passed the Insecticide Act, which led the EPA to finally ban DDT. The Endangered Species Act followed in 1973.

This period of environmental lawmaking has never been equalled in the United States, and certainly not by the Inflation Reduction Act of 2022, which squeaked through Congress on the narrowest of margins. It is hard to imagine such a breakthrough in the current political climate. Our grim prediction is that if this breakthrough does come, it will be driven by disasters that look like the Santa Barbara oil spill and the burning of the Cuyahoga, symbolic events that seize public attention dramatically enough to shift long-standing partisan views.

In September 2024 Sheldon Whitehouse trudged back on to the Senate floor to give his 294th 'Time to Wake Up' speech. In it, he recounted the economic risks climate change was creating for the United States. It wasn't just a problem for the flounder fishermen of Rhode Island, whose plight first drew Whitehouse's attention to climate change. Instead he described the woes of Florida homeowners, who faced the triple risk of rising sea levels, extreme precipitation and flooding, and intense hurricanes. Each of these individual risks is well known, and yet the United States Congress had done little about them.

Every Cassandra gets frustrated, and Whitehouse was no different. Speaking to the few of his colleagues who were actually present in the chamber, he said, 'I've been telling you for a while now. And I hate to say, "I told you so." But it's here now, and damn it, I told you so.'

The great irony of Sheldon Whitehouse's story is that he was only elected to the Senate in the first place because partisanship trumped environmental policy. Back in 2006, when he first ran for Senate in the heavily Democratic state of Rhode Island, Whitehouse's opponent was Republican Senator Lincoln Chafee. Unusually for a Republican, Chafee had a strong voting record in favour of environmental issues. Running against Whitehouse, Chafee was endorsed by the major environmental groups the Sierra Club and the League of Conservation Voters.

Progressive activists, however, argued that the green agenda would ultimately be better served by having a Democrat in the Senate, because that could contribute to a Democratic majority. On the back of that argument, Sheldon Whitehouse defeated Lincoln Chafee, and the voters of Rhode Island have re-elected him ever since. Those who live by the sword of partisanship sometimes die by the sword of partisanship.

The American public is cleaved in two by differing views on the urgency, and even existence, of human-made climate change.

In such a polarized environment, well-meaning leaders like Senator Whitehouse are not likely to change anyone's mind, no matter how many speeches they make. Even when the scandal of #ExxonKnew broke, confirming what Whitehouse had been claiming for years, few opinions moved. Democrats called for investigations, and Republicans shrugged and muttered that free speech is not a crime.

Weather calamities, like the ones that have regularly befallen hurricane-prone Gulf states and the wildfire-scarred parts of the western United States, have not been sufficient to move American public opinion. That does not mean that the persistent differences across Democrats and Republicans are immutable. Indeed, younger Republicans are more likely to believe that climate change is real, and to favour renewable energy, than older ones. Generational change might shift views in the Republican Party. For now, though, voters for the two parties remain far apart on the threat posed by climate change and what to do about it.

Climate change seems the hardest of issues for countries to solve. Reducing greenhouse emissions durably requires politically influential sectors like fossil fuels to accept changes they fiercely oppose. And it requires hard sacrifices of many countries around the world, with each having to solve the difficult political calculus of today for the benefit of future generations.

Yet from the perspective of today's American voters, climate change is the easiest of issues. It maps cleanly on to partisan identities. If a focusing event is going to bridge the gap between the voters of the two parties, it will have to be destructive enough to break down these well-trodden partisan cognitive pathways, which remain entrenched despite the increased frequency and severity of extreme weather episodes. Should such an event occur, it is likely to be an unspeakable tragedy.

Senator Whitehouse may yet have another chance to say, 'I told you so'.

7

FTX – Rashomon for the Crypto Era

> A hallmark of crypto is that it is largely unregulated
> – buyer beware.
> *NEW YORK TIMES*, 17 NOVEMBER 2022

> If the rise of Sam Bankman-Fried was a modern tale about cryptocurrency tokens and 'effective altruism', his fall seems to be as old as original sin.
> *WALL STREET JOURNAL*, 13 DECEMBER 2022

In the classic 1950 film *Rashomon*, director Akira Kurosawa tells the story of a potentially horrific crime from the vantage point of four different witnesses. Each has an interest in telling the story a particular way, and viewers leave not knowing which version of the story is the underlying truth. In filmmaking, this is known as the Rashomon effect.

On 11 November 2022, the world's second largest crypto exchange, FTX, declared bankruptcy, with $8 billion apparently missing from a firm that had once reached a stock market valuation of $32 billion.

The Rashomon effect is alive and well in the divergent interpretations of American media outlets as to why it is that Sam Bankman-Fried, the founder and CEO of FTX, committed such a staggering fraud.

The story of the FTX scandal starts with a cryptocurrency token. The easiest way to think of a crypto token is as a voucher that gets you a discount on crypto services. In the same way an airline voucher allows you to buy food at a discounted price in one place only – say, New York's John F. Kennedy Airport – FTX issued a token, FTT, that allowed people to trade at a discount on the FTX exchange. The tokens were valuable to those who wanted to buy and sell cryptocurrency on FTX.

On their own, FTTs had no intrinsic value. They did, however, have a market price. Unlike the $10 voucher you can use at Starbucks in Terminal 5 at Kennedy Airport, tokens like FTT are publicly traded. As more people used FTTs to trade crypto on FTX, the price of FTT went up. And as FTX made more money, the company bought back and destroyed FTTs, thus reducing the supply of FTTs and raising their market price. So long as people wanted to do business on the booming FTX exchange, the FTT token was valuable.

Before he founded FTX, Bankman-Fried – widely known as SBF – had founded a trading fund, called Alameda Research, through which he invested in crypto. That's how he got rich. Alameda used its stockpile of FTTs as collateral to borrow real money to finance its speculative trades. But those funds eventually weren't enough to meet Alameda's voracious need for capital. That's where Gary Wang, the co-founder of FTX and SBF's former college roommate at MIT, comes in.

Wang, FTX's chief technology officer, lived with Bankman-Fried and several other co-workers in a $35 million penthouse in the Bahamas, where the firm had moved in 2021. Their neighbours in the luxury compound included celebrities like Tiger Woods and Justin Timberlake. One of the penthouse residents was the CEO of Alameda Research, Caroline Ellison. Ellison was also Bankman-Fried's on-again, off-again girlfriend.

Wang was in charge of the underlying computer programming at the crypto exchange. In 2019, Bankman-Fried had asked his friend to create a secret backdoor to FTX that would allow Alameda virtually unlimited access to the funds of FTX customers. Alameda then used those funds to make trades in the crypto market. So long as the cryptocurrency market continued to go up, no-one would notice that SBF was taking the company's money to prop up his own investment fund.

Late in 2021, the price of the most important cryptocurrency, Bitcoin, started to decline, dragging the crypto market and the price of FTT down with it. As crypto prices continued to tank and Alameda's bets failed, Alameda increasingly held only one asset: FTT. And if it sold its large quantities of FTT, that would further undermine the price of the token.

On 2 November 2022, the cryptocurrency news site *CoinDesk* reported that Alameda Research was unusually dependent on FTT. A leaked copy of the FTX balance sheet showed the two companies were highly intermingled. It also showed that FTX appeared to have a huge hole in its balance sheet.

Changpeng Zhao was the head of Binance, the world's largest crypto exchange. He was also SBF's archnemesis. On 6 November, Zhao announced on Twitter that he was selling his substantial FTT holdings, which immediately caused the price of FTT to collapse. Crypto traders began withdrawing their money from FTX, leading to an outflow of billions of dollars from the crypto exchange.

On 8 November, FTX blocked further withdrawals. Zhao at first said he was going to buy FTX, then changed his mind the following day once he saw the books. Two days later FTX declared bankruptcy. A month after the bankruptcy, police in the Bahamas arrested Bankman-Fried and bundled him on to a plane to New York, where he faced federal charges of fraud and money laundering.

Creditors to the firm appointed John Ray as the new CEO. Ray's job was to recover the $8 billion that was missing from the FTX balance sheet.

Ray was no stranger to scandal – he led the energy firm Enron after its 2001 scandal and bankruptcy – but even he was shocked by what he found at FTX. 'Never in my career', he said after taking the helm of the crypto firm, 'have I seen such a complete failure of corporate controls and such a complete absence of trustworthy financial information as occurred here.'

Cryptocurrency is definitely not an 'easy' issue. Voters don't think they understand it, and they are correct about their lack of comprehension. Of the Americans we surveyed right after the FTX bankruptcy, 79 per cent said they had little or no understanding of crypto.

In a separate survey in March 2023, conducted four months after the bankruptcy, we asked a different group of Americans a simple knowledge question about cryptocurrencies like Bitcoin. Nearly three-quarters of them (70 per cent) got the answer wrong.

Cryptocurrency is a digital asset. It is protected by encryption software – thus the name 'crypto' – and depends on a decentralized accounting database called a blockchain. Thanks to this decentralized technology, crypto is not under the control of any government. It is not a coincidence that crypto was created in the wake of the financial crisis of 2008, when big banks and governments both fell into disrepute. Crypto requires neither of these institutions in order to function.

What it does require is a mindboggling amount of energy. That's because the cryptography on which cryptocurrency depends involves computers solving complicated mathematics problems to verify a transaction and add it to the blockchain. That computing power takes a lot of electricity. The largest cryptocurrency network, Bitcoin, consumes about the same amount of electricity in a year as the entire country of Poland.

We don't need to go deeper into the details of crypto, but suffice it to say that the FTX scandal presented voters with a very 'hard' issue. It also featured an intriguing anti-hero, Bankman-Fried, who appeared to have committed major fraud.

Yet even clearly transgressive tales can contain ambiguity. It was obvious to most people that Sam Bankman-Fried stole a lot of money from FTX customers. Where people could reasonably differ is in understanding why he did it. Did he steal the money because of a personal moral failing? Or did he instead steal the money because the rules governing private cryptocurrency exchanges allowed him to get away with stealing so easily? People's interpretation of Bankman-Fried's actions, in turn, coloured their understanding of the appropriate regulatory response to the scandal.

People are more open to information that conforms to their pre-existing ideas. That's called confirmation bias, and it affects how people on both the left and right interpret the world. For example, the views of individual Americans on economic performance depend on which party holds the presidency. If a Republican is president, Republicans tend to think the economy is doing better than when a Democrat is president, even if in the two cases inflation and unemployment are identical. And the same thing happens in reverse with Democrats. Partisanship even influences the way we learn from new experiences.

So how might partisan interpretations or partisan media coverage affect how people understood the FTX scandal?

Voters who are on the political right, and particularly the American right, believe in the responsibility of the individual. This emphasis on individual responsibility goes hand in hand with an emphasis on the importance of morality as a source of public order. For conservatives, this means that individuals who work hard and earn lots of money should be able to keep most of that money, rather than paying a large share of it in taxes.

This perspective also implies that individuals who steal from others primarily do so because of their own moral failings. Those who steal should face clear and public punishment because they have broken shared moral codes. The important thing, for those on the right, is that individuals are held accountable for their crimes to reinforce social order.

Those on the political left tend to weigh heavily the societal and structural conditions that enable or constrain the choices that individuals make. Considerations of social justice are the lodestar for those on the left, which means that it is the job of the state to compensate when market interactions do not produce just outcomes. Those on the left think that individuals who earn a lot of money should expect to pay more in progressive taxes, because they have benefited from the system.

A leftist who learns that someone has been caught stealing is less likely to see a failure of personal morality and more likely to see it as a failure of the system. Yes, the individual should be punished to dissuade others from a life of crime, but the system is at least as much to blame for the failure as the individual. To those on the left, not having the right set of rules and regulatory oversight made the theft much more likely.

These are gross oversimplifications of how those on the left and right understand theft. But they are consistent with biases shown by partisans in a variety of areas, including inequality. Because voters on the left prefer approaches that focus on inequality of outcomes, they gravitate towards policies that correct market outcomes. Voters on the right, in contrast, prioritize measures that establish equality of opportunity, even if not everyone takes equal advantage of that opportunity.

Just as individuals can impose a left or a right interpretation on events, so too can media outlets. For example, when a left-wing media news outlet such as MSNBC or the *Guardian* discusses a 'rigged system', it is generally referring to the rich setting rules in a system that is systematically biased in favour of people with lots of money. When a commentator on a right-wing broadcaster such as Fox News talks about a 'rigged system', they more likely have in mind the rigging done by bureaucratic actors – big business in cahoots with overzealous government regulators – to the detriment of the little guy.

In studying how the failure of the cryptocurrency exchange FTX affected public opinion, we would find abundant evidence of partisan interpretation, at the level of both individuals and the media. Republicans and Democrats were united in their disapproval of Sam Bankman-Fried's actions, but they failed to arrive at a shared interpretation of the scandal's consequences that typically give corporate scandals their political power. Our question was, why?

There is no more unlikely villain in this book than Sam Bankman-Fried. Bankman-Fried is a curly-haired graduate of MIT and the one-time wunderkind of crypto. He had appeared on stage with world leaders and celebrities. They wore suits, while he wore cargo shorts. He famously played video games while on investor calls about FTX, his crypto exchange.

Sam Bankman-Fried with supermodel Gisele Bündchen at a 2022 crypto conference.

Bankman-Fried captivated the chattering classes because he appeared to be a billionaire who did not care about money for its own sake. He was a devotee of effective altruism, a philosophical movement dedicated to employing cold hard reason and evidence to do good for the world. The effective altruism movement, led by Oxford philosopher William MacAskill, reflected an updated version of utilitarian theory, which advocates ethical action based on ensuring the greatest happiness for the greatest number of people. Its focus on unsentimental giving based on data proved attractive to Silicon Valley's super-rich, including Facebook co-founder Dustin Moskovitz and his wife Cari Tuna.

In 2013, while he was still at MIT, Bankman-Fried met MacAskill. MacAskill convinced the mathematically adept physics major that he should get a job in finance, because he could make a lot of money, which would allow him to do a lot of good for the world. Bankman-Fried followed that advice, joining trading firm Jane Street Capital just after graduating from MIT. He left Jane Street in 2017 to found Alameda Research. As a convert to effective altruism, Bankman-Fried wanted to make serious money to do serious good.

At Alameda, Bankman-Fried cashed in on the money-making possibilities of crypto. Specifically, he turned to arbitrage, taking advantage of the difference between the price of Bitcoin in Japan and the United States. In 2019, he founded his own crypto exchange, FTX. Two years later, the 29-year-old was worth $22.5 billion on paper. He was the richest person ever below the age of 30, except for Mark Zuckerberg. And he had succeeded in his goal of making serious money.

Unlike Zuckerberg, SBF was no shrinking violet. On several occasions, he was called to testify to Congress on crypto regulation — and he even wore a suit to do so. Bankman-Fried was the second-largest individual donor to the Democratic Party during the 2022 electoral campaign cycle. It later turned out he was also secretly funnelling money to Republicans as well, just to cover his bases.

Many of the corporate scandals we have discussed in this book — Dieselgate, PRISM, Cambridge Analytica — lacked an overtly partisan dimension. In contrast, Bankman-Fried's public prominence as donor to the Democrats created a partisan lens for media interpretation of the scandal.

In December 2022, shortly after the arrest of Sam Bankman-Fried, the *Economist* magazine commissioned a survey that asked Americans whether they thought SBF was guilty. Seventy-six per cent of those who voted for Democrat Joe Biden in 2020 thought Bankman-Fried should be convicted, as did 77 per cent of those who voted for Republican Donald Trump. SBF had acted so brazenly that even Democrats and Republicans could agree on his guilt. Americans clearly thought that what had happened at FTX was a scandal.

But we wanted to see how that scandal affected their views on crypto regulation. As we've already shown, most people don't understand the basics of cryptocurrency or its underlying blockchain technology. You may well be asking: how could people possibly have views on how to regulate crypto when they don't even understand how it works?

Just because they don't understand it doesn't mean Americans don't have an opinion about crypto. People can understand the issues that crypto poses for regulators in general terms without needing to understand the details. They know, for example, that they don't understand crypto. Should regulators therefore require cryptocurrency exchanges – like FTX – to provide their customers with information about the risks of investing in something that many people don't understand? That is a question of investor protection, and voters have opinions about it.

Similarly, people have opinions about whether digital currency should be under the control of a central bank, even if they don't understand how blockchain works. We found that their views across several different questions about regulating crypto were consistent. We could use surveys to measure how much crypto regulation people wanted, whether or not they had heard of Bitcoin.

Our next challenge was to figure out how knowledge of the FTX scandal affected their attitudes. We knew that the task would be conceptually messier than the survey experiments we discussed in previous chapters, because the real world is always more complicated than an experiment. One of the many reasons it's more complicated is that people learn about scandals from a variety of different news sources. Our survey experiments had only given them a single news story. Now we wanted to know if people learning about the news as it happened, from different news outlets in the real world, were affected by scandals in the same way as people in our survey experiments. We called this research project 'Scandals in the Wild'.

Our first job in 'Scandals in the Wild' was to figure out how to distinguish those who had heard about the FTX scandal from those who hadn't. We could of course just ask them whether they knew about the scandal, but then we would have to take their word for it. That's never a good idea in survey research. No-one likes to confess their ignorance, even on an anonymous survey.

We decided the best way to separate the knowledgeable from the blissfully ignorant was through a current events quiz. The quiz asked which of four plausible events had occurred recently. We listed the FTX scandal along three fictitious scenarios like, 'The FBI raided the offices of Wells Fargo after executives were accused of making significant transfers to Russian clients in breach of ongoing sanctions'. That one is not true, but to those not paying attention to the news no less believable than that FTX had filed for bankruptcy.

Two-thirds of people answered our quiz question correctly, suggesting how widely the media covered the news of the scandal. But the result also meant that 34 per cent of our survey-takers had not heard of the scandal. Armed with this knowledge, we could compare the regulatory preferences of those who had been exposed to the scandal – in other words, those who knew about it – with those who didn't.

To our surprise, we found that being exposed to the scandal affected Democrats and Republicans differently. Compared with Democrats who did not know about the scandal, Democrats who did know about it wanted *more* crypto regulation. But Republicans who knew about the scandal wanted *less* cryptocurrency regulation than Republicans who had not encountered it. Less than a month after the biggest cryptocurrency scandal in history, knowing more about the scandal was associated with wanting less regulation, among Republicans, but with wanting more regulation, among Democrats.

That was interesting. It is also consistent with the way that left-wing and right-wing news outlets in the United States covered the story of the FTX scandal. The quotations at the beginning of this chapter illustrate this difference. News outlets on the left, like the *New York Times*, highlighted that the field of cryptocurrency was in desperate need of regulation. Those on the right, like the *Wall Street Journal*, underlined the empty sanctimony of Sam Bankman-Fried, who vaunted his commitment to effective altruism while defrauding his own clients. They also often linked the scandal to Bankman-Fried's status as a large Democratic donor.

For example, just after the collapse of FTX, CNN (considered to be on the left) ran a story on its website that said the 'crypto market remains largely unregulated, making it the Wild Wild West of the financial world. And that leaves investors vulnerable when something breaks'.

MSNBC, again on the left, noted in one piece that 'a lot of the problems that arose out of the recent catastrophe are due to the lack of regulation of these products'. The *New York Times* harmonized seamlessly with the other left-wing news outlets, observing that 'Crypto went mainstream in the pandemic. Regulation has yet to catch up.'

Those news outlets on the right were less keen to jump to conclusions about the need for regulation, and more intrigued by the moral turpitude of Sam Bankman-Fried. Tucker Carlson, then the most prominent commentator on Fox News, posted a story in which he condemned the hypocrisy of the FTX founder: 'Effective altruism gives you a moral cover as you rip off investors in order to live tax-free in splendour in some beachfront paradise, as Sam Bankman-Fried did and to this day continues to do.' The *Wall Street Journal*, which like Fox News is owned by Rupert Murdoch and leans to the political right, piled on SBF along the same lines: 'there is no vaccine yet for this country's pandemic of moral vanity. Its latest victim is FTX founder Sam Bankman-Fried.'

Each side makes a valid argument, but they are very different points.

The gulf in journalistic coverage between media outlets of left and right left us with a question: did Republicans and Democrats think differently about the scandal as a matter of partisan perspective, regardless of where they got their news? Or did the way they thought about the scandal depend on the media outlet through which they learned about it? We rolled out another survey to find out.

We discovered that Democrats and Republicans did not, in fact, have completely different views of the cause of the scandal. Given the option 'systemic greed', 19 per cent of Democrats and 16 per cent of Republicans chose greed as a cause of the scandal. Not much difference there. Similarly, few respondents from either party blamed failures of regulatory agencies such as the Securities and Exchange Commission (SEC), with 8 per cent of Democrats and 5 per cent of Republicans blaming the SEC. Neither of these differences is statistically meaningful.

When asked about two other potential causes of the scandal, however, survey respondents from the two parties were far apart. When asked if the cause of the crisis was lack of sufficient regulation of the crypto industry, 31 per cent of Democrats agreed, while only 14 per cent of Republicans did. When asked if the cause was individual moral failings of the FTX leadership, the partisan differences were even greater. Forty-one per cent of Republicans pointed to moral failings, but only 18 per cent of Democrats.

Next we asked people where they had first heard about the FTX scandal. We classified their responses using a reputable site that tracks the characteristic biases of American media.

It turns out that where people got their news about the scandal matters as much as or more than their actual partisan affiliation when determining what people believe caused the FTX scandal. Take first the proposition that lack of regulation was the biggest cause of the scandal. Among people who self-identified as Democrats and who also got their news from a left-wing source like MSNBC, 42 per cent blamed lack of regulation for FTX's collapse. Among Republicans who got their news from a right-wing source like Fox News, only 12 per cent thought lack of regulation tempted Bankman-Fried into stealing from FTX.

As public opinion surveys go, a 30-point percentage difference is massive. When American partisans are getting their news from a like-minded media source, they really do see the world very differently than those on the opposite side of the political spectrum.

However, people who got their news from a source that leaned the *opposite* way from their political party affiliation had much more moderate views. People in the UK might think of these people as centrist dads. People in the United States might think of them as soccer moms. Whether dads, moms or neither, these are people who do not zealously ensure that their news source matches their political party.

Of the Republicans who learned about FTX through a left-wing source, like the *New York Times*, 25 per cent thought lack of regulation caused the crisis. That is exactly the same percentage of Democrats – 25 per cent – who thought lack of regulation was the root cause of the scandal, after learning about it from a right-wing source like the *Wall Street Journal*.

We observe exactly the same moderating pattern when looking at those who believe that individual moral failings caused the FTX scandal.

On this evidence, when voters of the left and right get their news from media on the other side of the spectrum, their views of scandals like FTX tend to be very similar. In other words, listening to the other side can moderate your views.

The FTX scandal was a corporate scandal, but its protagonist was also a prominent donor to the Democratic Party. Just as Republicans and Democrats had different opinions of the Clinton/Lewinsky scandal back in 1998, so too in 2022 had the polarized American media market given them two different narratives about the causes of the FTX scandal. That gave the scandal a partisan angle. It made for great copy, but it deprived the scandal of the bipartisan shared interpretation – why the scoundrel did it and what must be done in response – that generates the transformative force of many other corporate scandals.

On the facts of the case, the right and left were united: the FTX scandal was old-fashioned fraud, even though it featured a tech bro with sick gaming skills and took place in an industry so new that during the 2008 financial crisis it didn't even exist. Sam Bankman-Fried took the money of his FTX investors, gambled it away on investments through his trading fund Alameda Research, and just kept playing until the music stopped. For such a new financial industry, it was a very old-school crime.

If the FTX scandal is old-fashioned financial fraud, then the existing laws on securities regulation should be sufficient to prevent it from happening – if those firms register their cryptocurrencies and tokens as securities with the SEC.

This interpretation was not limited to the right-wing media. It was also the position of Gary Gensler, who is a Democrat. Gensler was the head of the SEC, the agency responsible for regulating financial markets, during and after the FTX scandal. In 2023, he described cryptocurrency as 'a field rife with fraud, scams, bankruptcies and money laundering'.

In the wake of the scandal, Gensler dismissed calls for new regulation. What he said was needed instead was enforcement of existing regulation about market manipulation. In Gensler's interpretation, tokens like FTT were simply micro-securities that need to be registered with the SEC to protect investors like those who got burned by FTX.

In 2023, Gensler took a record number of enforcement actions against crypto firms, including giant exchanges like Binance and Coinbase. Critics, such as billionaire Mark Cuban, lambasted Gensler's aggressive response, accusing him of 'perfecting regulation through litigation'.

In Congress, it is Republicans, not Democrats, who called for new rules for the crypto industry in the aftermath of the FTX scandal. However, they didn't want those rules to constrain crypto. Rather, they wanted to enable crypto to flourish. They argued that crypto is a technology, not a security, and thus not subject to the oversight of the SEC.

Throughout this book, we have seen that business often gets its way through lobbying and campaign donations. In the 2024 presidential election, the crypto industry lined up squarely behind Republican candidate Donald Trump. As a sector, crypto firms were the single largest corporate donors to politics in the 2024 campaign, donating $119 million.

That bet paid off handsomely when Trump won the election. President Trump named pro-crypto venture capitalist David Sacks his crypto czar, and he nominated the pro-crypto Paul Atkins to take over as head of the SEC. The Trump administration reversed the Gensler crackdown and created a more permissive environment for cryptocurrency. Donald Trump and his wife Melania didn't even wait for the presidential inauguration before each launched their own meme coin in 2025.

The conflict over American crypto regulation will continue to rage well after the publication of this book. The FTX scandal was the first big skirmish in that battle. The initial response of the US government under a Democratic administration was to tighten the screws by enforcing existing rules, not by writing new ones. The muscular enforcement reaction of the government was a natural response to a scandal in which massive majorities of Democrats and Republicans agreed that Bankman-Fried was guilty.

But the jury is still out on what Americans think about how tightly crypto should be regulated. This lack of consensus creates a permissive environment for the new Republican administration to deliver on President Trump's campaign promise to make the United States 'the crypto capital of the planet'.

However, in a striking contrast to what happened after the financial crisis, it turns out that crypto kings were not too big to jail.

On 2 November 2023, a New York jury took only five hours to deliberate over the guilt of Sam Bankman-Fried. For all the complexities of cryptocurrency, the FTX case was clear. In the words of prosecutor Damian Williams, 'this case has always been about lying, cheating, and stealing'. The jury convicted Bankman-Fried of all seven counts of fraud and money laundering the government had brought against him. The judge who sentenced Bankman-Fried to 25 years in prison in March 2024 said of the one-time whiz kid, 'He knew it was wrong. He knew it was criminal. He regrets that he made a very bad bet about the likelihood of getting caught, but he's not going to admit a thing.'

In late November 2023, just weeks after Bankman-Fried's conviction, Changpeng Zhao, the CEO of Binance, once known as the 'most powerful man in crypto', pleaded guilty to money laundering charges brought by the US government. He resigned his position and in April 2024 was sentenced to four months in prison. Binance agreed to intrusive future monitoring from the government, and the company paid a fine of $4.3 billion.

At least temporarily, the FTX scandal had a cathartic effect on the way American laws are enforced on crypto executives. The FTX scandal brought the attention of Americans to crypto in large numbers, and the majority judgement was that the sector is a scam.

That's what 64 per cent of respondents told us in the survey we fielded right after the scandal broke. Yet that effect is not uniform across voters from different parties, in large part because the media of the left reported the story differently than the media of the right.

The American media of the left and the right agreed Sam Bankman-Fried was a criminal, but they suggested very different reasons why he was guilty. The scandal will live on in American politics, because those distinctive partisan diagnoses of the scandal now inform the views of American voters on how the cryptocurrency market should be regulated.

Corporate scandals lead to the passage of new regulation when they tell a simple, shared story about the reasons for wrongdoing by big companies. Good stories have a clear moral: greed is bad, do the right thing, virtue is rewarded. Many of the stories in this book are of the David v Goliath character. We all know, without even thinking about it, that the moral of that story is that resourceful underdogs can beat giants.

Whatever else it is, the movie *Rashomon* is not a morality tale. When narrators disagree about important parts of the storyline, the story has no moral, except possibly that narrators could always be lying to you.

The partisan ambiguity of the media coverage of the FTX scandal suggests to us that in the coming years the conflict over crypto regulation will be won by whichever side tells a story about cryptocurrency that the American public actually believes.

8

Sasol and the Death of Mossville

Mossville, Louisiana, is an unincorporated area of five square miles on the western outskirts of Lake Charles, some 211 miles due west of New Orleans. Founded in 1790 by Jack Moss, a freedman, Mossville was one of the earliest established communities of free Blacks in the American South. Formerly enslaved people could settle on and acquire ownership of land through squatters' rights. Residents found fertile soil to farm rice, sweet yams and other foodstuffs. The lands were also plentiful with rabbits and other game animals, and the lakes and rivers full of catfish, crappie and mullet.

Through many decades, Mossville remained a self-sustaining, largely rural community. Its population grew after emancipation. According to locals, the place also provided refuge for Black families who faced extra-legal threats in the Jim Crow South. At its peak, some 8,000 people called Mossville home. It had its own churches, barbershops, a high school and a recreation centre with a swimming pool. Mossville even boasted a nightclub, the Paradise, where celebrated Black entertainers like Aretha Franklin, Otis Redding, Tina Turner and James Brown once performed.

Over time, Mossville also acquired neighbours. Westlake was one, named for its geographical location west of Lake Charles. Unlike Mossville, whose inhabitants were almost all Black, Westlake's inhabitants were mostly White. And unlike Mossville, which might have happily remained a rural outpost, Westlake welcomed the opportunities for economic development that came with the industrial age.

First incorporated as a town in 1945, Westlake's fortunes were transformed in the post-World War II years. The town, along with others like it in the Lake Charles area, became a major destination for the burgeoning petrochemical industry. Before long Mossville found itself surrounded by 14 such plants. These chemical and industrial plants came with jobs, jobs that soon became the primary source of employment in the Lake Charles area.

Westlake's fortunes became Mossville's fate as the economic benefits that resulted from these new plants came with environmental costs. The plants regularly pumped the surrounding land with a lethal cocktail of toxins. The Lake Charles region may not be as infamous as 'Cancer Alley', an 85-mile stretch of Louisiana snaking along the Mississippi River where some 200 chemical and industrial plants are sited. But the harms to residents in the area have been every bit as dire.

These toxins have put southwest Louisiana among the most polluted lands anywhere in America. The resulting health risks hit Mossville especially hard. A 1998 study by the Environmental Protection Agency found that toxins in Mossville were at levels 100 times higher than national safety standards. That same year, a group of residents who organized themselves as Mossville Environmental Action Now convinced an agency within the Centers for Disease Control and Prevention (CDC) to conduct blood tests. The CDC found that Mossville residents had levels of dioxin – a carcinogen that also carries reproductive, developmental and immunological risks – three times the national average. The toxicologist who conducted the tests stated, 'I am not aware of any other sites where we have found dioxin elevations of this magnitude.'

Mossville today is a ghost town, a dystopian industrial wasteland. Its population has collapsed to about 50 households. What few homes remain are surrounded by empty, weeded lots where homes once stood. Most of Mossville's residents have either died of causes linked to toxins in and around their homes, or sold their homes and left town.

The blight that beset Mossville came from years of industrial pollution. It also came from a corporation's aggressive campaign to buy families out of their homes, intended both as recompense for the environmental mess it had already made and to make room for future messes it was planning to make.

Yet not everyone left without a fight.

Some cases of egregious corporate misbehaviour never become scandals because they fail to capture widespread public interest and disapproval. Why is it that outrageous corporate action is sometimes met with public indifference, a collective shrug of the shoulders or turn of the cheek?

To answer that question, we need to revisit the distinction between hard issues and easy issues. Most types of corporate regulation, as we have noted, are hard issues for the average voter. Regulating business involves multiple, often cross-cutting dimensions, ranging from competing views on the role of government and the impact of rules and regulations on local economies, to differing views on particular firms. In many industries, regulatory questions also involve complicated, technical issues that are literally hard for ordinary voters to fully grasp – for instance, derivatives, shorts and hedges in financial regulation, or tracking technologies and data profiling in privacy policy and tech regulation.

In the heat of the moment, a scandal can simplify a hard issue for voters by concentrating their minds on particularly salient aspects. We have seen this dynamic repeatedly in previous chapters. Financial regulation becomes simplified when subpoenaed email records revealed that Goldman Sachs shorted securities they knew were a 'shitty deal' for their clients. Digital privacy becomes simplified when the Cambridge Analytica scandal exposes how Facebook collected and commercialized data on millions of unwitting users.

But a scandal's focusing effect is not a given. If the relevant events are reconstrued through the lens of a pre-existing, well-formed set of beliefs, a scandal may fail to materialize, or may materialize but fail to spark outrage. In our terms, this is when a hard issue gets interpreted through an easy issue.

In the United States, stories that can be retold and interpreted through the lens of race become 'easy issues'. They are not 'easy' because the topic of race is easy in the sense of comfortable, consensual or uncomplicated. Rather, issues that have a racial dimension to them are considered politically easy – perhaps paradigmatically easy – because they reduce the many, complex possible dimensions of choice on any given matter down to their racial or race-related dimensions, on which voters' beliefs are fully formed, easily accessible and fairly unshakeable.

In the same way that partisan identity shapes our interpretation of events, beliefs about race are stable predispositions that organize how Americans see the world. For Black Americans, social science research shows how racial cues can serve as mental shortcuts to forming judgements and making decisions quickly and efficiently. While the political viewpoints of Blacks are hardly monolithic, when faced with hard choices like who to vote for or which policies to support, Black voters hold a strong 'linked fate' orientation. That is, they ask, 'Will it benefit or harm Blacks in general?' to decide whether a given position benefits or harms them personally.

Whites, too, use racial cues to reduce complexity and shape judgements and decisions quickly and efficiently. But they do so differently from Black Americans, and their approach has changed over time. Where once large majorities of White Americans directly and overtly expressed their belief in invidious negative stereotypes about Black intelligence, motivation, criminality and the like, changing social norms and greater awareness now rule the day. Today, the vast majority of Whites reject such generalizations as inaccurate and harmful. Or at least, they are unwilling to agree with them in polite company.

The blatant prejudice of the past has been replaced with more indirect, implicit ways for Whites to express their negative beliefs about minorities like Black Americans. Whites use these more subtle expressions of antipathy to justify apathy no matter how shocking and scandal-worthy the plight of their Black neighbours. Whites today are more likely to express their antipathy as resentment than as outright bigotry. They express that resentment as a bundle of beliefs that racial and ethnic minorities are inadequately motivated to succeed, flout the rules of hard work, exploit public coffers, and unfairly 'jump the queue' of upward mobility.

Such beliefs turn out to be hugely influential in shaping the social and political views of White Americans. The extent to which White people hold these views predicts which candidates and parties they vote for, how they view anti-poverty and criminal justice policy, and even how they view issues that ostensibly have little to do with race, such as healthcare reform and corporate regulation.

This resentment can be blinding. In Louisiana, it has left many White people unable to see the myriad ways in which their well-being might be connected to the well-being of Black Louisianans. And this is exactly what happened in the Lake Charles area, where the White residents in Brentwood – a mostly White, unincorporated area just north of Mossville – failed to see how their fate was linked to that of their Black neighbours in Mossville.

In a growing number of places across the land – places where populist politicians have increasingly found favour – White Americans who feel passed over and left behind have turned to resentment. These voters feel left behind by globalization and de-industrialization and increasingly believe 'the system' is rigged against them. They believe themselves to be passed over by a government that is unfairly partial to the interests of liberal, wealthy, urban elites and racial and ethnic minorities. In particular, members of the White working class in America are aggrieved by a sense that they have lost their economic security, their social status and their political voice. In their place, they see themselves as targets of scorn and condescension from a mainstream media that portrays them as uneducated, racist rednecks.

This sense of loss and resentment is keenly portrayed in Arlie Hochschild's *Strangers in Their Own Land*. Hochschild, a self-avowed progressive and Berkeley professor, spent five years living in Lake Charles, Louisiana to research her book. She found there an 'empathy wall' – an 'obstacle to deep understanding of another person, one that can make us feel indifferent or even hostile to those who hold different beliefs or whose childhood is rooted in different circumstances'. This empathy wall stands as a barrier that leaves

White Louisianans indifferent, if not hostile, to the circumstances of their Black fellow Louisianans. This empathy wall divides the overwhelmingly White residents of Westlake and Brentwood from the overwhelmingly Black residents of Mossville.

Corporate decisions over where to conduct business affect both individuals and the communities they call home. Calcasieu Parish, where Mossville, Brentwood and Westlake sit, is ranked fourth highest among Louisiana's 65 parishes in terms of residential segregation. As a result, the parish's 14 industrial plants have produced decidedly unequal results for its White and its Black residents: jobs and a livelihood for some, pollution and peril for others.

Mossville is the setting for a story of man against machine. Like many such stories these days, machine wins. But why machine wins is important to this book.

The scandal here could have been the story of a South African corporation, an industrial vestige of its apartheid era, that chooses to build a massive and pollution-spewing complex in Mossville, rendering the community, once a refuge for freed slaves, into a ghost town. But that scandal never fully materializes. Companies that engage in reprehensible behaviour can avoid the withering scrutiny of a corporate scandal when a pre-existing, durable social division prevents an iceberg of public opinion from forming. In America, race is just such a pre-existing, durable social division.

The machine in this story is Sasol, South African Synthetic Oil Limited. Founded in 1950 as a domestic energy company that converted coal into synthetic fuel, Sasol's founding and success as an energy company was integral to sustaining South Africa's apartheid regime. As South Africa found itself increasingly isolated by the international community's condemnation of its ruthless segregationist rule, the state's access to energy and raw materials became central to its survival. Sasol thus started as a state-owned company.

By 1979, Sasol had been privatized. After the fall of apartheid roughly a decade later, the company began to expand heavily into petrochemicals. Before long, Sasol had grown into a multinational corporation with operations in 33 countries. Today, it is one of the largest corporate taxpayers in South Africa, with net revenues nearing $16 billion in 2024. Sasol is also one of the world's largest emitters of carbon dioxide. A single synthetic fuel plant in Secunda, South Africa, discharges some 60 million tonnes of carbon dioxide a year, making it the single largest emitter of greenhouse gases anywhere in the world.

Sasol's road to riches eventually ran through Mossville, Louisiana. Among its many global acquisitions was an existing chemical company in southwest Louisiana named Condea Vista, which Sasol bought in 2000. In the early 1990s, Condea Vista was routing toxic chemicals like ethylene dichloride, a known carcinogen, from the docks of the Calcasieu River to its chemical plant in Lake Charles, via an old and leaky pipeline. Subsequent clean-up efforts recovered 1.6 million pounds of ethylene dichloride in and around Mossville, with estimates of the total spillage amount ranging from 19 to 47 million pounds.

As a result of this and other toxic exposures, Mossville's residents suffered from elevated rates of cancer, liver disease and nervous system disorders. In 1998, Condea Vista agreed to pay $32 million as a settlement for a class-action lawsuit. This included a $14 million property buy-out fund. 'We've listened to the concerns of our near neighbours', the manager of Condea Vista declared, 'and we've structured this settlement to give them an opportunity to sell their property at a premium market value.' The 206 homeowners who accepted this buy-out made up the first major exodus of residents from Mossville.

Fast forward to 2012, at which point Sasol launched a major, $11–14 billion initiative to expand in the Lake Charles area. Specifically, Sasol aimed to build into Mossville and into adjacent Brentwood, a sparsely populated, mostly White community due north of Mossville. At a press conference filled with pomp, Louisiana governor Bobby Jindal pledged to provide Sasol with $115 million in incentives. He declared the initiative the largest single manufacturing project in Louisiana history. Sasol's planned expansion included a gas-to-liquids processing plant, a chemical plant, a refinery and a separate ethane cracker to produce solvents and plastics.

To secure Sasol's commitment to this new facility, the state issued regulatory waivers authorizing the company to release up to 10.6 million tonnes of additional greenhouse gas emissions and 3,275 tonnes of volatile organic compounds annually. The expansion threatened to pump toxic ethylene oxide, benzene, chlorine and other products into the area. Under the plan, Sasol would become the biggest producer of carbon emissions in Louisiana, a state that in 2018 was the seventh largest source of greenhouse gas emissions in the US. But Jindal and Louisiana's business leaders didn't mention the potential downsides, focusing instead on claiming their share of the credit for negotiating a deal that promised 1,200 permanent jobs and 7,000 construction jobs.

The sweetheart corporate deal here wasn't the scandal story lurking in Mossville. Rather, it was the profit-seeking decision of a corporation to expand its operations, impervious to the destructive impact that decision would have on the very life of a once-thriving community.

Stacey Ryan next to a fence along his parcel, with Sasol's Mossville plant in the background.

This is where Stacey Ryan enters our story. Ryan is a long-term resident and a direct descendant of Mossville founder Jack Moss. A tall, burly, soft-spoken man, Ryan describes himself as a bookworm who dreamt of becoming an astronaut when he grew up. Ryan is also the main protagonist in Alexander Glustrom's award-winning 2019 documentary, *Mossville: When Great Trees Fall.*

At the time the movie was filmed, most of Ryan's neighbours had already resigned themselves to playing the only card dealt them by Condea Vista and then Sasol. They had sold their property and left town, accepting meagre sums for their homes that rarely allowed them to purchase another home elsewhere. According to one report produced by an environmental justice NGO, sales of properties outside Sasol's Voluntary Property Purchase Program garnered a price that was 82 per cent higher than in Mossville. In neighbouring Brentwood – a community that is 90 per cent White – sale prices of homes were 88 per cent higher than in Mossville.

Ryan was among the few Mossville stalwarts who refused to sell. He brought the demeanour of a gentle giant and the resolve of an old oak tree to the fight. Like many of the former residents who accepted the buy-out offers, Ryan was born and raised in Mossville. And like too many others, Ryan had been directly affected by the ravages of industrial pollution.

Both of Ryan's parents died of cancer at relatively young ages, 54 and 61. His aunts and uncles also died young, of cancer, respiratory illness and liver disease. Ryan himself suffered various chronic illnesses, ailments that forced him to retire early after working as a plant operator at Condea Vista and another chemical company in the area. As Ryan put it, 'My family's been pretty much wiped out'.

In 2011, Ryan moved on to a plot of land in Mossville that his family owned. When he moved in, the property had electricity, working sewers and access to well water. Ryan grew vegetables, raised chickens and kept a horse on his postage-stamp-sized lot. Ryan's parents had sold half of their property back in 1998, but they kept this eighth of an acre to run the father's auto mechanics shop.

Despite Sasol's very public promise that its buy-out offers would be 'the most generous of its kind ever executed', the company initially offered $2,000 for Ryan's family property. At that price or any other, Ryan resolved to remain in Mossville. He vowed to be buried in Perkins Cemetery in Mossville, alongside his mother and father, his aunts, uncles and grandrelatives, where most Mossville residents were buried.

Ryan had promised his parents that he would remain in Mossville and fight for the community. He not only refused to sell to Sasol, but also joined in organized efforts to resist its planned expansion. 'People need to know what's going on', he said, 'and the things industry will do to get its way. As long as I'm here, Sasol can't emit the amount of pollution that the EPA will allow it to emit. Someone needs to take a stand and let this be known.'

But Sasol's campaign to buy out property in Mossville proved relentless. In little time, Sasol successfully bought out all of Ryan's neighbours. Ryan's trailer home at 3009 5th Avenue was the last lot remaining on that street in Mossville, an island surrounded by lots that Sasol had bought, razed and then left undeveloped.

Stacey Ryan's property in Mossville.

'I was told by my own district representative that I would be a casualty of war', Ryan recounted: 'just swept aside because I was holding up progress.' Being 'swept aside' by Sasol looked cold, coordinated and pitiless. The local power company, Entergy, took down the power lines to his home because of 'non-use'. When Sasol's construction work damaged the local sewer system, it was left unrepaired. Vandals destroyed his well. Calcasieu Parish refused his petition to have a water line to his home or to repair the sewer system. Sasol trucks regularly clogged the roadway to his home. The Parish even explored the option of seizing his land through eminent domain, despite the absence of a clear public use justification.

Ryan steadfastly refused offers to sell his family's lot, even as Sasol eventually raised its bid up to $40,000. He resisted and persisted, in his own words, 'like a flea on a dog'. He dug out his own septic system, installed solar panels for power, and brought water in by the barrel from another property in Mossville where his mother had lived. In time, the solar panels were stolen from his roof and the Parish rejected his application to replace them. According to Ryan, someone broke into his property and stole his refrigerator, his oven and even his horse. Ryan said his house had even been hit by shotgun slugs. 'I don't accuse Sasol, but I've caught Sasol people on my property.' 'Whoever's left here needs help', he added. 'Sasol picked the right spot in Louisiana in terms of having a free ticket to do whatever they want, and the local government is going right along, tossing our community into the trash.'

As we have seen again and again, activists can often bring attention to stories that the media has ignored. And Stacey Ryan was not without help. The local group we mentioned earlier, Mossville Environmental Action Now, joined forces with the Sierra Club, a national environmental NGO, and the Louisiana Green Army, a grassroots organization.

The Louisiana Green Army was led by Russel Honoré, a retired Army lieutenant general who became nationally renowned for coordinating military relief efforts after Hurricane Katrina struck New Orleans and its environs. 'I spent over 37 years of my life protecting American democracy all over the globe', Honoré said of Mossville. 'Then I retired and came back to Louisiana and found that the oil companies had bought the democracy in Louisiana.'

Their efforts would not be enough. In this story of Stacey Ryan against Sasol, man against machine, the immoveable object finally relented to the unstoppable force. After years of holding out and after filing a lawsuit against Sasol, Ryan's indomitable spirit finally broke. By 2016, he agreed to sell. Sasol had convinced a sibling who co-owned the property to sell and he, too, ultimately capitulated.

Ryan imagined using the buy-out money to move to a more halcyon life in Helotes, Texas. He wanted to go far away from Lake Charles, where he could raise his children free from worry about toxins in the air and soil. But in another of life's cruel twists, Ryan ended up resettling just across the river from Mossville. Most of his buy-out settlement funds went to pay for his medical bills.

The cavalry did eventually show up in Mossville. Sort of. In 2021, President Joe Biden appointed Michael Regan as the first African American to head the US Environmental Protection Agency. Regan had the president's full endorsement to take seriously the issue of environmental justice, and announced a 'Journey to Justice' tour through Mississippi, Louisiana and Texas to see first-hand and raise public awareness about the environmental impact of industry on historically Black communities. This journey to justice brought Regan to Mossville.

After his visit, Regan's response was unsparing. 'I can tell you', he said, 'being on the ground here, seeing it for myself, talking with the community members, it's just startling that we got to this point . . . It's our responsibility to protect every person in this country, no matter the colour of their skin, how much money they have in their pocket or their ZIP code.'

These words of course came too late for Mossville, as the damage had already been done. By the time Regan had come to visit, only about 50 households remained in Mossville. In a scene from Glustrom's documentary, a long-term Mossville resident walked her dog alongside a deafening convoy of Sasol construction trucks. 'You don't see any traces of us anywhere', she lamented. 'To everyone else, all they see now is Sasol. It doesn't look like we were here. They're erasing everything. Everything.'

In Mossville, we see many elements of a corporate scandal of the sort we have written about throughout this book. There is obvious corporate wrongdoing. Sasol is an archetype villain straight out of Hollywood, with origins as a state enterprise founded to preserve apartheid rule in South Africa. There is a lionheart of an everyday hero in Stacey Ryan, who stands up to Sasol. Mossville residents, with NGOs, organize efforts to raise public awareness and mobilize opposition.

Yet a full-blown scandal of the sort that might transform corporate policies and practices and shape their oversight and regulation failed to materialize. Why? Was this just a matter of a dominant industry getting its way in a state dependent on and eager to lure more business from that industry?

In part, yes. Large companies were once the economic anchor and civic lifeline in American cities like Detroit with the Big Three automakers, Pittsburgh with the steel industry, and Rochester with the tech giants of yesteryear, Kodak and Xerox. Today, large companies can bulldoze a population without public outcry.

Chemical and energy industries are decidedly powerful economic actors in Louisiana. In 2013, chemical manufacturing industries in southern Louisiana alone employed more than 250,000 workers, producing more than $60 billion in outputs, or 27 per cent of the region's economic output. States regularly compete with one another for major capital investments, and in Louisiana Sasol found an eager and willing partner. The proposed new Sasol facilities represented jobs and economic growth to a state that, in 2012, had a 23 per cent poverty rate (above the national average of 15 per cent) and a GDP growth rate of just 1.4 per cent (lower than the 2.5 per cent average for the United States).

Was Sasol simply 'too big to scandalize'? We find that reasoning incomplete. For one thing, Sasol is far from alone among big global corporations that hold sway with national and subnational governments. All the companies in this book share that aspect, so sway by itself does not bestow immunity or gift a 'get out of jail free' card.

To understand why Sasol's operations in southwest Louisiana failed to result in a major scandal, we return to the three key ingredients that give scandals their power to transform: emotions, information and existing public opinion. We need to ask, why were Mossville's neighbours in Brentwood and Westlake not more outraged by Sasol's actions? Why did the media coverage at the time focus chiefly on a massive capital investment in Louisiana and not on the collateral damage that investment would surely bring? Why did existing opinion – in southwest Louisiana or in the United States for that matter – not object to a foreign corporation with a chequered history destroying a beloved local community?

The fate of Stacey Ryan and the Black residents of Mossville brings us back to easy and hard issues. It turns out that scandal-worthy corporate behaviour can fail to catalyse public opinion into outrage if there is an underlying racial dimension in play. Large companies like Sasol are especially likely to fell a healthy community with impunity if the population they raze is not seen as 'one of us'.

We mentioned earlier Arlie Hochschild's book, *Strangers in Their Own Land*. Hochschild describes driving around Lake Charles and finding that 'reminders of the racial divide were everywhere'. Starting at the old Calcasieu Parish Courthouse, Hochschild encounters a statue of a Confederate soldier and beside it a Confederate flag; the list goes on.

In southwest Louisiana, the reservoirs of latent opinion Hochschild finds do not tap into the injustices of petrochemical companies making clear-eyed calculations for financial gain that put all Louisianans, Black or White, in harm's way. Rather, for White Louisianans, the 'Deep Story' – Hochschild's term for what we call latent opinion – is one of resentment, grievance and the injured state of being unseen.

As Hochschild describes the Deep Story that resonates with White working-class Louisianans,

> You're a compassionate person. But now you've been asked to extend your sympathy to all the people who have cut in front of you. So you have your guard up against requests for sympathy. People complain: Racism. Discrimination. Sexism. You've heard stories of oppressed blacks, dominated women, weary immigrants, closeted gays, desperate refugees, but at some point you say to yourself, you have to close the borders to human sympathy.

Whether in Mossville, Louisiana, or Anytown, USA, White Americans' racial resentments and feelings of being left behind can upstage the focusing power of scandalous corporate behaviour. As we noted earlier, the ways White people express their resentments need not even be explicit to have material consequences. Failure to become outraged can be as seemingly harmless as believing that if Stacey Ryan and his ancestors had worked harder, they would have worked their way out of Mossville and away from the land and air ravaged by Sasol and other petrochemical plants around Lake Charles.

There is a term for how the consequences of industrialization and economic development are distributed unequally: 'environmental racism'. When coined in 1982 by civil rights activist Benjamin Chavis, the term rallied protesters who objected to a plan to site a hazardous waste landfill in a predominantly African American community in Warren County, North Carolina. In the years since, the term has been developed in scholarship and policymaking to describe decisions that result in a disproportionate environmental impact on the communities where racial and ethnic minorities reside.

The 'racism' in the term often polarizes, as it implies that the disproportionate impacts were either known, or should have been known, yet the decisions were made without regard for the affected communities. There can be little dispute, however, that the impacts of industry and business decisions are not equally shared. The few who make decisions over where to site fossil fuel extraction and processing plants, and hazardous waste sites more broadly, generally also have the means to decide where to live. They typically choose to live a safe distance from any negative consequences of their siting decisions. The many who are subject to the consequences of those siting decisions generally lack the means to decide where to live. They just have to put up with it.

In the United States, race forcefully shapes where one lives and where one works. Decisions like where to build a new petrochemical plant or where to site a new landfill are made against a terrain of race and residential segregation. Nelson Mandela is said to have once commented, 'Where you stand depends on where you sit.' The corollary to this adage in the United States today is, 'Tell me your zip code, and I will tell you how much you earn, the quality of your education, your probability of going to jail, what illnesses you face, and even how long you can expect to live'.

Scholars of racial segregation – its roots and its role in perpetuating racial inequalities – often home in on America's cities and metropolitan areas. Yet the relationship between where racial minorities live and their life prospects is ubiquitous. Companies have every incentive to build and operate their plants where land is cheap, and where political opposition to their siting is likely to be weaker and less organized, if not actively disenfranchised.

In the United States, that has always meant that pollution-producing plants are likelier to be sited closer to where poor people and racial minorities live. And, as Hochschild noted from her time in Lake Charles, there is an impenetrable 'empathy wall' in America that divides the 'haves' from the 'have-nots', and Whites from Blacks. It is a wall that all too often impedes the surge of anger and action that shapes the iceberg of public opinion.

For a long time, political scientists have debated the extent to which race is a central feature of American politics and whether the United States is 'exceptional' among the rich democracies in that aspect. In fact, Taeku recently published a book on this debate. In our research for this book, everywhere we have conducted surveys on racial resentment, whether about attitudes towards Blacks in Great Britain, North Africans in France, Turks in Germany and Switzerland, or Indigenous Australians, we find extensive evidence of White resentment.

The mix of anti-minority sentiments and the conviction that minority groups don't play by the rules is consequential. Not just in the United States, and not just when the minority group is African American. That racial considerations and empathy walls can disrupt the power of a good scandal is also not uniquely American. We go next halfway around the world, to Australia, to see again the difference between instances of corporate malfeasance that became scandals and those that did not.

Noel Stevens was an unlikely face of Australian anti-bank outrage. Stevens, a 49-year-old scaffolder who enjoyed his beer in the evenings, had little savings. His one significant financial investment was an almost A$300,000 life insurance plan.

In 2010, Stevens received a cold call from a teller at the local branch of Commonwealth Bank of Australia (CBA), the country's largest bank. The teller suggested he should come in and see a CBA financial planner. That planner convinced him to abandon his old life insurance policy and sign up for the CBA plan instead. The transaction netted the teller a referral fee of A$445 and the planner A$815.

It was not such a good deal for Noel Stevens.

A year later Stevens was diagnosed with terminal pancreatic cancer, which can cause shooting pains in the stomach and back. When he attempted to arrange for the policy to pay out to his only daughter, Teghan Couper, the CBA refused the claim – two days before Christmas.

Bank employees had scoured his monthly statements, cataloguing the alcohol purchases. They could prove that he was a heavy drinker, but then they already knew that. At the time of his application, the bank had received notes from his doctor observing that he drank eight 'stubbies' – the Australian term for a short bottle of beer – nightly. The bank was aware that Stevens had been counselled about alcohol consumption.

The bank denied Stevens's insurance claim, but it nonetheless continued to charge him his annual premium. He took the CBA to court, giving testimony from his hospital bed while on pain-dulling morphine. Stevens finally won the case in July 2012 just days before he died. As his daughter was making funeral arrangements for her father, her lawyer contacted her to let her know the bank was appealing the court's ruling. Couper eventually won the appeal case too. She got her money, but the bank had spent more on legal fees fighting the claim than she was actually paid.

Noel Stevens was no anti-bank activist, and his daughter's story attracted limited attention at the time of his death. But it did catch the attention of Adele Ferguson, a reporter for the *Sydney Morning Herald*. The story of how Noel Stevens was treated by CBA formed the centrepiece for a report by Ferguson, broadcast in 2014 on the investigative television programme *Four Corners*, which attracted more than one million viewers in a country of fewer than 24 million people.

The episode, entitled 'Banking Bad', was a public relations disaster for the Commonwealth Bank of Australia. The public anger unleashed by the interview with Stevens' daughter reached a crescendo in 2017 in the appointment of the Banking Royal Commission. The final report of the Commission, headed by the fearsome judge Kenneth Hayne, raked all four major Australian banks over the coals for their repeated exploitation of customers, including charging fees to dead people. Australian banks were forced to implement changes in how they treated their customers that would have prevented the Noel Stevens scandal.

The Hayne inquiry into financial malpractice in Australia in 2017 also discovered other victims whose stories had drawn less public interest than that of Noel Stevens. Unlike Stevens, who was White, many of these other victims were Indigenous Australians.

The Aboriginal Community Benefit Fund (ACBF), which later became the Youpla group, was established in 1992 by a White New Zealander named Ron Pattenden to sell funeral insurance to Indigenous Australians. Funerals are particularly culturally significant to this community, and Aboriginal mourning and burial ceremonies can last between days and months. The fund immediately came under scrutiny for not operating according to the rules of the New South Wales government. Over the years regulators repeatedly charged the fund with selling a poor-quality insurance product and using predatory sales tactics, as well as deliberately misrepresenting itself as an Aboriginal organization.

One victim, Tracey Walsh, paid A$10,000 in premiums for a policy which would only ever pay out A$8,000. Moreover, the firm had a reputation for not paying out claims. Regulators from the state of New South Wales and the federal Australian Securities and Investment Commission went after the company repeatedly for causing 'financial detriment' to its clients and continuing to misrepresent its links with the Indigenous community. Yet, absent any pressure from the public, these charges were repeatedly dismissed.

The Banking Royal Commission used ACBF-Youpla as one of its case studies of abusive practices by financial organizations. In his interim report, Commissioner Kenneth Hayne castigated the company for falling below community standards in a number of respects, including by selling insurance policies to children. The report also noted that customers of ACBF-Youpla received only 13 per cent of the premiums they paid, the lowest percentage discovered in an industry-wide survey.

On the heels of this high-profile reprimand, regulatory authorities closed in on ACBF-Youpla. Eventually, in March 2022, the company collapsed into insolvency. The bankruptcy left many Indigenous families unable to pay the funeral expenses of their deceased relatives, leaving their bodies stranded in morgues for months.

Australian Indigenous families had ultimately lost A$174 million in payments to the company, while its founder, Pattenden, had received almost A$21 million – tax-free. Pattenden had structured his ownership of ACBF-Youpla in such a way that his dividend payments functioned as a loan repayment between his companies. This sort of loan repayment was not legally subject to tax in either Australia or New Zealand.

Samantha Rudolph is the Aboriginal Policy Officer for the Consumer Action Law Centre in Melbourne. She offered a scathing critique of the history of regulatory failures that ultimately produced Youpla's collapse: 'If this was a mainstream insurer that had policyholders from the mainstream population, we believe that it wouldn't have gone on for 30 years, the government would have stepped in and shut it down, perhaps within five years.'

The story of ACBF-Youpla illustrates that scandals that disproportionately affect racial minorities sometimes fail to cause widespread outcry, or that outcry happens only in the wake of scandals that also affect members of the majority population. The Youpla case is every bit as outrageous as the abuses the Commonwealth Bank of Australia visited on the family of Noel Stevens. The story nonetheless did not gain traction in the media, despite repeated regulatory challenges and court cases. That is because its overtones of racial exploitation did not resonate with members of the majority White community in Australia.

What resonates with the public is tied up with issues of race and identity. And when race becomes the defining character of a scandal — as, for example, in issues of mortgage redlining, where minorities are disproportionately excluded from access to credit markets — a scandal may lose its capacity to generate outrage across the broader population.

Race is of course not the only reason that outrageous corporate behaviour fails to get picked up by the media and turned into a scandal, just as southern Louisiana is not the only place in that state despoiled by the petrochemical industry. We should know. Pepper was born in northern Louisiana, and his entire family hails from Ouachita Parish, in the northeastern corner of the state.

Ouachita Parish is in some unhappy ways the northern twin of Calcasieu Parish, where Stacey Ryan comes from. It's the third most residentially segregated parish in the state, just in front of Calcasieu. In 2016, Ouachita Parish was the 29th most toxic county in the country, in terms of chemicals released into the environment. Calcasieu Parish was 27th in this list of infamy.

The single largest source of these toxins in Ouachita Parish is the big Angus petrochemical plant, located in the town of Sterlington. The facility in Sterlington has long brought good jobs to an area that doesn't have many. When he was at university back in the 1960s, Pepper's father worked there one summer as a carpenter's assistant, at a carbon black plant on the site. Carbon black is a stiffening agent for tyre rubber.

The way Pepper's dad tells it, it was a well-paid job, but hellish: the inside of the plant was kept at 120 degrees Fahrenheit. He would return home every day covered from head to toe in fine carbon black powder, which would then ooze out of his skin again shortly after he'd taken the first of his multiple post-work showers.

The carbon black section of the plant closed in 1977, but the Angus facility carried on with a variety of chemical functions, including the production of nitroparaffin, a solvent used for pharmaceuticals and cosmetics. In 1991, an explosion in a compressor at the plant killed eight workers and injured 128 workers and residents. The explosion caused extensive property damage in the town of Sterlington, half of whose population of 1,200 had to be temporarily evacuated.

When the Assistant Secretary of the US Department of Labor visited the scene of the blast, he was horrified. 'It took metal beams and twisted them like pretzels. It penetrated stainless-steel tanks like throwing rocks through cardboard', he told the Associated Press.

The explosion in Sterlington briefly made the news, particularly because it was one of a series of deadly accidents at American petrochemical plants that occurred just as the industry was cutting costs, with the implication that safety was one of them.

The Occupational Safety and Health Administration (OSHA) quickly reached the then-largest settlement in its history – $10 million – with the company. As part of the settlement, Angus agreed to safety improvements. Two months before the Angus explosion, OSHA had reached the same sort of 'no blame settlement', for a slightly lower amount, when an explosion at a Citgo refinery in Calcasieu Parish killed six workers.

In both cases, unions representing plant workers complained that the rapid settlements, which required no admission of guilt from the companies, were outrageous, because they deprived workers harmed by the explosions of the opportunity to pursue further damages in the civil courts. Robert Wages, the aptly named president of the Oil, Chemical and Atomic Workers union, slammed the Angus settlement as a 'scandalous, sleazy manoeuvre'.

Readers may be thinking, 'Well, that's what union leaders always say'. The job of a union representative is after all to defend workers. However, economist Kip Viscusi, an expert in cost-benefit and regulation analysis, agreed with Wages' assessment. Economists tend to focus on efficiency rather than workers' interests, yet in a 2020 article, Viscusi named the Sterlington settlement as an egregious example of a settlement too small to incentivize the company to take safety seriously. The Angus settlement really was a rip-off, and at the time no-one but the union seemed to care.

Predominantly White communities like Sterlington can suffer a corporate injustice that fails to catch the public imagination, just as predominantly Black communities like Mossville do. We relay the story of Sterlington and the realities of life in rural Louisiana to remind readers that the public can disregard the consequences of corporate injustice for many reasons. Racial boundaries are a powerful and recurring reason. But they are not the only type of boundary that allows hard issues, like petrochemical safety, to avoid the broad public scrutiny that scandals bring.

The ability to sew a thread of common cause is a key to collective outrage and political action. Whether we are in Calcasieu Parish or Ouachita Parish, Louisiana or Australia for that matter, citizens everywhere are often divided by identities that create empathy walls. We have seen in this chapter how members of the voting public can see incidents of outrageous corporate behaviour as 'not my problem' and their victims as 'not one of us'.

This is a problem for all of us, when we allow our identities and our resentments to avert our gaze from injustices visited on our fellow citizens. And it is a problem when journalists, presuming our indifference, fail to report on such events because they think no-one will care. As we have seen over and over in this book, scandals only become scandals when the media seizes on an issue and refuses to let it go.

On this point, Russel Honoré, the Louisiana native and leader of the Louisiana Green Army, is more eloquent than we are about the duties of the media. Speaking to the Society of Environmental Journalists in 2014, Honoré expressed his disgust over an earlier session featuring a communications executive from BP, the British oil giant. In 2010 BP was responsible for the Deepwater Horizon disaster and oil spill in the Gulf of Mexico, which killed 11 workers and devastated the local economies of the Gulf States, which depend on fishing and tourism.

Referring to the oil and fuel industry, Honoré said, 'They have hijacked our damn economy'. While accepting that fossil fuels were necessary for energy, he added that 'it does not give the industry the right to destroy where we live'. Then Honoré turned to the ballroom full of journalists: 'There is never a time the world needs you more . . . Do your damn job!'

PART FOUR

The Renovation Project

9

The Fall of a Samsung Prince

The titans of the corporate world all start somewhere. For the Samsung Group, that origin story begins in Uiryeong, a sleepy and sparsely populated agrarian town in South Gyeongsang Province, between Daegu and Busan.

Uiryeong is the birthplace to Lee Byung-chul, born in 1910 into a wealthy *yangban* family, by tradition the highest non-royal social class in Korea. The privileges of pedigree, however, were precarious in Lee's time. Korea in the first decades of B. C. Lee's life fell under Japanese colonial rule, where tumult and inconstancy ruled the day even for landed gentry like Lee's family. Property rights were routinely ignored as land and businesses were usurped. Labourers and 'comfort women' were forced into servitude by the Japanese military. Korean culture itself was a target of Japan's imperial ambitions, as Japan sought to remake Korea in its image by banning the teaching of Korean language and history in schools, destroying historical documents and artefacts, and even coercing Koreans into adopting Japanese names.

Into this milieu, Lee set out to make a mark not just for himself, but also for a Korea that seemed hopelessly under Japan's thumb. After a brief stint at Waseda University in Tokyo, a training ground at the time for Korea's aspiring elite, Lee returned to Korea to start his own business. His first venture, a rice polishing mill in Masan, sputtered. Then in 1938 Lee settled on a grocery and trading company in Daegu. This new enterprise, which specialized in noodles, vegetables and dried fish and shipped products to China and Manchuria, proved far more successful. Lee named his company Samsung Sanghoe, or the Three Stars Shop. Lee's choice of moniker bore an uncanny likeness to one of Japan's largest *zaibatsu* (conglomerates), Mitsubishi (the 'three diamonds' or 'three chestnuts'). The name reflected Lee's keen and lifelong attention to Japan as an archetype of personal and national achievement.

Today we know this trading company as the Samsung Group, the largest conglomerate in South Korea. In *Samsung Rising,* Geoffrey Cain recounts his visit to Daegu to the site of B. C. Lee's trading shop, which had since been razed. In its place, Cain finds a replica of the original building's façade. One of the several plaques memorializing the company's history catches Cain's eye. The plaque is etched with the following quote from Lee: 'I think people are most happy when they know what gives their life purpose. I am unshakeable in my faith that strengthening the nation through business is the path I must walk.'

Strengthening a nation through business is not the typical motivation for a corporate tycoon. But this quote encapsulates South Korea's path to modernization, where a small trading company like Samsung that once exported noodles and dried fish grows into one of the world's leading corporate brands.

That transformation is not just a story of personal triumph and ballyhooed success. There is also a story involving scandals. In fact, if we were to don Mad Scientist white coats and head to our secret Scandal Lab to design an especially hard test case for our account of scandals and democratic backlash, it would look a lot like South Korea.

It would be a country that had only recently made the leap from poverty and underdevelopment to advanced capitalism, and from rule under dictatorship to stable democracy. It would be a country in which corporations were the conquering heroes in a national story of success, from economic backwater to industrial titan and technological dynamo. It would be a country whose citizens linked their interests and those of their country inextricably to the interests of its largest, most profitable corporations.

In other words, it would be a country where one might say, 'What's good for Samsung is good for South Korea'.

We shall see that in such a hard test case as South Korea, the misbehaviour that rises to the level of a major scandal is as surreal as it is shameful. Yet, the bigger they come, as they say, the harder they fall. And the scandal we describe in this chapter ultimately takes down both a sitting president of South Korea and the anointed prince of Samsung. In this instance, what was bad for South Koreans turned out to also be bad for Samsung.

None of this was prefigured in 1948 at Korea's independence and birth as a modern nation. Even into the early 1960s, South Korea's per capita income was at or below that of Haiti, Yemen and Ethiopia. Its capital city Seoul was still a place of hand-drawn carts, 'moon villages' (slums populated by post-war refugees and rural migrants), the thick smell of crude diesel engines and an infrastructure inadequate to a rising wave of mass migration.

Over the next several decades, South Korea achieved what many still refer to as the 'miracle on the Han River', a reference to Seoul's main waterway. The gross national income per capita in South Korea grew from $67 in the early days of independence in the 1950s to $33,745 by 2023. Between 1962 and 1996, South Korea's gross domestic product grew an average of more than 8 per cent each year, from a GDP of $4 billion to $610 billion. Today, Korea's nominal GDP is a soaring US$1.7 trillion, ranking 14th in the world.

This transformation did not occur overnight, nor did the 'miracle' happen by dint of ambition, hard work and ingenuity alone. It happened largely by design, a result of explicit government intervention and state planning in the Korean economy that yoked the fledgling nation's economic future to the prosperity of a select few private enterprises, the *chaebol*. More on the *chaebol* in a moment.

Other factors were of course also at work. In its early years of independence, South Korea was among the world's largest recipients of foreign aid. The lion's share came from the United States, which saw Korea as a strategic ally and bulwark against communism. Despite the rampant political corruption in these years, this aid created the foundation for long-term economic development planning. Foreign aid also enabled South Korea to invest heavily in human capital, from primary education to technical training to administrative expertise, all critical resources for an aspiring economy.

It nevertheless took a coup d'état for South Korea's economic fortunes to take a dramatic turn upwards. On 16 May 1961, an army general named Park Chung-hee led a military coup that seized power from the then-democratically elected government. President Park is remembered by many today as a heroic, historic figure who turned a poor Korea into one of Asia's 'Four Tigers'. He is also remembered for his pitiless rule over the Korean people, subjecting them to years of arbitrary, ruthless and deadly repression. In exchange, Park promised economic growth and relentlessly pursued Korea's independence from its status as a de facto financial ward of the United States.

To keep that promise, Park jettisoned South Korea's floundering industrialization policy based on import substitution for a series of five-year economic development plans that targeted labour-intensive, export-oriented industrialization. This was a hard pivot to infrastructure and investments in export industries and the production of capital goods. In some instances, that pivot entailed directly manipulating Korea's fledgling market economy by helping to found powerful companies like Pohang Iron and Steel Company. The pivot also required strong-arm tactics to secure buy-in from South Korea's industrialists and business elites.

Like B. C. Lee.

Park Chung-hee unceremoniously and publicly paraded Lee and many of Korea's wealthiest men as corrupt cronies of the previous Syngman Rhee administration, threatening jail and forfeiture of their assets. In private, however, Park quietly extracted their commitments to redirect their manufactured capital and human capital towards his new five-year plans. In return, Park aggressively directed government funds and favours to the chosen few companies that backed his economic agenda, protected them from any real market competition and mostly played the disinterested spectator while these companies ran roughshod over workplace labour standards and the right to organize.

These chosen few companies would become what we today know as *chaebol*. Chaebol – which literally translates into 'rich family' or 'financial clique' – are large, diversified, family-owned conglomerates, much like Japanese *zaibatsu* of the pre-war era. Chaebol are not only massive corporations notable for their centralized ownership, but also remarkably diversified in the number and range of economic activities of their subsidiaries. The Samsung Group, for instance, has nearly 80 affiliates. In addition to Samsung Electronics, for which it is best known, Samsung also has its hands in shipbuilding, construction, life insurance, advertising, biopharmaceuticals, luxury hotels, theme parks and golf courses, to name only its highest-profile affiliate companies.

Over the last half century, many chaebol have come to exercise an outsized influence on South Korea's economy. In 2022, the total assets of Korea's five largest chaebol were responsible for 61 per cent of the entire nation's GDP. The Samsung Group alone made up 22 per cent. The largest of these family-owned conglomerates like Hyundai, LG (Lucky-Goldstar), Lotte and Samsung are household names not just in South Korea but throughout the world.

But, like B. C. Lee and his trading company in Daegu, Korea's chaebol and their founders started as very different, much smaller-scale enterprises. The Lotte Group started out as a chewing gum confectionary in Japan. The LG Group began as a cosmetics manufacturing business that made it big with a facial cream called Lucky. The Hyundai Group began as a small automobile repair shop in Seoul before Hyundai was launched as a construction firm.

The humble-origins, rags-to-riches folklore surrounding these companies and their billionaire founders is etched into South Korea's consciousness. They are an indelible source of national pride and identity. For many Koreans, the economic vitality of South Korea marches in lockstep with the financial successes of its chaebol. According to a 2023 poll reported in the *Korea Herald*, 60 per cent of Koreans hold a favourable view towards chaebol, 88 per cent credit them with Korea's economic growth, 74 per cent with investment, 71 per cent job creation, 71 per cent innovation, and 63 per cent increasing income nationally.

Beyond the polling numbers, a job with a chaebol is a career ambition for Korea's most highly trained and talented. The larger the chaebol, the greater the status that comes with the job and the more desired that career. In addition to status and salary, jobs with chaebol are also highly sought after because many act as a de facto 'shadow welfare state' with generous benefits packages for their employees. For instance, the benefits package for a Samsung employee may cover not just health insurance and an annuity plan, but also coverage for wedding and funeral expenses as well as family educational expenses from kindergarten to university.

Becoming a 'Samsung man' has particular cachet as a marker of prestige and prosperity. In 2014, some 200,000 hopeful employees took the 'Samsung SAT', a lengthy test of aptitude in mathematics, sciences, history, logic and analytical reasoning. That number represented some 30 per cent of all college graduates in South Korea that year, many of whom had prepared through toil and tears for years for a mere 5 to 10 per cent chance of passing the exam and being offered a career with Samsung.

With the chaebol wielding this kind of power over a country and its people, one would hardly expect South Korea to be a place where a corporate scandal could activate a mass backlash. President Park Chung-hee's initial favouritism towards B. C. Lee and other chaebol leaders gave them every reason to expect that they could

Samsung man

behave badly with impunity. With the additional vaunted standing in Korean society that came with its rising economic fortunes, the chaebol seemingly enjoyed the additional bulwark of support from public opinion.

And yet the Korean public eventually became properly angered and mobilized. What came to be known as the Choi Soon-sil

Scandal, and the groundswell of popular anger it sparked, represent a singular moment in recent Korean history, one that through the main characters involved connects the past to the present. This would be corporate scandal wrapped inside a political scandal, and the moment culminates in the downfall of a nation's president and the discredit to the heir to its largest conglomerate.

The main characters of the past are Park Chung-hee, the former president and dictator credited for leading Korea out of its poverty-stricken past; B. C. Lee, Samsung founder who profited from Park's economic development plans; and Choi Tae-min, a third gentleman we have not yet been introduced to. The main characters of the present are Park Geun-hye, daughter of Park Chung-hee who had won office as president in the 2012 national elections; Lee Jae-yong (J. Y. Lee), grandson of B. C. Lee who was groomed to succeed B. C. Lee's son and his father, Lee Kun-hee, as chairman of the Samsung Group; and Choi Soon-sil, daughter of Choi Tae-min and the spark that ignited the scandal in this chapter.

But we are getting a bit ahead of ourselves. To appreciate how we got to the Choi Soon-sil scandal, we need to describe the circumstances of Park Geun-hye's early life and how she and her father became acquainted with Choi Soon-sil's father, Choi Tae-min.

If growing up as the child of a president is never easy, Park Geun-hye's early years were especially eventful. When she was still at the tender age of 11, her father, Park Chung-hee, engineered a military coup and eventually seized the presidency. Then, at 22, she endured her mother being killed by an errant bullet in a failed assassination attempt on her father. By the time she was 27, Park's father was killed in a second assassination attempt – this one successfully executed by her father's close friend and then director of the Korean Central Intelligence Agency.

Formative years so filled with chaos, terror and loss could understandably have led Park Geun-hye to seek a quiet life away from the limelight. Yet immediately after her mother's death Park found herself in an even more visible and vulnerable position, as she was expected to take on the role and duties of South Korea's First Lady herself. Where a father might have stepped in to gently guide his child into the withering glare that came with this title, Park Chung-hee, by his own admission, was a detached and disinterested parent.

This is where Choi Tae-min enters the story. Choi Tae-min was a somewhat sinister religious figure who led a cult-like Christian sect called the Church of Eternal Life and once proclaimed himself a 'Future Buddha'. Choi had made President Park Chung-hee's acquaintance and would seize on personal tragedy to insinuate himself fully into the young Park Geun-hye's life.

After Park Chung-hee's wife was killed, Choi Tae-min sought and received Park's approval to take on the role of spiritual mentor to his daughter. Choi claimed powers of necromancy that enabled him to communicate with Park Geun-hye's dead mother in his dreams. And in those dreams, Choi claimed, the mother pleaded with him to look after her orphaned daughter.

Written accounts show that in this role Choi held a Svengali-like influence over the young woman, an influence he exploited to extract bribes to fill his personal coffers. As the then US Ambassador Alexander Vershbow wrote in a diplomatic wire in 2007 after Choi died, 'Rumours are rife that the late pastor had complete control over Park's body and soul during her formative years and that his children accumulated enormous wealth as a result.'

Choi Tae-min's relationship to both Park Chung-hee and Park Geun-hye saw him come to be referred to as a 'Korean Rasputin'. One theory holds that Choi's influence over both father and daughter was so prepotent that it was the motive behind Park Chung-hee's assassination by his own intelligence chief.

It is after Choi Tae-min passes away in 1994 that his daughter, Choi Soon-sil, enters the story. Through her father, Choi Soon-sil had become a trusted friend of Park Geun-hye's. The connection might have waned after her father's death, but instead it deepened. So much so that when Park Geun-hye suffered a knife attack at a political rally in 2006 in an apparent assassination attempt, Choi Soon-sil tended to her recovery. By then, Choi Soon-sil had fully assumed the father's role as Park Geun-hye's spiritual guide.

Over time Choi Soon-sil too came to be seen as a Rasputin-like, occult figure who held Park Geun-hye totally under her control. This relationship between Choi Soon-sil and Park Geun-hye is the foundation stone of the scandal, alongside the clandestine access to the innermost corridors of power in Korea that Choi exploited as a result.

Such private, privileged entrée and influence is jealously guarded and kept sub rosa. Corruption and unscrupulous connections do not always mature into ripe scandals. South Korea and the world may never have known about Choi Soon-sil but for another affair. This one did not conjure shamans and necromancers. It involved a puppy.

'Puppygate', as the affair was called in Korea, involved Choi Soon-sil and her entanglements with a man named Ko Young-tae. Twenty years her junior and endowed with matinee idol looks, Ko was rumoured to work as a gigolo at a 'host bar'. He was hungry to launch a fashion accessory brand, saw Choi as a means to do so, and charmed his way into a relationship that eventually led him to be dubbed as Choi Soon-sil's 'boy toy'.

Through Choi, Ko became the unofficial clothier to President Park Geun-hye, and the pair grew thick as thieves. So much so that Choi regularly entrusted her daughter's puppy to Ko's care. Then, in a quintessentially Korean twist, one fateful day Ko apparently left the puppy to go off and play a round of golf. Choi found the puppy abandoned and flew into a fit of rage. This set off to a massive fight after which, per Ko's testimony before South Korea's National Assembly, 'she treated me like a slave, swearing at me many times'.

Ko's indignation at being mistreated fuelled a thirst for vengeance. He began to secretly collect evidence of Choi Soon-sil's insider's access to Park Geun-hye, including CCTV footage of Choi bossing Park's presidential aides around like her own lackeys. Ko handed this evidence over to a broadcast station, TV Chosun.

This evidence might have broken the Choi Soon-sil scandal open but for yet another unexpected turn. A rival station, JTBC, scooped TV Chosun's plan to run the story on 25 October 2016 by running its own exposé a day earlier, on 24 October. JTBC had something juicier than CCTV footage. A JTBC reporter had got their hands on a Samsung Galaxy tablet belonging to Choi Soon-sil. It turned out that Choi had hastily fled South Korea to Frankfurt in Germany after sensing an impending media feeding frenzy around her relationship to Park Geun-hye. And in her haste, Choi had left behind the tablet, unencrypted.

The tablet's files contained a treasure trove of evidence, revealing lurid details of Choi Soon-sil's intimate ties to President Park Geun-hye. They also included evidence of corruption and improper influence: a private citizen's possession of the president's calendar; the president's confidential briefings for cabinet meetings; intel on potential presidential appointments; perhaps most incriminating of all, dozens of draft presidential speeches marked up in red by Choi.

The bombshell shocked the nation. As a candidate for president, Park Geun-hye had run on an anti-corruption platform. While campaigning, Park publicly proclaimed that because she had no husband and no children, her power as president could not be exploited and she was therefore incorruptible. Now the Samsung Galaxy tablet's content laid bare the extent of Choi Soon-sil's influence.

President Park was evidently both highly exploitable and corruptible. This was now a full-bore scandal.

Further investigations in the weeks that followed – both by journalists and then the Korean parliament – unearthed layers upon layers of further intrigue. President Park, who already had a reputation as an enigmatic and aloof leader, soon had to confront rumours of other covert confidantes with an outsized influence on the Blue House. Rumours swirled of a secretive clique of 'eight fairies' that Choi Soon-sil had created to be puppet-masters, wielding control over Park Geun-hye and her decisions as Korea's president.

Most damning were discoveries of the Park government's quid pro quo trafficking in influence and favours with chaebol. A sordid political scandal was quickly becoming a juicy corporate scandal. Choi Soon-sil's influence, presumably with President Park's knowledge and approval, extended to brokering backroom deals between the Park government and chaebol executives. There was literally a backroom: on the top floor of the Testa Rossa, an unassuming Italian café under Choi's ownership in the posh Gangnam district of Seoul. At the other end of these clandestine café meetings were two sham foundations Choi had set up to receive and pass through millions in 'donations' from chaebol in exchange for political favours.

A fever-pitched, mediatized dragnet ensued. By 6 December 2016, the Korean National Assembly had summoned chief executives from Samsung, Hyundai, SK, LG, Lotte and other chaebol to answer questions about their involvement in under-the-table arrangements with Choi Soon-sil. By 2017 it appeared that Choi's foundations had received some $70 million in corporate donations, and some 50 different chaebol were implicated in such influence-peddling. The parties found guilty included the Lotte Group and its chairman, Shin Dong-bin, who was sentenced to two-and-a-half years for transferring about $7 million in exchange for favourable licensing of Lotte's duty-free businesses.

The biggest fish, however, was the Samsung Group. Samsung and its future leader, Lee Jae-yong, were found guilty of paying or promising roughly $38 million to Choi's foundations and funnelling additional millions of dollars to Choi's daughter – including a horse valued at more than $700,000. In exchange, Samsung expected to receive favourable government approval of a proposed merger of two of its affiliates, Samsung C&T Corporation and Cheil Industries. The merger's intended effect was to make Lee the dominant shareholder of the Samsung empire. Thus, it held the key to Samsung's succession plan for Lee Jae-yong.

'Jay Y.', as he is popularly called, is Park Geun-hye's counterpart in this scandal. He is the grandson to Samsung founder B. C. Lee and the only son of Lee Kun-hee, who followed B. C. Lee as chairman of the Samsung Group. Jay Y. not only held the status of heir to the throne by blood lineage, but he also looked the part of a corporate prince. Educated at Seoul National University, Keio and Harvard, the perfectly coiffed, alabaster-complexioned and sartorially splendid Jay Y. had been groomed for accession through several management positions created for the purpose.

The expectations put on Jay Y.'s shoulders were heavy. His father, Lee Kun-hee, was the stuff of legend. Unsatisfied with the Samsung his father (B. C. Lee) had built, Lee Kun-hee sought to transform Samsung from a brand known for producing lower-quality consumer products at cheap prices into a global conglomerate at the leading edge of technological innovation. As the lore goes, to achieve that vision Lee Kun-hee famously sequestered Samsung's top brass at a retreat in Frankfurt, Germany and commanded, 'If you are to change, change completely . . . Change everything except your wife and kids.' Lee Kun-hee's gambit was a thumping success.

Now, by 2016, he was hospitalized and recovering from a heart attack. As we noted earlier, Samsung accounts for roughly 20 per cent of Korea's GDP. All eyes in Korea were thus fixed on how and when Samsung would transfer power and leadership to Jay Y. Lee. Geoffrey Cain's *Samsung Rising* quotes a former Samsung senior vice-president's observation that 'He's sort of like a god inside the company. Every little thing he does is analysed, and it becomes basically an edict right away.'

It was in this context that the Choi Soon-sil scandal evoked a deafening public roar that ultimately galvanized a legislature and judiciary to respond. High-level senior officials and management were held to account, including the summary dismissals of Park Geun-hye's closest government advisers and vice-presidents at Samsung. Under ordinary circumstances or in a run-of-the-mill scandal, that level of accountability might have closed the book on the affair. However, this was no ordinary scandal.

Importantly, the dramatic consequences that this scandal precipitated – the impeachment and imprisonment of a sitting president and the criminal investigation, arrest and conviction of a chaebol heir – did not result from the routine application of laws and regulations designed to rein in cronyism and corporate malfeasance. Korea had enacted such restraints starting in the 1990s, but old ways can be stubbornly resistant to change. Corporate scofflaws and backroom deals that disregarded well-intended corporate oversight largely continued to thrive.

Rather, the scandal's power came from a hidden force: decades of anger and unrest that had been simmering beneath the surface as South Korea modernized its economy at great social cost. In this chapter, we see the difference democracy makes.

The Choi Soon-sil scandal touched a raw nerve with South Koreans. What might have been a tale of malfeasance followed peremptorily by a speedy and sweeping repression of public outrage to protect privileged insiders – like we saw in Chapter 1 with Sanlu in China – instead resulted in the largest demonstration in the nation's history. Between October 2016 and April 2017, roughly 16 million South Koreans – nearly a third of the population – participated in what came to be known as the 'Candlelight Protests'.

For weeks and then months, massive crowds gathered around Gwanghwamun Square, by the Royal Palace, demanding nothing less than the ousting of President Park and the wholesale reform of politics and business–government relations. Participants burned candles to 'give light to the darkness' the Choi Soon-sil scandal symbolized: an unwelcome reflection of Korea's past, and a return to corruption, authoritarianism and cronyism between government and the chaebol that many Koreans saw as an enemy of the people and a barrier to better days ahead. On a single day alone, 3 December 2016, nearly two million Koreans braved the cold and gathered in downtown Seoul, raising their candles to demand accountability from the highest levels of government.

The turn in public sentiment against Park Geun-hye and Korea's chaebol stretched far beyond the millions who participated in the Candlelight Protests. It also registered resoundingly in presidential approval ratings. In the first year of her presidency, Park Geun-hye regularly enjoyed support from a majority of South Koreans, with ratings that at times exceeded a fulsome 60 per cent. That would not last. By mid-2016 President Park's approval had already dropped down to about 30–35 per cent, after Park's Saenuri Party suffered

Candlelight rally at Gwanghwamun Square, Seoul.

a major setback in the general election that year. When the Choi Soon-sil scandal hit, however, the bottom fell out. By November 2016, Park's approval ratings plunged to a shockingly low 4 per cent.

This is how the iceberg of public opinion can emerge out of a scandal. Faced with previous corruption scandals, South Korea's parliamentary and judicial institutions had often looked the other way or slapped wrists. Now an outraged public demanded swift and sure action. The sheer brazenness of the wrongdoing, the scale of the protests it precipitated, the bottomed-out public approval ratings, all converged to produce the kind of iceberg that can take down a government.

By 9 December 2016, about a week after more than two million protesters gathered in Seoul with their candles, the National Assembly voted to impeach the president by an overwhelming 234–56. Not three months later, on 10 March 2017, the Constitutional Court unanimously upheld the National Assembly's decision. Park then faced criminal proceedings, for which she was given a 24-year prison sentence and a $16.8 million fine. Choi Soon-sil, for her part, received a 20-year sentence for influence-peddling, corruption, soliciting favours illegally and abuse of power.

Importantly, what began as a tale of political corruption also turned into one of corporate misconduct. The effigies of Park Geun-hye the Candlelight Protest participants paraded up and down Sejongno boulevard included chaebol logos lassoed around her waist. Participants waved flags and placards that declared, 'Arrest Lee Jae-yong!'

The Choi Soon-sil scandal thus also led to the criminal conviction in August 2017 of the Samsung dynast Jay Y. Lee on charges of bribery, embezzlement and perjury. Lee received five years in prison. To experts, the criminal conviction of a chaebol leader – of the Samsung Group, no less – represented a watershed in democratic accountability for South Korea. 'Until now', declared Jong-il You, an economist and reform advocate who would become dean of the country's elite KDI School of Public Policy and Management, 'Samsung has always been considered above the law in South Korea. This marks a big stride in establishing judicial justice in the country because it has kept failing before Samsung.'

This defining moment had been a long time coming. One could say, in a manner befitting a Victorian novel, that the fall of Park Geun-hye and Jay Y. Lee was foreshadowed from their ancestors' beginnings.

For Park Geun-hye's part, the ghosts of her father's past were inescapable. Park Chung-hee's conviction that Korea's economic fortunes required a ruthless disregard for human life and citizens' rights ultimately instilled a spirit of resistance in the Korean people that presaged the Candlelight Protests. During his reign, Park and his police state apparatus forcefully quashed any opposition and demonstrations, notwithstanding the economic achievements the regime ushered in for Korea. Thus, his legacy has always deeply divided the nation.

The brutal tactics of the 1970s and 1980s gave rise to strong civil society associations that cultivated dissent and nurtured demands for democracy. By 1987, labour, Christians, farmers, students, scholars and journalists allied and organized to successfully transform Korea from an authoritarian state into an electoral democracy. Those same engines from civil society also sparked a tradition of peaceful assembly by candlelight to protest against perceived injustices. Candlelit demonstrations were held in 2002 when US soldiers were exonerated after two female students had been run over and killed by their armoured vehicle. They broke out too in 2008 after the South Korean government's decision to continue to import United States beef despite instances of 'mad cow disease' being contracted from them.

By the time the Korean public learned the details of Choi Soon-sil, Park Geun-hye and Jay Y. Lee's transgressions in 2016, these candlelit protests had hardened into a full-blown iceberg of public opinion. Over 20 successive Saturday nights, thousands and then millions of South Koreans rallied and railed against President Park and a broken system of cronyism, brandishing placards that declared, 'The people are sovereign!' And after the nation's constitutional court upheld Park's impeachment, tens of thousands gathered again in a 'Celebration of Democracy' on 11 March 2017 in a festival-like atmosphere, replacing their candles of sombre protest with a revelry of firecrackers, live music, cosplay and Korean flags.

For Jay Y. Lee's part, the ghosts of his grandfather's past, too, were inescapable. While B. C. Lee's commitment to wed his personal business ambitions to the nation's economic prosperity makes for a good *Bildungsroman*, Samsung today is no different from other chaebol or any other corporation in its pursuit of profit. The profit motive, especially in the context of global competition, ultimately fed a more ominous side to B. C. Lee's legacy, and that of his fellow chaebol founders. That is the legacy of steep and sobering social externalities that continue to haunt South Korea.

Today South Korea has the highest suicide rate among OECD countries, at nearly 25 suicide deaths per 100,000 persons. Among Koreans aged 10 to 39 suicide, the ultimate death of despair, is the leading cause of mortality. South Korea also has the world's lowest fertility rate, dropping down to 0.72 in 2023, or less than half the average fertility rate among OECD countries. If this rate remains unchanged, by 2100 South Korea's population is forecast to be roughly half its current number, a demographic time bomb that has reached crisis proportions.

These distressingly high suicide rates and low fertility rates are symptomatic of a deeper, brewing despair and anger among South Koreans, stemming from myriad sources, including stagnating wages, rising costs of living, demanding work cultures, shifting gender roles and attitudes towards marriage, a hyper-competitive bottleneck for upward mobility, and a general resentment among Korea's 'have nots' towards the 'haves'.

Such a grim portrayal may seem incongruous, given the current global fascination with *Hallyu*, the wave of Korean culture from K-pop and K-drama to skin care and the unapologetically spicy and punchy flavours of Korean cuisine. Yet beneath the catchy beats of 'Gangnam Style' and the love harmonies of BTS lie other cultural outputs that augur a far less promising portrayal of everyday life in Korea.

Consider *Squid Game*, a Netflix series and dystopian thriller that depicted the Hobbesian daily nightmare facing its characters. This hell on earth set in South Korea compels the show's characters to engage in mortal combat for the slim chance of winning a jackpot in a sadistic tournament that only one competitor will survive. Or consider *Parasite*, the Oscar-winning feature film that unflinchingly showed the deceitful and desperate hunger poorer Koreans have for a taste of the good life, as well as the cruelty and indifference of Korea's wealthy class towards the plight of the less fortunate.

Both *Squid Game* and *Parasite* compel as high art and riveting drama, but also as scathing commentaries on inequality, class tensions and the pitiless consequences of South Korea's 'miracle on the Han River'. While Samsung founder B. C. Lee's vision and raison d'être of 'strengthening the nation through business' was instrumental to this 'miracle', the scions of chaebol founders like his grandson Jay Y. Lee are still haunted by the systemic ills and societal disquiet that have come with and been born of that miracle. As William Faulkner famously observed, 'The past is never dead. It's not even past.'

We close this chapter with two stories involving two Kims. We have seen throughout this book that when icebergs of public opinion crash into corporate titans, there is almost always a policy entrepreneur or political activist at the leading edge. In the case of Samsung and South Korea, it was these two Kims.

First, there is Kim Sang-jo. An economist and university professor at Hansung University, Kim was dubbed the 'chaebol sniper' for a career devoted to exposing the excesses of the South Korean state's cozy, cronyist relations with chaebol. For decades he toiled in the trenches for Solidarity for Economic Reform, an NGO that led minority shareholder campaigns and took chaebol to court, winning landmark cases against firms like Hyundai Motors and Samsung Electronics.

The Choi Soon-sil scandal that led to Park Geun-hye's impeachment and ushered in a new president also quickly redefined Kim's status and terms of engagement, from outsider activism to insider advocacy. Politically, the scandal put reform of the chaebol at the top of the agenda of all candidates vying to succeed Park in the 2017 election. The winner, Moon Jae-in, confronted the issue directly in his inaugural speech to South Korea's National Assembly. 'Under the Moon Jae-in government', he declared, 'politics–business connections will disappear ... I will lead the reform of the chaebol.'

Reading the room of South Korean public opinion, Moon brought Kim Sang-jo into his administration and appointed him antitrust czar. With the formal titles of Chief Presidential Secretary for Policy and Chair of the Fair Trade Commission, Kim had effectively transitioned from outsider to insider policy entrepreneur.

The extent of chaebol reform to date has dashed some of the hopes raised during the 2017 election. Yet by 2020 the Moon government had passed a slew of changes into law. These directly targeted financial and corporate governance of the nation's largest chaebol, including Samsung. They revised existing laws on commerce and monopoly power. They limited major shareholders' voting rights. They introduced outside auditors to some chaebol. Six companies identified as financial conglomerates, Samsung among them, were targeted for tighter oversight and regulations.

The momentum to continue tightening the screws on chaebol governance, however, slowed to a grind with the onset of COVID-19 and the grim economic challenges that accompanied the pandemic.

The second Kim at the sharp edge of public opinion is Kim Yong-hee. This Kim is a former Samsung employee turned outsider entrepreneur. Where Kim Sang-jo's was the story of a corporatist democracy at work, Kim Yong-hee's saga represents the depths of desperation plumbed in trying to scandalize public opinion at the practices of a corporation like Samsung.

Kim Yong-hee's story starts in 1982, when he was hired by Samsung's aerospace division. He became known as a spirited labour organizer, a zeal for which, according to Kim, he paid the price of being physically attacked and subsequently fired on trumped-up charges of sexually assaulting a co-worker. Kim successfully sued for wrongful dismissal, only to be rehired on the condition that he agree to be reassigned to a Samsung construction subsidiary in Russia.

From Russia, Kim wrote to his family about being tied up, beaten and harassed by fellow Samsung employees who accused him of being a North Korean spy and demanded that he renounce his activism. In 1991, Kim's father went missing, never to reappear, allegedly leaving behind only a letter asking his son to abandon his union organizing efforts.

By 1995 Kim was jobless and vengeful. He spent the next 25 years on a singular mission to publicize Samsung's intimidation, retaliation and other outrageous practices. This period included his participation in the Candlelight Protests of 2016, as well as sit-ins and hunger strikes aimed at Samsung. However, Kim's efforts were repeatedly disregarded, thwarted or vanquished, to the extent that in June 2019 when, as he recounted in an interview, 'a Samsung security guard as young as my sons spat in my face', he had an

Kim Yong-hee gesturing to supporters from his CCTV tower.

epiphany. 'That was the moment I realized that I had done everything I could on the ground.'

Kim's next step was to climb up a CCTV tower near Samsung's Seoul headquarters at the city's busiest junction, some 25 metres (82 feet) above ground. For the next 355 days, Kim Yong-hee would live atop this tower, unfurling a banner of protest against Samsung. Supporters would bring bento boxes of food, bags of clothing and charged batteries for his electronics, which Kim would pulley up to the top of the tower, pulleying down dirty clothing and any waste he had produced. He described his quarters as too small to even stretch his legs: 'I suffered panic disorder and had to constantly fight the urge to jump off.'

After steady pressure from the media coverage of Kim's protest and sterner pressure from a Seoul High Court judge, who threatened additional jail time for Jay Y. Lee, in May 2020 Samsung finally responded. Jay Y. Lee formally apologized for the conglomerate's failure 'at times' to comply with the law, and for its harsh labour practices. Lee specifically referenced 'all those who have been hurt in labour issues' and Samsung's 'failing to promptly solve the issue', nearly 30 years after it first fired Kim. Jay Y. Lee further announced that Samsung's tradition of passing the reins to one's children would end with him, although whether that happens remains to be seen.

For his part, Kim Yong-hee descended from the CCTV tower, telling news reporters, 'I hope my struggle helps Samsung build a new management–labour relationship.'

The Choi Soon-sil scandal and the fate of Samsung illustrate how, even in the most unlikely cases, scandals can ignite latent opinion and catalyse transformative political change. The dreadnoughts of the Korean economy crashed into an iceberg their captains, like Jay Y. Lee, had not seen on the horizon until it was too late: an activated Korean public that had over time turned against the chaebol and their corrupt ties to politicians.

Sceptics of our view of scandal accountability might point out that by August 2022 the tide had turned, as South Korea's then President Yoon Suk-yeol pardoned Jay Y. Lee, Shin Dong-bin (chair of the Lotte Group) and other business leaders caught in the dragnet of the Choi Soon-sil scandal. This pardon seemingly returned Korea to the status quo and a continuation of South Korea's custom of leniency towards chaebol misconduct.

President Yoon has since paid dearly for his indulgence of corporate bad behaviour. In the most recent parliamentary elections in April 2024, Yoon's conservative People's Power Party suffered a startling, stinging defeat, winning only 108 out of the 300 seats in the National Assembly. The election was widely seen as a referendum on Yoon's presidency, and soon followed by Gallup approval ratings for Yoon that by May 2024 plummeted to 21 per cent.

The nosedive in approval ratings proved a harbinger for President Yoon's astonishing downfall. Adding to public anger at his acquiescence to chaebol power were broad accusations of economic and governance failure and mounting scandals of his own, largely stemming from his wife's alleged misconduct. Dubbed a Lady Macbeth by the Korean press, she was accused of everything from influence peddling, stock manipulation and plagiarism to accepting a $2,200 Dior handbag in violation of Korea's anti-graft laws.

On 3 December 2024, Yoon, increasingly isolated, cornered and seemingly without any runway to resurrect his political career, fatefully chose to declare martial law. In 1980, the last time martial law was declared in South Korea, then General Chun Doo-hwan unleashed the full force of Korea's military to violently suppress pro-democracy forces, including a brutal massacre of several thousand participants in the Gwangju Uprising. Fast forward to 2024, and Yoon's shocking move was swiftly thwarted by the mobilization of the opposition party and an outpouring of protesters outside the National Assembly and throughout major cities, gathered in candle-lit vigils to demand Yoon's resignation.

Yoon's brazen manoeuvre swiftly led to his impeachment by South Korea's parliament, subsequently upheld by the nation's Constitutional Court.

Niels Bohr, a pioneer of quantum physics, is reputed to have said that the 'opposite of a correct statement is a false statement. But the opposite of a profound truth may well be another profound truth.'

We conclude our global tour of corporate scandals in South Korea because it is here that we find the timeworn struggle between two opposite but profound truths. The first is that when large firms dominate the economy in democratic countries, they will exercise enormous political power. In no democracy is that truer than in South Korea, where to this day the chaebol exert an outsize influence on the country's politics.

Yet a second truth is starkly revealed by the Choi Soon-sil scandal. Even in a country that rode from grinding poverty to great prosperity on the back of chaebol innovation, voters in a democracy get to have their say over how much cronyism, corruption and abuse of power they are willing to tolerate. In South Korea, democracy has been a laboured achievement, won only after decades of mass protest, often at great cost to human lives.

A result of this history is that Koreans have muscle memory for mischief and corruption, whether from politicians, corporations or both. The muscles of activated latent opinion in Korea are flexed repeatedly, and can fell presidents and industrial titans alike. As Jay Y. Lee and his Samsung minions learned, the jolt of an angered public is what a billionaire backlash feels like.

Yet the reform we have seen from mass backlashes the world over is never a one-way street. In every country we have visited on our scandal tour, the politics of corporate regulation remains dynamic – popular victories imposing new rules on companies are followed by periods in which governments move back in a deregulatory direction. In an increasing number of democracies around the globe, frustration with this dynamic has helped to fuel pernicious populist impulses.

As we argue in our final chapter, however, the clash of profound truths – the disproportionate influence of large corporations that can lead to scandalous misconduct and the democratic exercise of voices against it – does not have to lead to bad populism. We invite readers to imagine with us instead the possibilities for a good populism.

10

Good Populism

Upton Sinclair, whose book on the horrors of a Chicago slaughterhouse knocked the American meat industry flat on its back, regarded the book's runaway success as a political failure. Sinclair was a committed socialist. He wrote the novel to focus the American public's attention on the dehumanizing conditions facing workers that he called the 'wage slaves' of the midwestern stockyards, in the hope that, upon seeing the reality of capitalism, many Americans would turn into socialist voters. He did not expect his book's primary legacy to lie in the non-revolutionary domain of food safety regulation. 'I aimed at the public's heart', he reflected bitterly, 'and by accident I hit it in the stomach.'

As history has shown, in the early twentieth century the American public did not turn en masse towards socialism. But people were ready to turn against the robber barons of Gilded Age capitalism. The publication of *The Jungle* informed them and enraged them; it confirmed their worst suspicions about the big meatpacking companies, whose food they ate every day.

The book did not, however, change the minds of American voters. It just concentrated their attention and anger on the politicians that had allowed the Beef Trust to get away with selling rancid meat. The American regulatory state's rapid expansion following the book's publication was only possible because of the unleashed power of latent public opinion.

Latent opinion is that bundle of fundamental beliefs and preferences people hold about politics. It is the iceberg that lurks beneath the visible surface, making politicians and business elites alike anxious.

From the shitty deal of Goldman Sachs to the PRISM leaks of Edward Snowden to Facebook's wanton disregard of its users' privacy, scandals bring to light the political power of targeted public anger. Each of these defining events of this new age of corporate scandal released the force of a latent public concern. Each case touched off a democratic response to corporate capture. Reforms that business lobbyists had once vigorously blocked became law, imposing rules on big corporations unused to being constrained by democratic politics.

Scandals can galvanize pre-existing latent opinion into a force strong enough to cut through the interest group capture of political systems. It is a force strong enough to forge bonds of common cause across polarized partisan divides. Scandals reveal an undervalued resource for good politics. That resource is latent opinion.

In this book, we have focused more on scandals themselves, and less on latent opinion. This is somewhat akin to writing a book about earthquakes and only mentioning in passing the theory of plate tectonics.

Earthquakes are moments of profound readjustment on the earth's surface. They are a product of the underlying forces driven by a system of interconnected massive plates that rub against each other at different rates. A book about earthquakes gains its narrative appeal from the drama of pent-up power they unleash on people and nature with little warning. But it is incomplete without an exploration of the underlying forces themselves.

In this chapter, we shift our attention from the energy released to the source of that energy itself: the iceberg of latent public opinion.

We began this book with Upton Sinclair because all the advanced capitalist countries today stand where the United States stood at the beginning of the twentieth century. As in that earlier era, technological change has ushered in breakthrough innovations that have improved the overall standard of living for many. And yet, once again we live in an era of gaping inequality, swelling popular disaffection and power concentrated in the hands of unaccountable giant corporations.

Citizens today demand more from their politicians than did voters in Sinclair's time. They ask for government to protect them from the vagaries of international markets and from a variety of other risks, from crime to the soaring cost of living. Yet governments strangled by interest group capture and divided by polarization are unable to deliver. People everywhere are angry. The sad irony is that the less able governments are to respond to people's demands, the more public anger is directed at governments themselves.

The social contract between states and their citizens feels shredded. In 2024, voters in more than 60 countries went to the polls. And every governing party in rich countries that held elections saw its vote share decline. That has never happened before, ever.

The term many increasingly use to describe the mood of our time is populism. Typically, it is a term of disparagement and is a cause for consternation. The populism we see today often fuels the rise of extreme nationalist candidates and parties who menace long-standing democracies. Voices of despair look at today's politics and see the 1930s, when fascists overthrew several democratic regimes. We look at today and see instead the 1900s, the period when the Progressive movement built a new regulatory framework that aimed to undercut the tyranny of big companies and widespread corruption.

Hours after the inauguration of Donald Trump in January 2025, the world's richest man – Elon Musk – took a sledgehammer to the financial plumbing of the American Treasury, through his Department of Government Efficiency (DOGE). In the first months of the new administration, DOGE's team of young engineers fanned out across the offices of the American government and seized control of payments across departments. DOGE shut down the Consumer Financial Protection Bureau (CFPB), one of the prize creations of the Dodd-Frank Law whose passage Carl Levin enabled with his congressional hearings on the shitty deal. The forceful action of these shock troops of Silicon Valley seemed to signal that the era of government watching out for the little guy was over, and that regulation was for losers.

Given what we have seen in public opinion, our bet is that this hubristic attack on government institutions is not the beginning of oligarchy but the catalyst for sustained popular pushback against it. That's because the populist rage that drives DOGE and the demand for regulation of big companies we have chronicled come from the same place: an activated, angry public. Latent opinion fuels the anti-incumbent, populist moment we are currently living through. That same latent opinion, properly activated, can also fuel different kinds of transformations, and not just right-wing populists.

That was also true of the public anger in Upton Sinclair's time. The Progressive movement of the early twentieth century succeeded where earlier populist political programmes had failed by proposing broadly popular solutions to economic disruption: regulate business, don't destroy it; create countervailing power in the economy by empowering labour unions; and break the grasp of corporations on legislatures so that people can exercise a meaningful voice in democracy.

The American Progressive movement found success by following the contours of American latent opinion in its time, which favoured fair, free and competitive markets. It advocated reforms that responded to the plight of the masses and not the privilege of the elites. Democrats and Republicans disagreed about other important matters, but they agreed on reforms that built upon these core foundations.

While populism comes in different varieties, populist impulses across the rich democracies of today share common elements that tell us a lot about the nature of latent opinion today. Populists are anti-elite and anti-establishment. They are pro-popular sovereignty and favour majoritarian solutions, even if they infringe on the rights of minorities. Populists dismiss expertise. Populist solutions to complex policy problems are often simple or simplistic, depending on your point of view.

One significant concern of both Sinclair's time and ours is the overriding role of large corporations in corrupting democracy and undermining the vitality of capitalism. Elon Musk paid almost $300 million to get Donald Trump elected and then immediately used DOGE to undermine the regulators that challenged his businesses. That concern about big business buying political influence is a thread woven through scandals from the United States and the United Kingdom to the European Union, South Korea and Australia. We wager that a policy programme that broadly attacks issues associated with corporate domination of democracy responds to the populist impulses of today, even outside the moment of any particular scandal.

Some readers, and many of our ivory tower colleagues, will surely object, 'Now is hardly the time for more democracy! We have seen quite enough seismic shifts in democratic politics recently.' The rise of populism could portend a slide to authoritarian rule and a dismantling of the very guardrails necessary to keep corporate domination of democracies in check.

The anti-incumbent rage of recent elections suggests that voters do not care whether the party or candidate they voted for will actually deliver what they say they want: curbs on inflation, secure jobs at living wages and a social safety and pensions net they can count on. Many seem hellbent on merely burning their political houses down as the only recourse to a system they have come to see as rigged in favour of the elite class and broken for ordinary citizens.

Other voters see the same lack of responsiveness from their governments, but are nevertheless prepared to double down on making the system work. They hold to Winston Churchill's precept that 'democracy is the worst form of government except for all those other forms that have been tried from time to time'. Activists on the extremes of the political system are disappointed when they don't get everything they want from politics. We think that's just the way democratic politics works.

We ally ourselves not with the hard left nor the hard right, but with the hard hats renovating existing democratic systems. We choose not to call in the wrecking ball, but to get to work afresh with bricks and mortar. Renovating an old house with draughty windows, creaky floorboards and leaky plumbing is slow and arduous work. But ultimately, building a house of government of the people, by the people and for the people is what makes a system democratic.

This is where we lean into the idea of good populism. The latent anger and frustration that fuel populist movements is the same force whose breathtaking power we observed through the scandals in this book. That power has the potential to strong-arm governments into being more responsive and accountable to voters. Yes, populist movements can have deeply detrimental effects on the democratic project. They can polarize polities and turn citizen against citizen. They can exile reason to the dusty attics as demagoguery and fear-mongering rule the day. But they can also compel governments to disregard influential industries and embolden them to heed voters instead.

Democracies are better than other forms of government that have been tried through history because they are designed to respond to the interests of citizens, and their institutions require citizen voice to speak about what those interests are. We saw in the scandal of Sanlu baby formula how the Chinese government, intent on dodging any responsibility for its regulatory failures, undermined the belief of the Chinese people in the safety of their own food industry. In France, by contrast, the government was accountable to public anger over the Lactalis scandal, which ultimately shored up the regulatory shortcomings revealed.

Enabling capitalism, with its competitive private markets, is vital to citizens' interests in democracies. Yet the excesses of the drive for profit must be tempered so that corporations neither control politics nor strangle innovation. Markets do not govern themselves. Market failures require regulation to solve them, as any first-year economics textbook will tell you. If corporate excesses are not counterbalanced by citizen voice, we get neither good politics nor good economics. We get fat cats and protests in the streets.

Good populism is thus *good* in the sense that it redirects the power of popular sentiments to require governments to be more responsive to voters' interests or to hold governments accountable when they are not. The collective outrage at scandalous behaviour is one way good populism might make itself known, but not the only way. Achieving a form of government both accountable and responsive to voters requires more than just electing the right slate of candidates and entrusting our representatives to do the right thing. It also requires, from time to time, an earthquake powered by latent opinion to shake loose the stubborn residue of corporate influence that inevitably calcifies in the halls of power.

We see good populism as a set of demands from politics that has the potential to both respond to the most salient concerns of latent public opinion and enhance the capacity of democratic governments to act effectively. Scholars of modern politics often point to the trade-off between responsive and responsible government. This is the tension between doing the voters' bidding, no matter the consequences, and doing what is in the best interest of the voters, the economy and the political system that supports them.

Populism is often impugned because doing the voters' bidding can appear ill-conceived and short-sighted, if not outright dangerous. In the United States, for example, the second Trump administration's actions in its first few months were justified as delivering on an electoral mandate. Yet these actions also threaten to bulldoze the infrastructure of the federal government itself and jettison America's constitutionally established checks and balances.

A prerequisite for good populism is a programme that makes politics more responsive without undermining the capacity of government to deliver on the things that are vital, even if a populist majority may not want them. The populist wave is born of the inability of states to do things their citizens demand and need, which then fires up voters to launch the electoral wrecking ball at governments. Good populism can only work by increasing the capacity of states to do those things citizens demand and need.

If states can successfully respond to voters' demands while also exercising responsible governance, we see a potential for leaders championing good populism to peel voters away from bad populists. People who were once willing to elect politicians promising vengeance and destruction on government itself may come to recognize good populist leaders who strive to meet their demands and fashion a politics that works in their interests. Such voters may update their vision for politics and put on the hard hats of renovation.

Let us be clear what we think is dangerous in what we call 'bad populism'. First, populist appeals rest fundamentally on the distinction between 'the people' and the elites. Sometimes, the focus on 'the people' demonizes minority groups, such as immigrants or religious minorities. That is the rotten heart of bad populism. Secondly, majority rule often means trampling on minority rights. Thirdly, the insistence on simple solutions for the people rejects independent regulators, and expertise in general, as sinister agents of a bureaucratic deep state. Evidence-driven and rule-based policy? No thanks!

What, then, are the elements of a programme for good populism? We see at least three key ingredients. While there is a case to be made for good populism more broadly, we focus on those elements that would bring a renewed vigour to reforming and regulating the corporate domination of governments.

The first involves a broader definition of 'the people'. Bad populism defines the people exclusively – not *all* the people, just 'us' and not 'them'. 'Them' can be people who don't look or talk like we do. But 'them' can just as well refer to elites, whether they are in universities or in government.

Populism gone bad fails to focus on the common interests that all voters share. For instance, against an establishment agenda that prioritizes the needs of large corporations over those of individual workers, consumers and small business entrepreneurs. It instead seeks scapegoats, often minority groups. Yet an alternate agenda based on common interest is possible when latent opinion can sustain demand for governments to represent the interests of voters as a whole rather than large corporations.

Such a sustained demand is populist in the sense that it distinguishes the people from the elites, but elites here are defined by virtue of their alliance with large corporations. Where government operates in cahoots with those corporations, they too are part of that elite. When he was running for president in 2011, American politician Mitt Romney once told a hostile audience at the Iowa state fair that 'corporations are people'. Romney was wrong about that, and that is why he sits on the dust heap of failed politicians.

Corporations are not people. Corporations are an efficient way of organizing contracts for productive, profitable ends. Some of them, including the ones whose dirty laundry we have aired on the previous pages, have been stupendously successful at creating innovations that people want and need. But as they have grown more successful, they have invested ever more heavily in lobbying to bend politics in the service of their business interests. They should stick to what they are good at: delivering innovation that people want and will pay for. In contrast to their goods and services, very few people want to buy the self-serving policies their lobbyists are selling.

'Us' versus 'them' – having a common foe – reminds people what they share: their standing as equal citizens. People also share a vulnerability to unbridled corporate power. This is not a partisan programme. Some people want to limit the influence of corporations because they don't like the woke politics and the nanny-state bureaucratic programmes for diversity and inclusion they mandate. Others don't like the ability of companies to pay exploitative wages or impose difficult conditions on their workers. Many have more personal complaints – about increasing prices, decreasing quality and reliability and the surrendering of personal information.

Not everyone has the same complaint about corporations, because people have legitimate political differences over these questions. But it is a broadly popular view that, in a democracy, these questions should be the subject of informed debate between voters, not determined by the whims of the leaders of large companies.

The next element of good populism is the use of majoritarian devices to achieve its ends. Whereas with bad populism, majorities can run roughshod over the rights and interests of minority groups, so the majoritarian aspect of good populism depends on our first element, where 'the people' are defined inclusively around shared experiences and common interests. Viewed in this way, majoritarianism in democracies can disrupt the cozy ties and excessive influence of large corporations on legislatures and political parties.

This is not an endorsement of the referendum as an all-purpose tool of collective decision-making, as it too often sacrifices good policy on the altar of simplicity. Indeed, there is a tendency with authoritarian populist leaders to use plebiscites – take-it-or-leave-it referenda – to cover up or extend their abusive patterns of rule. In 2009, for example, Hugo Chávez used a referendum to abolish term limits on himself in Venezuela. The use of such devices ties the leader directly to the people, in an attempt to disempower representative parties.

Good populism refocuses our concern away from disempowered parties and on to empowered citizens. The difference here is one of context. The top-down referenda used by populists like Chávez suppress challenges to the political status quo. They are majoritarian devices that undermine competitive democracy. In contrast, the bottom-up referendum is a tool for citizens fed up with unresponsive politicians who bow to the interests of large corporations.

When the threat to democracy comes from demagogues, majoritarianism is a risky gambit. But if the greatest threat to democracy is instead the capture of legislatures, regulators and governments themselves by industry lobbyists, majoritarianism starts to look a lot more appealing. And because good populism defines the cleavage of politics as running between 'we the people' and 'they the big corporations', it prompts voters to understand the stakes when anti-corporate measures come to their attention.

Populism is often defined as the evil twin of pluralism. Yet if people can be persuaded to see themselves as democratic citizens first, citizens who share a common foe of misbehaving large corporations, the most ominous threats to pluralism are avoidable. Good populism organically builds solidarity across lines of racial and partisan identity. For instance, a banner like 'the people against Facebook' unifies majorities with outsiders against a common foe, rather than pitting them against one another or enabling those in power to scapegoat and sacrifice minorities at risk.

The third and final element of good populism is to rebuild trust in independent regulatory agencies, which are essential to enable governments to deliver on their promises to voters. Yet these agencies also bear some responsibility for the distrust of the public. To overcome this, they need to justify their policies in terms of their benefit to the citizen, as opposed to the consumer or the functioning of markets. This plain-language justification is no more onerous than having to write an executive summary for each policy, but it sets citizens in a democracy at the core of regulatory action – both for the agency that has to write it and the citizens who may read it. This may seem like a cheap gimmick, but it actually goes to the heart of popular disaffection with expert agencies, which frequently defend abstract ideas like markets rather than people, who are the constitutive members of any political community.

Research routinely finds what most voters already suspect: bureaucracies and agencies do not simply implement the 'will of the people' as legislated by politicians or directed by presidents. Rather, they enjoy wide discretion and autonomy to interpret and implement laws and directives, and voters are wary of abuses of that latitude. Discretion and autonomy in polarized polities with plummeting levels of political trust is why bad populist leaders can dismiss government agencies as inefficient, ideological and corrupt. The point of reorienting agency policymaking around citizen benefit is to instil in government norms of transparency and justification that prioritize people and not just markets.

We citizens are all consumers. But in our consumer identity, we predictably optimize for the best quality products at the cheapest price and the highest level of convenience. These are metrics on which the largest corporations have excelled in bringing us unparalleled wonders. Need a new iPhone by tonight? Amazon Prime can deliver that for you!

Good populism reinforces the citizen identity, reminding citizens that they don't only care about cost and convenience. They also care about the process by which Apple provides the iPhone and the social costs we may all bear as a result. As we see it, citizens as good populists span the ideological spectrum, from those concerned with the offshoring of jobs and fair competition for local businesses to those focused on the impact of corporate practices on everything from food safety and clean air to pension funds and data privacy.

Democracies that are responsive to voter demands need capable regulators. Good populism does not assume the worst of government agencies. In this sense it is clearly distinct from bad populism. The Dieselgate scandal was brought to light after an American regulatory body, the Environmental Protection Agency, paid attention to the information that activist John German had passed on, ultimately lowering the boom on the fundamental fraud of Volkswagen's 'clean diesel' scam.

This faith in regulators is conditional. Corporate lobbyists won't stop pressing their case just because regulators are tasked with justifying their actions in terms of citizen, not consumer, benefit. Our leaders and institutions will continue to be fallible and subject to corporate capture. Adopting the norm of justifying policies by their benefits to citizens just makes it that much easier for citizens to see when the political elites are adopting policies that move away from their interests.

Good populism is not something we just dreamed up. We have seen it in action in the workings of successful activists in this book. People like Alastair Mactaggart in California. The three principles we've just enumerated ran like silken twine through Mactaggart's long-shot battle to get privacy regulation adopted in California.

In talking to us about why his campaign resonated with the people of California, Mactaggart counterposed the interests of the people against those of corporations so vast that he referred to them as nation-states:

> I think people are increasingly getting uncomfortable with the notion that these 'nation-states', essentially, are [so] powerful … We've always kind of grown-up thinking of the big bad wolf – Standard Oil trust, US Steel trust, the kind of things that started antitrust. We're like, 'Wait, that was nothing. This

is really actually serious.' But because they've been so effective and because, by and large, the people who run them have been, 'Hey, we're just like you, we're good liberal Democrats, too. You know, we all want the same thing', there hasn't been this perception of 'Wait, that's power that could be used against us.'

This counterbalancing of the people against the powerful corporations underlay Mactaggart's strategy. It wasn't an anti-capitalist strategy. As Mactaggart told us, 'I'm not a fan of regulation for the sake of regulation. [But] sometimes it's necessary because, human nature being what it is, power corrupts.'

To combat this power, Mactaggart followed the second principle of good populism by using an initiative – a type of referendum – to break through an uncompetitive status quo in the California legislature, which was dominated by the Big Tech companies. Mactaggart took the privacy battle to the companies by saying, 'Let the people of California decide'. He used the device of the initiative once in 2018 to get the legislature to pass a law on digital privacy. When Big Tech came after that law with amendments in 2019, he went back to the people of California in 2020 with another initiative. In each case, Mactaggart's objective was to open up a system clogged by lobbying, and he succeeded by getting the people on his side. That's what good populist majoritarianism looks like.

Finally, Mactaggart followed the third principle of good populism when his 2020 initiative created a regulatory agency, the CCPA, to enforce the provisions of the new law. He knew that existing state authorities – the attorney general's office – were overstretched. Without the requisite policy expertise and resources, they would be unable to keep up with Big Tech's attempt to evade the law. For that you need a knowledgeable enforcer.

'The administration [of the CPPA] is where the point of the spear is going to be', said Mactaggart in 2021. 'So clearly the most important job is going to be hiring the executive director.' Ashkan Soltani, the former chief technologist for the US Federal Trade Commission, became the first head of the agency, and the sharp point of the spear Mactaggart had sought to defend the newly established privacy rights of Californians.

Consider the contrast between the CPPA and the 'bad populist' DOGE initiative of Elon Musk, which indiscriminately weakened state capacity. That included undermining even the basic capacity of the American state to collect income taxes, but also attacking regulators who had challenged Musk's companies: the Federal Aviation Administration which regulated SpaceX, and the National Labor Relations Board, which challenged workplace practices at Tesla. Mactaggart's building of the CPPA shows that he understood the mantra of good populists everywhere: for a government to solve problems and stand up for the citizen against big companies, it needs bureaucratic capacity. That's what independent agencies deliver.

The proposed programme of good populism will not repair all that ails modern democracies. Like this book, the programme closely targets a specific aspect of the problem of voter disaffection with democratic politics: a sense that corporate power is out of control. The key elements just enumerated provide a template for evaluating policy proposals in terms of their likelihood of countering corporate power, and for thinking about how to make those policies more responsive to voters in every democracy in the current moment.

It would be a rich irony, in a book about democracy and latent public opinion, if two professors from elite universities finished with a tidy set of policies to solve all our problems. Such answers should not come from us. They should come from citizens and political parties and be the subject of robust political debate. That said, we do have some ideas to start the conversation about what good populist reforms will look like.

These proposals directly address some of the problems we have identified, and respond to voters' demands while simultaneously reinforcing the ability of governments to exercise control over the companies on which voters depend for their livelihood. In some sense, that is the acid test of any set of reform proposals – that they reinforce the capacity of our democratic home to repair itself.

Our first proposal involves increasing the transparency of private companies – those that are not publicly listed on a stock exchange. Elon Musk controls the private company SpaceX. Musk currently owns about 40 per cent of the company's shares, but he has super-voting rights which maintain his absolute control of the company. SpaceX competes with Boeing and Lockheed Martin to work with NASA, the American space agency. Boeing and Lockheed Martin are both publicly listed companies on the New York Stock Exchange.

SpaceX is an extraordinarily successful company. In the past few years, SpaceX has been running rings around the launch activities of Boeing, an aerospace company wrecked by scandals of its own in recent years. SpaceX has been far more proficient in launching rockets than Boeing.

The success of SpaceX doesn't stop there. SpaceX owns Starlink, which controls a network of satellites that provide broadband internet coverage to poorly served locations. One such location is Ukraine, which Russia invaded in 2022. In his biography of Elon Musk, Walter Isaacson reported that Musk refused Ukraine permission to use Starlink to launch a submarine drone attack on Russian forces in the illegally annexed Crimea. In declining to make Starlink available, Musk was effectively operating his own foreign policy. A businessman has used his control of a private company to usurp powers that democracies entrust to elected governments.

The rockets of SpaceX and the satellites of Starlink provide crucial state capacities, in the United States and elsewhere. Nor is SpaceX the only private company providing defence technologies. Anduril, a private company founded by billionaire Palmer Luckey (inventor of the Oculus virtual reality headset), designs and sells stationary platforms and drones to the American border security forces. Anduril also supplies missiles, drones and even small submarines to Ukraine and several NATO governments.

Private companies like Anduril and SpaceX can make rapid progress and solve formidable challenges in part because they don't have to deal with the onerous requirements for disclosure that come with being publicly listed. For starters, the CEO doesn't have to disclose his salary. These companies are also not required to supply externally audited financial accounts to the market.

But private companies enjoy more consequential privileges compared to their public competitors, such as not making public information about big potential failures. In the first half of 2025, SpaceX tried to launch four of its upgraded Starship rockets. Three of those vessels exploded spectacularly in the sky, and a fourth went up in flames on the ground. SpaceX was happy to launch rockets, knowing they could well explode, because there were no shareholders breathing down the neck of Elon Musk about the risk/reward trade-off involved in each launch.

In public companies, boards of directors provide oversight of the CEO. The exact structures of control in private companies are murky. And we know nothing about the conflicts of interests of directors of such companies, such as their independence from the controlling owner. If board members are entirely financially dependent on the CEO, they are unlikely to stand up to decisions they don't like.

Disclosure requirements form the backbone of public oversight of listed companies in capitalist democracies. Yet SpaceX, which exercises fundamental powers formerly held only by nation-states, is not even subject to the accounting disclosures and shareholder votes required of its hapless but publicly listed rival Boeing. Musk may not need to go to capital markets, which is what usually forces companies to go public. From the citizen's perspective, it is fair to ask: should the United States government outsource so much of its space program to a financially opaque private corporation like SpaceX, which is ultimately subject to only one man's control?

We would answer no. Good corporate law is certainly not sufficient to keep democracy functioning. But requiring large companies that supply crucial state functions to open themselves to public scrutiny is a necessary step for democracies to hold these companies to account in politics. The power of the public to check excesses depends on such mundane disclosures.

In a market economy, private companies should never be forced to go public. Yet the provision of public services, even those as exotic as spaceflight, should always be justifiable in terms of their benefit to the citizens. Those citizens have an interest in the public accountability of the corporations that deliver government policy. It follows that in democracies, private companies above a certain value threshold that do not open themselves to public scrutiny equivalent to that required of publicly listed companies should not be allowed to compete with those public companies for state contracts.

Our second proposal addresses the common informational sphere on which democracy depends: the media, including social media. Two examples highlight a critical issue that democracies need to address. First, Elon Musk owns X – formerly Twitter – which in recent years has played an outsize role in public discourse in many democracies. After Musk intervened in the 2024 presidential election by endorsing Donald Trump, research suggests that he altered the algorithm of the site to favour his own posts even more egregiously than he had previously. He is the most followed person on X by far, with more than 200 million followers, and he has repeatedly posted disinformation related to politics, in both the United States and Europe.

Our second example involves the *Washington Post*. The venerable *Post* remains perhaps best known for breaking the story of what would become the Watergate scandal in 1972, a scandal that would eventually force the resignation of an American president, Richard Nixon.

At that time, the *Post* had just gone public after being run as a family-owned business for nearly four decades. The *Post*'s current owner is Jeff Bezos, another of the richest men in the world. Bezos bought the *Post* in 2013 and converted it to a private company.

Less than two weeks before the 2024 US presidential election, the *Post* announced that it would not endorse a candidate for president, even though it had regularly endorsed candidates since 1976. Bezos personally overruled an editorial team that had already written an endorsement for Kamala Harris. Bezos offered a principled defence of his intervention, but to many it looked as if he feared angering the eventual winner, Donald Trump. Among Bezos's other, less principled possible sources of anxiety was a $3.4 billion contract his aerospace company, Blue Origin, secured with NASA.

In February 2025, Bezos declared that the *Post* opinion pages would henceforth only publish op-eds that supported 'personal liberties and free markets', in what observers widely saw as a capitulation to the agenda of President Trump.

The very rich have long owned media outlets around the world. This is neither new nor particularly concerning on its own. What is concerning today is the convergence of two trends on the supply side of our information ecosystem – corporate consolidation and media fragmentation.

First, media ownership has experienced a long-term trend of consolidation that has affected the production of political news through legacy media outlets. Six giant companies now own 90 per cent of the American media. Three companies control 90 per cent of the national newspaper market in the United Kingdom.

These trends affect most of the world's rich democracies. The effects of this concentration of media ownership on the news we receive include a sharp reduction in the number of independent outlets investigating and publishing news, a consequent reduction in the diversity of news content, and the constant worry of censorship or distorted coverage of news that is detrimental to business interests.

Secondly, the digital revolution has produced an exponential increase in the number of outlets for political information. Traditional news outlets today are competing with influencers on platforms like TikTok and YouTube. This proliferation is not in itself bad.

Even so, it has opened the floodgates to misinformation and disinformation. We live in a world of increasing media fragmentation. The sheer volume of outlets and content today makes it challenging for the modern peers of the muckrakers to break stories that can reach the broader public, unless they can get on the Joe Rogan Experience podcast.

The role of scandals in tapping into latent opinion is an informational one: the media tells us what is going on, and it's even worse than we thought. It's how Upton Sinclair roused Americans to control the beef trusts, and how Edward Snowden's leak of the

PRISM programme rescued European privacy regulation. But that only works if we all hear about the scandal and believe it.

With democratic publics ever more siloed in the information to which they are exposed, the familiar risk of billionaires demanding favourable coverage from their pet newspaper has been conjoined to a newer worry – that they can now sow immediate doubt about the scandals that once would have reined them in.

When the public sphere was more fact-based, and information sources were limited to major networks, there was only so much variation in the stories to which people were exposed. Today, as we saw in the case of Sam Bankman-Fried's bankrupt crypto exchange FTX, multiple stories circulate about why people acted the way they did, and the interpretive stories and their factual basis may diverge more than they overlap.

The profit motive once constrained a finite number of news outlets from moving too far away from what the public was interested in. If they did, they would lose readers or viewers, and therefore advertising revenue. They were interested in getting the scoop, because they were in a competitive marketplace. Nowadays, the profit motive matters for today's embattled news outlets, but it may not matter as much to their billionaire owners.

Many billionaires don't depend on their media assets for their fortunes. These assets function more like accessories – gaudy jewellery that flaunts their status. The *Washington Post* lost 10 per cent of its subscribers after Bezos refused to allow it to endorse Kamala Harris. That is a severe blow for the *Post*, but one that has no effect on Bezos's fortune. Whether they mobilize their media jewels politically, like Musk, or demobilize them politically, like Bezos, there is always the risk these once-democratic pillars of the media are just being used for business ends.

And for billionaires, scandals that affect them are always bad for business.

Americans who write about the media sometimes lament the lack of public sector broadcasters as the root problem. Yet the situation is scarcely better in the UK, where the BBC is a once-revered public institution that has come under heavy fire for being part of what some Americans like to call the lamestream media. Voices on both the left and the right have accused the BBC of systematic bias, and the previous Conservative government repeatedly vowed to reduce its funding. Public broadcasting networks in the UK and continental Europe face many of the same problems as media outlets in the United States.

Public financial support for quality journalism is a good thing for democracy, to be sure. Aggressive cuts to federal funding for public media by the Trump administration and Congress have increased the burdens on an already strained system. This risks further reducing the breadth and quality of information available to the American public. But alone, neither public funding nor philanthropic intervention will be sufficient to solve the failings of the currently broken information ecosystem.

The good populist solution to this problem is to use the threat of government intervention to compel a more truth-based public sphere. To be crystal clear: it is not the government's job to fact-check media. That would take us further away from the democratic ideal, not towards it.

But what the government could do is require major networks and news websites to develop their own classification scheme for news outlets themselves, including a 'deliberate distortions of the truth' scheme. Governments could appoint an independent regulator to randomly sample news articles and video clips for the top 20 most viewed sources of news to assess them according to this scheme – which, remember, would have been created by news outlets themselves. The results could produce monthly report cards for each news site, which sites would be required to post in a prominent place on their site – much like the grades for sanitary conditions for restaurants posted in the UK and in some American states and cities. Truthfulness in our shared public sphere is, after all, a matter of democratic hygiene.

A functional system for rating the reliability of news sites already exists in the private sector. It is called NewsGuard, and it was founded by former journalists from the *Wall Street Journal* and the *New York Times*. NewsGuard demonstrates that such a system is feasible and not necessarily partisan. However, NewsGuard is a for-profit company. Good populism holds that core features of democratic functioning – such as ensuring a truth-based public sphere – are something government cannot leave to the private sector, where conflicts of interest always have the potential to undermine its credibility.

To reiterate an important point, the system we propose is *not* government fact-checking. It is a light-touch intervention to remind people that some news is distorted, and they should think about that before reading and sharing news. Research has shown that light-touch interventions like these are more successful than onerous fact-checking regimes in getting news consumers to think about whether what they are seeing on social media is true, and whether they should share it.

Nor does such a scheme violate principles of freedom of speech. News sites can publish whatever they want, within the existing law. But their freedom of speech does not mean that citizens do not have a right to a statement of fact-based reliability about sites. Citizens can indeed choose, informed by such a system, which news to consume. Because we believe in the power of competition to make markets work better, we think news sites that do systematically well on this score will figure out how to employ it to ratchet up their readers or viewers.

Our report card will not solve the deeper problems plaguing the supply side of news. The problems of journalism are dire in every democracy we study. Pepper's oldest daughter is a journalist, so he hears a report from the trenches every week. Journalism is increasingly an endangered profession that has yet to figure out how to replace the advertising income that underwrote most for-profit outlets prior to the rise of the internet. They now compete in a fragmented attention economy where few people will pay for news. Local, independent news sources are particularly on the endangered list.

A vibrant journalism is the air that breathes life into the ability of voters to hold big business, and the wayward politicians who work for them, to account. Bad populism feeds off toxic air in which truth is questioned, if not deliberately distorted, and unverified click-bait is consumed as reality. Good populism could thrive in renovated public spaces for truth, evidence and political debate based on shared facts – be those shared spaces on social media or on network television, where many people still get their news.

It is in such public spheres that the inheritors of the muckrakers today stand their best chance of informing us about what's really going on with big business. Even, indeed especially, when it exceeds our worst fears.

The success of reforms like these depends vitally on having champions inside the system. Good populism makes an unlikely bet: that dry regulatory policy can be the stuff that makes ordinary people remember their links to each other, and that their interests differ from the corporations that dictate many of the conditions of their lives. The details are boring, but with the right explanation, tighter regulatory policy can tap into the mighty vein of incensed opinion. Making that connection is the job of political leaders.

In 2010, Carl Levin put on a masterclass of how to do that. He worked together with Republicans on his committee to explain the financial crisis to the American people. In so doing, he broke the story of the Goldman Sachs scandal, which in turn broke the logjam that had prevented American financial reform from passing Congress. Our job, as observers of politics, is to make sure that leaders understand just how rich this seam of discontent is. It can be mined for either good or bad populism.

A tenet of good populism is that voters need to keep a perpetual and persistent eye on their representatives and regulators, with news media as their sentinel. But such vigilance to ensure accountability is tiring and slow work. The changes we have written about have only taken place thanks to the work of motivated insiders, people like Margrethe Vestager, Kim Sang-jo and Lina Khan.

These are not superheroes avenging evil forces of capitalism. They are extraordinary everyday champions who are willing to bear more than their share of abuse from lobbyists – and sometimes politicians, peers and even the public posting on X – in order to win a right-sized relationship between the citizen and big companies.

The fate of good populism depends on them, and on the countless public servants like them whose names we don't know.

Speaking of extraordinary people, we should not forget the obsessive outsiders who drove these campaigns for their own idiosyncratic reasons. Max Schrems got a bee in his bonnet about privacy. Inspired by the European success on privacy, California real estate developer Alastair Mactaggart decided to take on the tech giants who lived just across the Bay from him. Kim Yong-hee took even longer odds than Mactaggart, sitting on a CCTV tower in Seoul for almost a year to protest against the biggest company in Korea.

Their motivations were all different. Each person struggled within flawed democratic systems in different ways. Yet the ability to organize, to protest and to believe, perhaps foolishly, that one individual can make a difference, ties this Austrian and American and Korean together. Schrems, Mactaggart and Kim also shared an unusual willingness to take on the certainty of short-term risks for that slim chance at long-term reward. In the words of Mactaggart, 'It's like that Buddhist thing, where you walk past a mess and a mop, and say, "Someone ought to clean up that mess". And eventually you realize you have to pick up the mop.'

We never know who will be the one to pick up the mop. But we do know that civic duty and vigorous civil societies underlie the ability of democracies to correct their own failings. We saw in Chapter 1 that authoritarian rulers fear scandals, and that makes autocracies weaker. The same is true for civil society, which autocrats often try to weaken in order to secure their own power. A public in which anyone can pick up a mop at any time to clean up the mess is a dangerous thing for those who prefer order over democratic accountability.

Reining in private greed for the public good is not always pretty, and the project is often incomplete. The changes made after the last scandal do not foreclose future scandals, and lobbyists slowly chip away at the last round of reforms. The struggle tends to be a series of pitched battles, with victories followed by defeats followed by stalemates. It is seldom a stirring story. Still, what we are observing in the wake of big corporate scandals is in fact democracy in action.

Many fellow citizens look at our current democracy and see a glass that is half-empty. But we hope instead that we have shown you a glass half-full, and that we have demonstrated reasons to expect it to get fuller, not emptier, if latent opinion around the world can be activated to demand good populism, not bad.

The populist tide in this moment is not likely to subside. The question we have tried to address is how that anger and pent-up demand for change in so many countries can be harnessed in the service of restoring democracy, not tearing it down.

The rebuilding project will be a long one. Those looking at today's blocked democratic politics can be forgiven for wanting to just tear the whole damn thing down and start over.

We believe that a flawed democratic house is far superior to a shiny authoritarian mansion on a hill or an imagined democratic house of our dreams. The dream house doesn't exist. In the despot's mansion, the big companies and the political leaders call the shots. At least in our house, we the people do.

Acknowledgements

Over the decade that led to this book, our colleagues, friends and families have endured a lot. It is one of the great joys of finishing it to be able to thank them, however inadequately, for their support.

We would first like to express our gratitude to those who have worked with us on the various seams of research that we have woven together in this book. We were lucky to be able to benefit from the keen insights and help of the gifted young scholars affiliated with the Banklash research programme at the Blavatnik School of Government at the University of Oxford: Jae-Hee Jung, Ryan Shandler, Tom Nicholls, Harry Begg, Robin Hsieh, and Clemence Hautefort. Together with them we have worked out many of the scholarly underpinnings of our claims about scandals and political accountability, and this reflects only a small part of what we have learned from them. We have likewise benefited from the help of talented research assistants over the years, including Julie Bernard, Kristine Kay, Sunmin Kim, Mika Erik Moeser, and David Weisstanner. We are also indebted to Gavin Ellison at YouGov, our partner in collecting the bulk of our public opinion data. Part of what we learned came through a series of interviews over the years, and we thank those interviewees, many of whom requested anonymity. Among interviewees we can name we would like to acknowledge Alastair Mactaggart, Margrethe Vestager and Barney Frank, each of whom has shown that individuals can make a difference in the world.

Hayley Pring was our research assistant extraordinaire, and we are hugely in her debt. There is not a chapter in this book that is not better because Hayley went the extra mile to find information, put our data into digestible form, or indeed insist that we follow up on a particular story that she had discovered. She has read every page and helped us check facts. Any errors that remain are ours alone, but the book in your hands would be a lesser thing but for the inspiration and dedication that Hayley poured into it. Thank you!

We are likewise grateful to the colleagues, students and friends who read parts of the manuscript or advised us on their areas of expertise. Among these we would especially like to thank Ben Ansell, John Armour, Stephen Chaudoin, Henry Farrell, Jonas Fischer, Ben Franta, Archon Fung, Irem Güçeri, Jennifer Hochschild, Torben Iversen, Katerina Linos, Jenny Mansbridge, Ciaran Martin, Elsa Massoc, Anthony Maton, James Morone, Paul Pierson, Tom Simpson, Marco Steenbergen and Nicholas Ziegler, as well as participants at the Banklash/Wealthpol conference held at Nuffield College in 2022. Other colleagues at Berkeley, Harvard, the European University Institute and Oxford have listened patiently to these ideas as we have developed them, challenging us along the way. We are grateful to them collectively, and to the congenial intellectual environments these institutions have provided us over the years.

This book is the culmination of a long research trajectory. That research has been funded at times by the Russell Sage Foundation, the EUI Research Council, and especially the European Research Council, which funded the Banklash programme under the European Union Horizon's 2020 programme (grant agreement no. 787887). The scholarly output so generously supported has come in the form of journal articles and working papers over the years. The stories this book tells rest on this research bedrock.

Readers will be the judge of whether we have made the relationship between corporate scandals and public opinion riveting. But if we have missed the target, it's not for want of tremendous help along the way. Together with many friends in VC Jericho, Rory

ACKNOWLEDGEMENTS

Carnegie listened to the gestation of this book over long hours on the byways of Oxfordshire, and he never stopped insisting that we tell a good story. Michael Holmes was a formidable devil's advocate. Audra Wolfe was our development editor and first Outside Reader, and she sometimes understood what we were trying to do better than we did. The final architecture of the book owes much to her. Matthew Rice inspired us with possible visual intersections of billionaires and icebergs. Our most enthusiastic advocate, relentless defender, and constructive critic has been our agent Doug Young from PEW Literary. Tomasz Hoskins from Bloomsbury Continuum saw the appeal of a big ideas book, and he and Octavia Stocker shrewdly helped us polish the prose and structure of each chapter so the ideas could sparkle. Lora Findlay designed a brilliant cover. The entire Bloomsbury team – Graham Coster on copyediting, Sarah Jones on project editing, and Sarah Head and Jessica Gray on marketing and publicity – have helped us shine the brightest possible light on the book.

There is no-one happier than our families that this book is now finished, so that there can perhaps be other topics of dinner table conversation than corporate scandals. Mary Louise Culpepper and Shirley Lee have read draft after draft of this book, reining in our rhetorical excesses in just the right places. And that does not even begin to scratch the surface of our gratitude to these two women, of whom we continue to be in awe. They remind us every day that there is so much more to life than our work.

Finally, we thank our children. Sophie, Savannah, and Saralynn all settled their withering gaze on their father's overwritten text and improved it, and Sebastian stands ready to write the musical score for the film version. Ella and Linus tolerated their father's dreadful dad jokes, far more so than they tolerated his lazy arguments and florid prose in earlier drafts of these pages. If our book makes a bet, it is on the future generation. We therefore dedicate it to our children – in hopes of brighter days ahead.

Notes

INTRODUCTION

1 **The book sold out:** Philip J. Hilts, *Protecting America's Health: The FDA, Business and One Hundred Years of Regulation*, UNC Press, 2003, pp. 49–50.

1 **Prevented all but a handful:** Thomas A. Bailey, 'Congressional opposition to pure food legislation, 1879–1906', *American Journal of Sociology*, vol. 36, 1930, pp. 52–64; Shaun P. Kennedy, 'History of food fraud and development of mitigation requirements and standards', in *Food Fraud*, Academic Press, 2021, pp. 9–22; John L. Gignilliat, 'Pigs, politics, and protection: the European boycott of American pork, 1879–1891', *Agricultural History*, 35, pp. 3–12.

2 **34 separate corporations:** Michael McGerr, *A Fierce Discontent: The Rise and Fall of the Progressive Movement in America*, Oxford University Press, 2003.

3 **Critics on the political left:** Claire Provost and Matt Kennard, *Silent Coup: How Corporations Overthrew Democracy*, Bloomsbury Publishing, 2023; Tim Wu, *The Curse of Bigness: How Corporate Giants Came to Rule the World*, Atlantic Books, 2020.

3 **Those on the right:** Sohrab Ahmari, *Tyranny, Inc.: How Private Power Crushed American Liberty – and What to Do About It*, Forum Books, 2023; Michael Lind, *The New Class War: Saving Democracy from the Managerial Elite*, Penguin, 2020. For an empirical analysis of the leftward political shift of senior American corporate executives and the woke corporation, see Reilly Steel, 'The Political

Transformation of Corporate America, 2001–2022', *American Political Science Review*, forthcoming 2025.

4 **Scandals concentrate public attention:** Scholars call singular events that rivet the public, like scandals and disasters, 'focusing events'. Thomas A. Birkland, *After Disaster: Agenda Setting, Public Policy and Focusing Events*, Georgetown University Press, 1997; John Kingdon, *Agendas, Alternatives and Public Policies*, Brown and Company, 1984.

5 **Much safer now:** Daniel K. Tarullo, 'Financial Regulation: Still unsettled a decade after the crisis', *Journal of Economic Perspectives*, vol. 33, 2019, pp. 61–80.

5 **A consequence of the political backlash:** Adam Tooze, *Crashed: How a Decade of Financial Crises Changed the World*, Allen Lane, 2018.

5 **Corporate capture:** the literature on corporate capture and the power of business in democratic capitalism is massive. Notable classic works include Charles E. Lindblom, *Politics and Markets: The World's Political-Economic Systems*, Basic Books 1977, and George Stigler, 'The Theory of Economic Regulation', *Bell Journal of Economics and Management Science*, vol. 2, pp. 3–21, 1971. Contemporary examples include Alexander Hertel-Fernandez, *State Capture: How Conservative Activists, Big Businesses and Wealthy Donors Reshaped the American States – and Nation*, Oxford University Press, 2019; Daniel Carpenter and David A. Moss, eds, *Preventing Regulatory Capture: Special Interest Influence and How to Limit It*, Cambridge University Press, 2014; and Pepper D. Culpepper, *Quiet Politics and Business Power: Corporate Control in Europe and Japan*, Cambridge University Press, 2011.

6 **Worst bad dream:** Bethany McLean and Peter Elkind, *The Smartest Guys in the Room: The amazing rise and scandalous fall of Enron*, Portfolio, p. 245.

6 **The company's stock was overpriced:** Bethany McLean, 'Is Enron Overpriced?', *Fortune*, 5 March 2001.

6 **Those employees lost $2 billion:** McLean and Elkind, 2003, p. 401; Levin Center, 'Portraits in Oversight: Congress and the Enron Scandal', https://levin-center.org/what-is-oversight/portraits/congress-and-the-enron-scandal/#ftn.

7 **Sarbanes-Oxley law:** Bryan D. Jones and Frank Baumgartner, *The Politics of Attention: How government prioritizes problems*, University of Chicago Press, 2005, pp. 72–76.

CHAPTER 1 SCANDALS AND PUBLIC OPINION

11 **8,500 cats and dogs:** Abigail Goldman and Don Lee, 'Reported Pet Deaths at 8,500, FDA Says', *Los Angeles Times*, 4 May 2007.
11 **10,000 tons of formula:** Jim Yardley, 'Chinese Baby Formula Scandal Widens as 2nd Death is Announced', *New York Times*, 15 September 2008.
12 **A new initiative:** Andrew Jacobs, 'China Sentences Activist in Milk Scandal to Prison', *New York Times*, 10 November 2010.
12 **Food safety was a problem:** 'Growing Concerns in China about Inequality, Corruption', Pew Research Center report, 16 October 2012: https://www.pewresearch.org/global/2012/10/16/growing-concerns-in-china-about-inequality-corruption/.
12 **The Chinese public today:** John K. Yasuda, *On Feeding the Masses: An anatomy of regulatory failure in China*, Cambridge University Press, 2018, p. 2.
13 **The ones who should take responsibility:** David Barboza, 'Death Sentences in Chinese Milk Case', *New York Times*, 22 January 2009.
13 **36 infants were sickened:** Sybille de la Hamaide, 'The Baby Milk Scandal Stalking France's Lactalis', Reuters, 1 February 2018: https://www.reuters.com/article/business/the-baby-milk-scandal-stalking-frances-lactalis-idUSKBN1FL5WT/.
13 **35 hearings:** 'France Needs "Food Safety Police" to Avoid New Lactalis Crisis: Report', *Straits Times*, 19 July 2018: https://www.straitstimes.com/world/europe/france-needs-food-safety-police-to-avoid-new-lactalis-crisis-report.
13 **Opened criminal investigations:** https://www.lemonde.fr/en/france/article/2023/02/16/french-company-charged-over-baby-milk-salmonella-scandal_6016092_7.html.
16 **Already declining dramatically:** Henry E. Brady and Thomas B. Kent, 'Fifty Years of Declining Confidence and Increasing Polarization in Trust in American Institutions', *Daedalus* vol. 151, Fall 2022, pp. 43–66.
18 **983 sub-postmasters**: 'Post Office Horizon scandal: Why hundreds were wrongly prosecuted', BBC, 30 July 2024: https://www.bbc.co.uk/news/business-56718036.
18 **Widespread public outrage:** Stephen Barber, 'Post Office scandal: what the lack of action tells you about Britain's polarised politics',

NOTES 233

      The Conversation, 11 January 2024: https://theconversation.com/post-office-scandal-what-the-lack-of-action-tells-you-about-britains-polarised-politics-220958.

18 **Most trusted brand:** Grace Augustine, Jan Lodge, Mislav Radic, 'Mr Bates vs the Post Office depicts one of the UK's worst miscarriages of justice: here's why so many victims did not speak out', *The Conversation*, 4 January 2024: https://theconversation.com/mr-bates-vs-the-post-office-depicts-one-of-the-uks-worst-miscarriages-of-justice-heres-why-so-many-victims-didnt-speak-out-220513.

19 **What's good for GM:** The famous epigram is actually a misquotation of Charles Wilson, the CEO of General Motors nominated by Dwight Eisenhower to be Secretary of Defense in 1953. Wilson owned an enormous amount of GM stock, which became an issue at his Senate confirmation hearing. When asked at the hearing if he could imagine making a decision as Secretary of Defense that went against the interests of GM, he responded that such a scenario was implausible, 'because for years I thought what was good for our country was good for General Motors, and vice versa'. See Historical Office of the Secretary of Defense: https://history.defense.gov/Multimedia/Biographies/Article-View/Article/571268/charles-e-wilson/.

CHAPTER 2   FROM WATERGATE TO DIESELGATE

24 **Los Angeles to Seattle:** Jack Ewing, *Faster, Higher, Farther: The Volkswagen Scandal*, W. W. Norton and Company, 2017, pp. 164–72.

24 **Shocked and astounded:** Harry Kretchmer, 'The Man Who Discovered the Volkswagen Emissions Scandal', BBC News, 13 October 2015: https://www.bbc.com/news/business-34519184; Elizabeth Wason, 'The LSA Alum Who Exposed Volkswagen', University of Michigan 'In the News', 5 October 2015: https://lsa.umich.edu/lsa/news-events/all-news/search-news/the-lsa-alum-who-exposed-volkswagen.html.

24 **Immediately suspicious:** Ewing, 2017, pp. 173–4.

24 **'Acoustic function':** Ewing, 2017, pp. 176–80.

25 **VW had a chance to fix the problem:** Rupert Neate, 'Meet John German: the man who helped expose Volkswagen's emissions scandal', *Guardian*, 26 September 2015.

25 **Fines and recalls:** 'Volkswagen Says Diesel Scandal Has Cost It 31.3 Billion Euros', Reuters, 17 March 2020: https://www.reuters.com/article/business/volkswagen-says-diesel-scandal-has-cost-it-313-billion-euros-idUSKBN2141JA/.

25 **1,200 premature deaths:** Guillaume P. Chossière, Robert Malina, Akshay Ashok, Irene C. Dedoussi, Sebastian D. Eastham, Raymond L. Speth and Steven R. H. Barrett, 'Public health impacts of excess NOx emissions from Volkswagen diesel passenger vehicles in Germany', *Environmental Research Letters*, vol. 12, 2017.

26 **Matter of trust:** Valerie Hamilton, 'VW owners in California feel "ripped off" by cheating', dpa-AFX International ProFeed, 25 September 2015; retrieved using Nexis UK, Lexis Nexis.

27 **An initial transgression:** Our three features are inspired by those enumerated in Ari Adut, *On Scandal: Moral disturbances in society, politics and art*, Cambridge University Press, 2008, pp. 12–16; for another, broader definition, see John B. Thompson, *Political Scandal: Power and visibility in the media age*, Polity Press, 2000, pp. 13–25.

28 **Gossip made tedious:** Adut, 2008, p. 8.

28 **Many scholars believe:** Robert Entman, *Scandal and Silence: Media responses to presidential misconduct*, Polity Press, 2012; Brendan Nyhan, 'Scandal Potential: How political context and news congestion affect the president's vulnerability to media scandal', *British Journal of Political Science*, vol. 45, 2015, pp. 435–66.

30 **Acquaintanceship:** Mark D'Arcy, 'Mandy Rice-Davies and a Classic Westminster Scandal', BBC News, 19 December 2014: https://www.bbc.co.uk/news/uk-politics-30546514.

30 **Second-order transgressions:** Our interpretation of the Profumo scandal, including the limerick that illustrates it, follows the account in Thompson, 2000, pp. 17–20.

31 **Increasing polarization of Americans:** On the relationship between the occurrence of political scandals and how partisan opponents view presidents, see Nyhan, 2015. On the growth of partisan polarization in the United States, see Geoffrey C. Layman, Thomas M. Carsey and Juliana Menasce Horowitz, 'Party Polarization in American Politics: Characteristics, causes, and consequences', *Annual Review of Political Science*, vol. 9, 2006, pp. 83–110.

33 **Half the overall health costs:** Chossière et al., 2017.
34 **Newspapers on the left:** Riccardo Puglisi and James M. Snyder Jr., 'Newspaper Coverage of Political Scandals', *Journal of Politics*, vol. 73, 2011, pp. 931–50.
35 **On the same page:** James Walsh, Naomi Vaida, Alin Coman and Susan T. Fiske, 'Stories in Action', *Psychological Science in the Public Interest*, vol. 23, 2022, pp. 99–141.
36 **German car manufacturers:** Rüdiger Bachmann, Gabriel Ehrlich, Ying Fan, Dimitrije Ruzic and Benjamin Leard, 'Firms and Collective Reputation: A study of the Volkswagen emissions scandal', *Journal of the European Economic Association*, vol. 21, 2023, pp. 484–525; Vanitah Swaminathan and Suyun Mah, 'What 100,000 Tweets about the Volkswagen Scandal Tell Us about Angry Customers', *Harvard Business Review*, 2 September 2016.
37 **Transgressions define the boundaries:** Andrei S. Markovits and Mark Silverstein, eds. *The Politics of Scandal: Power and process in liberal democracies*, Holmes & Meier, 1988.
38 **Use of defeat devices:** Markus Becker, 'EU-Kommission wusste früh von Abgasmanipulationen', *Der Spiegel*, 14 July 2016: https://www.spiegel.de/auto/aktuell/volkswagen-abgasskandal-eu-kommission-wusste-frueh-bescheid-a-1102967.html.
38 **New Deal for Consumers:** Mateusz Grochowski, 'European Consumer Law after the New Deal: A tryptich', *Yearbook of European Law*, vol. 39, 2020, pp. 387–422; Katharina van Elten and Britta Rehder, 'Dieselgate and Eurolegalism: How a scandal fosters the Americanization of European law', *Journal of European Public Policy*, vol. 29, 2022, pp. 281–300.
38 **Volkswagen accounted for 8 per cent:** See https://www.best-selling-cars.com/brands/2024-full-year-global-volkswagen-group-electric-car-sales-worldwide-by-brand-and-model/.

CHAPTER 3 GOLDMAN SACHS'S SHITTY DEAL

43 **Causes of the financial crisis:** Goldman was one of four case studies undertaken by the PSI, each targeted at a particular aspect of the crisis. The three other case studies were of Washington Mutual, to investigate why banks turned to high-risk lending; the Office of Thrift Supervision, to understand why federal regulators

did not intervene to stop high-risk lending; and the credit rating agencies Moody's and Standard and Poor's, to understand why the rating agencies gave triple-AAA ratings to investment products with risky mortgages. See Permanent Committee on Investigations (PSI), 'Wall Street and the Financial Crisis: Anatomy of a Financial Collapse', United States Senate Report, 13 April 2011 (hereafter cited as PSI, 2011).

44 **Paulson made over $1 billion:** PSI, 2011, pp. 560–74.
44 **More and more leverage:** 'Ex-Goldmanite "Fabulous Fab" Tourre Takes the Heat as Jury Finds Him Liable for Securities Fraud', *Forbes*, 1 August 2013. In the text we have corrected the spelling of monstrosities, which the Frenchman Tourre originally wrote as 'moustruosities'.
44 **$550 million fine:** 'Goldman Sachs to Pay Record $550 Million to Settle SEC Charges Related to Subprime CDO', press release, US Securities and Exchange Commission, 15 July 2010. See https://www.sec.gov/news/press/2010/2010-123.htm.
45 **Levin's team had to scramble:** Elise J. Bean, *Financial Exposure: Carl Levin's Senate Investigations into Finance and Tax Abuse*, Palgrave Macmillan 2018, p. 278.
45 **Scariest seat in Washington:** Kelsey Snell, 'Corporate World Won't Miss Levin', *Politico*, 11 September 2014.
46 **Goldman's Top 10 Excuses:** Katya Wachtel, 'The Best Goldman Jokes of All Time', *Business Insider*, 21 January 2011.
46 **CDOs:** A synthetic CDO is a structured financial product built from derivatives, which are securities based on the price of underlying assets. The assets sold by Goldman were related to mortgages, and the CDO enabled Goldman and its clients to bet on the price of mortgage bonds. Bean, 2018, pp. 278–9.
46 **'Hard sell' tactics:** PSI, 2011, p. 390.
47 **Interests were aligned:** PSI, 2011, pp. 390–2.
47 **$1.7 billion profit:** PSI, 2011, p. 9.
47 **Real bad feeling:** PSI, 2011, p. 508.
48 **What a shitty deal:** Joseph Cotterill, 'Goldman in DC: A blogger round-up', *Financial Times*, 28 April 2010.
49 **'Hard' and 'easy' issues:** Edward G. Carmines and James A. Stimson, 'The two faces of issue voting', *American Political Science Review*, vol. 74, 1980, pp. 78–91.

49 **Abortion an 'easy' issue:** We do not mean that the politics of abortion are easy or that the issue is straightforward to design policy around. In that sense, few issues are 'easy'. Politically, abortion has long been and continues to be a flashpoint in the US, dividing the cultural right from the cultural left. In terms of policy, writing laws to fit the politics around abortion rights is complicated, not easy. European countries, too, have widely varying rules on the gestational age at which abortion is legal, and what considerations override that general rule.

50 **Regulatory policy positions:** Pepper D. Culpepper, Jae-Hee Jung and Taeku Lee, 'Banklash: How media coverage of bank scandals moves mass preferences on financial regulation', *American Journal of Political Science*, vol. 68, 2024, pp. 427–44.

50 **Facing the country:** The countries we surveyed were the US, UK, Switzerland, Germany, France and Australia.

52 **Generated a profit:** Pepper D. Culpepper and Raphael Reinke, 'Structural Power and Bank Bailouts in the United Kingdom and the United States', *Politics & Society*, vol. 42, 2014, pp. 427–54.

53 **The draft bill:** The law is called Dodd-Frank in honour of its champions in the two houses of the American Congress: Representative Barney Frank and Senator Chris Dodd.

54 **One Senate staffer:** Pepper D. Culpepper and Taeku Lee, 'The Art of the Shitty Deal: Media Frames and Public Opinion on Financial Regulation in the United States', *Socio-Economic Review* 2022, p. 643.

55 **What is a bank?:** John Cassidy, 'The Volcker Rule', *New Yorker*, 19 July 2010.

55 **Volcker rule:** 2018 reforms under the Trump administration weakened some of those limits for smaller banks, but they remained in force for all large banks with assets of $250 billion or more.

55 **Safer than before 2008:** Aigbe Akhigbe, Anna D. Martin and Ann Marie Whyte, 'Dodd-Frank and Risk in the Financial Services Industry', *Review of Quantitative Finance and Accounting*, vol. 47, 2016, pp. 395–415; Aaron M. Levine and Joshua C. Macey, 'Dodd-Frank is a Pigouvian regulation', *Yale Law Journal*, vol. 127, 2017, pp. 1336–1415.

55 **Republicans saw political peril:** David M. Herszenhorn and Edward Wyatt, 'Republicans Allow Debate on Financial Overhaul', *New York Times*, 28 April 2010.

56 **Public opinion drove that bill**: Robert G. Kaiser, *Act of Congress: How America's essential institution works, and how it doesn't*, Vintage Books, 2014, p. 327.

57 **More news you consumed:** Pepper D. Culpepper and Taeku Lee, 'The Art of the Shitty Deal', pp. 635–57.

58 **Significantly change:** As in a medical trial, our experiment works because of the properties of random assignment. Our survey contained 1,000 people, selected to be representative of the American population. By randomly assigning participants to treatment and placebo groups, we ensure that the average attitude in one group should be equal to the average attitude of the other group, so long as the groups are sufficiently large.

Any difference in the attitudes of the two groups can only be due either to randomness or to the one thing that we know differs between the two groups: the articles we had them read. We use statistical techniques to take account of the possible effect of random variation. That leaves us with what we call the treatment effect, where the 'treatment' is reading the 'shitty deal' article.

Readers may worry that, unlike in drug trials, it is possible that some members of our placebo group remember the details of the scandal, and that they have therefore been 'pre-treated'. Given that six years had passed between the original scandal and our survey, we are confident the details of this scandal were not widely known when we fielded our survey. However, if some members of the placebo group did in fact remember those details, that that would mean that our survey actually *underestimates* the effect of the scandal, since this knowledge would bias upwards our measurement of control group attitudes – anger, blaming banks for the financial crisis, and preferences for more financial regulation – diminishing their apparent difference with the treatment group. For details of the full experiment, see Culpepper and Lee, 2022.

59 **Investment banks:** The exact wording of our survey item was this: 'Investment banks, which raise capital for corporate clients, should be entirely separate from ordinary banks'. Respondents then indicated their agreement or disagreement on a scale ranging from 1 to 5.

59 **Bank banned employees:** Courtney Comstock, 'Goldman Sachs's New Rules on Swearing in Emails, Texts and Ims', *Business Insider*, 29 July 2010.

NOTES 239

59 **Only a single banker went to jail:** Jesse Eisinger, 'Why Only One Top Banker Went to Jail for the Financial Crisis', *New York Times*, 30 April 2014.
60 **Central counterparties:** Central counterparties are financial institutions that serve as intermediaries for all derivatives trades. They monitor risk and can demand collateral. They can net out the positions of traders on opposite sides and make the level of systemic risk more transparent to regulators.
61 **Dude, I owe you:** 'Eagle Fried', *Economist*, 27 June 2012. BBC economics correspondent Andy Verity has argued that the traders convicted for these email exchanges were victims of a rigged system, in which they were simply following practices that were not illegal, created no victims and paled in comparison to some of the rate rigging sought by their superiors and by officials at the Bank of England. See Andy Verity, *Rigged: The incredible true story of the whistleblowers jailed after exposing the rotten heart of the financial system*, Flint, 2023.
61 **LIBOR:** Matt Taibbi, 'Everything is Rigged: The Biggest Price-Fixing Scandal Ever', *Rolling Stone*, 5 April 2013.
62 **High-voltage shock:** 'Ring-Fence Needs Electrification, says Banking Commission Report', UK Parliament, Parliamentary Commission on Banking Standards, 21 December 2012: https://committees.parliament.uk/committee/284/parliamentary-commission-on-banking-standards-joint-committee/news/180152/ringfence-needs-electrification-says-banking-commission-report/.
64 **Ban on proprietary trading:** Note that the regulation proposed by the European Commission already constituted a watering down of the Liikanen group's proposals, particular with respect to ring-fencing. See David R. Sahr, 'Does Volcker + Vickers = Liikanen?', Harvard Law School Forum on Corporate Governance, 8 March 2014: https://corpgov.law.harvard.edu/2014/03/08/does-volcker-vickers-liikanen/.
64 **European banks dismissed:** David Howarth and Scott James, *Bank Politics: Structural reform in comparative perspective*, Oxford University Press, 2023, pp. 240–73.
64 **A gruesome end:** Jim Brunsden, 'European Commission Withdraws Bank Separation Proposal', *Financial Times*, 24 October 2017.

CHAPTER 4 EUROPE V FACEBOOK

65 **PRISM revelations**: Glenn Greenwald and Ewen MacAskill, 'NSA Prism program taps into user data of Apple, Google and others', *Guardian*, 6 June 2013.
66 **Tempora**: Ewen MacAskill, Julian Borger, Nick Hopkins, Nick Davies and James Ball, 'GCHQ taps fibre-optic cables for secret access to world's communications', 21 June 2013.
66 **Leaks kept coming**: David E. Sanger and Eric Schmitt, 'Snowden Used Low-Cost Tools to Best NSA', *New York Times*, 8 February 2014.
66 **Story has fundamentally changed**: George Packer, 'Big Brother and Silicon Valley', *New Yorker*, 17 June 2013.
68 **1,222 pages of information**: Julia Prummer, 'Max Schrems, the Man Who De-Friended Facebook', *VoxEurope*, 27 April 2012.
69 **Only way she could communicate**: James Jacoby, interview of Max Schrems, *PBS Frontline*, 28 March 2018.
71 **You know in a click**: Craig Timberg, 'Facebook Privacy Targeted by Austrian Law Student', *Washington Post*, 19 October 2012.
72 **Next big thing**: Today, Facebook's parent company Meta is the sixth largest company in the world. It is preceded on this list by five American tech companies.
72 **FaceMash**: Sheera Frenkel and Cecilia Kang, *An Ugly Truth: Inside Facebook's Battle for Domination*, Hachette, 2021.
72 **Explicitly selected**: Frenkel and Kang, 2021, p. 63.
72 **Privacy is the vector**: John Hudson, 'The Future of Facebook', *Atlantic*, 22 April 2010; Marshall Kirkpatrick, 'Facebook Says the Age of Privacy is Over', *New York Times*, 10 January 2010.
74 **1995 Data Protection Directive**: Abraham L. Newman, *Regulating Personal Data in the Global Economy*, Cornell University Press, 2008.
74 **Updating its privacy law**: Moritz Laurer and Timo Seidl, 'Regulating the European Data-Driven Economy: A Case Study on the General Data Protection Regulation', *Policy & Internet*, 2020, p. 265.
74 **Pugnacious**: Michelle Cini, 'Women and Leadership across the EU Institutions: the case of Viviane Reding', in Henriette Müller and Ingeborg Tömmel, eds, *Women and Leadership in the European Union*, Oxford University Press, 2022, pp. 95–111.

NOTES 241

74 **Villain of the year:** See: https://www.theregister.com/2007/02/21/ispa_villain_internet/#:~:text=Register%20www,to%20UK%20internet%20service%20providers.

74 **A law Reding initiated:** The law was fought tooth and nail by European telecoms companies, and it only came into force in 2017. Michelle Cini and Marián Šuplata, 'Policy Leadership in the European Commission: the regulation of EU mobile roaming charges', *Journal of European Integration*, vol. 39, 2018, pp. 143–56.

74 **How to use it:** Ioanna Schimizzi, 'Viviane Reding reflects on political career and looks ahead', *Delano*, 21 September 2022: https://delano.lu/article/viviane-redingreflects-on-euro.

75 **Top of her list:** Laurer and Seidl, 2020.

75 **Example of Schrems:** 'Safeguarding Privacy in a Connected World: A European data protection framework for the twenty-first century', Communication from the European Commission, 2012: https://eur-lex.europa.eu/legal-content/en/TXT/?uri=CELEX-%3A52012DC0009.

76 **Amazon and Facebook:** Agustín Rossi Silvano, 'Internet Privacy in the European Union and the United States', PhD thesis, European University Institute, 2016, pp. 48–49.

76 **Never experienced such lobbying:** James Fontanella-Khan, 'Brussels: Astroturfing takes root', *Financial Times*, 26 June 2013.

76 **AmCham hosted several conferences:** Rossi 2016, pp. 43–56.

78 **Chernobyl of data protection:** Hannah Kuchler, 'Max Schrems: the man who took on Facebook – and won', *Financial Times*, 5 April 2018.

78 **European political conversation:** Nikhil Kalyanpur and Abraham L. Newman. 'The MNC-Coalition Paradox: Issue Salience, Foreign Firms and the General Data Protection Regulation', *JCMS: Journal of Common Market Studies* vol. 57, no. 3, 2019, pp. 455–60.

78 **Those who knew about the Snowden leaks:** 'Data Protection', Special Eurobarometer, 431, June 2015.

79 **Europe's answer:** 'Informal Justice Council in Vilnius', *EU Monitor*, 19 July 2013: https://www.eumonitor.eu/9353000/1/j9vvik7m1c3gyxp/vjbgkg36dazx?ctx=vhkejco8liwc&start_tab0=1020.

79 **Countries in favour:** Agustín Rossi, 'How the Snowden Revelations Saved the EU General Data Protection Regulation', *International Spectator*, vol. 53, 2018, pp. 95–111.

79 **The bill passed:** 'Progress on EU data protection reform now irreversible following European Parliament vote', European Commission press release, 12 March 2014.

79 **Mass transfers violated European privacy law:** EVF lodged the same formal complaints against Apple, Microsoft, Skype and Yahoo, all of which had been exposed as being part of the PRISM programme. Natasha Lomas, 'Facebook, Apple, Microsoft, Skype & Yahoo Hit with Prism Data Protection Complaints in Europe', *TechCrunch*, 26 June 2013.

80 **Industry-developed solution:** Damon Greer, 'Safe Harbor – A Framework that Works', *International Data Privacy Law*, vol. 1, 2011, p. 143.

81 **Court's findings:** Henry Farrell and Abraham L. Newman, *Of Privacy and Power: The Transatlantic Struggle over Freedom and Security*, Princeton University Press, 2019, p. 149; Judgement of the ECJ: https://eur-lex.europa.eu/legal-content/EN/TXT/?uri=CELEX%3A62014CJ0362.

81 **Digital dark ages:** Farrell and Newman, 2019, p. 151.

81 **Altered the balance of power:** Farrell and Newman, 2019, p. 158.

82 **Localizing the data:** Anu Bradford, *Digital Empires: The global battle to regulate technology*, Oxford University Press, 2023, p. 230.

82 **Europe fit for the digital age:** 'The European Commission's Priorities': https://commission.europa.eu/strategy-and-policy/priorities-2019-2024_en.

83 **A second charge:** Rowland Manthorpe, 'Europe vs. Silicon Valley: Behind enemy lines with the woman deciding Google's fate', *WIRED*, 27 June 2017: https://www.wired.com/story/who-is-margrethe-vestager/.

83 **Framework for other investigations:** Mark Scott, 'Google Fined Record $2.7 Billion in E.U. Antitrust Ruling," *New York Times*, 27 June 2017. The fine was €2.4 billion, which at 2017 exchange rates was $2.7 billion, but at the 2025 exchange rate used throughout this book is equal to $2.5 billion.

84 **Gatekeepers:** The companies designated as gatekeepers were Alphabet (Google's parent), Amazon, Apple, Meta (Facebook's parent) and Microsoft, along with TikTok's owner, ByteDance. See 'The EU's New Competition Rules are Going Live', *The Verge*, 6 March 2024: https://www.theverge.com/2024/3/6/24091592/

eu-dma-competition-compliance-deadline-big-tech-policy-changes; EU press release: https://ec.europa.eu/commission/presscorner/detail/en/ip_23_4328.

84 **Audits on disinformation:** Catherine Hoeffler and Frédéric Mérand, 'Digital Sovereignty, Economic Ideas, and the Struggle over the Digital Markets Act: a political-cultural approach', *Journal of European Public Policy*, vol. 31, 2024, pp. 2121–46; Johann Laux, Sandra Wachter and Brent Mittelstadt, 'Taming the Few: Platform regulation, independent audits, and the risks of capture created by the DMA and DSA', *Computer Law & Security Review*, vol. 43, 2021, pp.1–12.

84 **Companies ferociously lobbied:** Javier Espinoza, 'Internal Google Document Reveals Campaign Against EU Lawmakers', *Financial Times*, 28 October 2020.

84 **Never seen this kind of money:** Adam Satariano and Matina Stevis Gridneff, 'Big Tech turns its Lobbyists Loose on Europe, Alarming Regulators', *New York Times*, 14 December 2020.

84 **Apple nearly doubled:** Pietro Lombardi, 'Big Tech Boosts Lobbying Spending in Brussels', *Politico*, 22 March 2022: https://www.politico.eu/article/big-tech-boosts-lobbying-spending-in-brussels/.

84 **Largest single lobbying spender:** 'Lobbying Power of Amazon, Google and Co. Continues to Grow', Corporate Europe Observatory, 8 September 2023: https://corporateeurope.org/en/2023/09/lobbying-power-amazon-google-and-co-continues-grow.

85 **Details of its strategy**: Corporate Europe Observatory, 'Big Tech brings out the big guns in fight for future of EU tech regulation', 11 December 2020: https://corporateeurope.org/en/2020/12/big-tech-brings-out-big-guns-fight-future-eu-tech-regulation; Emmanuel Berretta and Guillaume Grallet, 'Comment Google veut faire plier Bruxelles', *Le Point*, 28 October 2020.

85 **Huge majorities:** The DMA passed with 588 votes in favour, 11 opposed and 31 abstentions; the DSA passed with 539 votes for, 54 against and 30 abstentions.

86 **DPCs are captured:** Tuulia Karjalainen, 'The Battle of Power: Enforcing Data Protection Law Against Companies Holding Data Power', *Computer Law & Security Review*, vol. 47, 2022, pp. 1–10.

87 **Enforcement issues:** '5 Years of the GDPR: National Authorities Let Down European Legislator', NOYB: https://noyb.eu/en/5-years-gdpr-national-authorities-let-down-european-legislator.

87 **Fines on tech companies:** See https://www.enforcementtracker.com/?insights.

87 **Regulatory superpower:** Anu Bradford, *The Brussels Effect: How the European Union rules the world*, Oxford University Press, 2020.

CHAPTER 5 CAMBRIDGE ANALYTICA AND THE TECHLASH

89 **I'm a businessman:** We discovered the story of Alastair Mactaggart thanks to the outstanding article by Nicholas Confessore, from which this quotation comes. Nicholas Confessore, 'The Unlikely Activists Who Took on Silicon Valley – and Won', *New York Times Magazine*, 14 August 2018.

90 **Referendum:** The referendum process is a related tool for collecting citizen signatures to allow a popular vote to overturn a law passed by the legislature.

90 **The Octopus:** Rebecca Solnit, 'The Octopus and its Grandchildren', *Harper's Magazine*, August 2014: https://harpers.org/archive/2014/08/the-octopus-and-its-grandchildren/.

92 **Donations:** Eric Preizkalns, 'Telcos and Internet Giants Join Forces to Fight Californian Privacy Law', *Commsrisk*, 6 July 2018: https://commsrisk.com/telcos-and-internet-giants-join-forces-to-fight-californian-privacy-law/.

92 **Limiting our choices:** Press statement by the Committee to Protect California Jobs, 3 May 2018: https://www.prnewswire.com/news-releases/statement-by-the-committee-to-protect-california-jobs-on-submission-of-signatures-for-internet-regulation-ballot-measure-300642494.html.

93 **Greyball:** Mike Isaac, 'How Uber Deceives the Authorities Worldwide', *New York Times*, 3 March 2017; Rob Davies and Johana Bhuiyan, 'Uber used Greyball fake app to evade police across Europe, leak reveals', *Guardian*, 12 July 2022.

93 **Through the app:** Ruth Berins Collier, Veena B. Dubal and Christopher L. Carter, 'Disrupting Regulation, Regulating Disruption: The politics of Uber in the United States', *Perspectives on Politics*, vol. 16, 2018, pp. 919–37; Kathleen Thelen, 'Regulating Uber:

The politics of the platform economy in Europe and the United States', *Perspectives on Politics*, vol. 16, 2018, pp. 938–53.

94 **Platform power:** Pepper D. Culpepper and Kathleen Thelen, 'Are We all Amazon Primed? Consumers and the Politics of Platform Power', *Comparative Political Studies*, vol. 53, 2020, pp. 288–318.

94 **Influence on the cheap:** The one exception to this lack of lobbying expenditure was Microsoft, which the US government had sued for abusing its dominant position in 1998. Given that it faced intense regulatory scrutiny earlier than the other Big Tech companies, Microsoft ramped up its lobbying spending in the 1990s and has never looked back. The data in the US lobbying graph come from OpenSecrets: https://www.opensecrets.org/.

94 **50 times the size:** Germán Gutiérrez and Thomas Philippon, 'How EU Markets Became More Competitive than US Markets: A study of institutional drift', National Bureau of Economic Research working paper 24700, June 2018, p. 28.

96 **Self-made rules:** This is the same 'safe harbour' approach to self-regulation that was rejected in Europe, as discussed in Chapter 4.

96 **Privacy advocate:** The privacy advocate was Jeff Chester, executive director of the Center for Digital Democracy. Brendan Sasso, 'Obama's "Privacy Bill of Rights" Gets Bashed from All Sides', *Atlantic*, 27 February 2015.

97 **Cow Clicker:** Ian Bogost, 'My Cow Game Extracted Your Facebook Data', *Atlantic*, 22 March 2018.

97 **Unattributable, untrackable:** 'Exposed: Undercover secrets of Trump's data firm', Channel 4 News Investigations Team, 20 March 2018: https://www.channel4.com/news/exposed-undercover-secrets-of-donald-trump-data-firm-cambridge-analytica.

98 **Confidence Poll:** Jonathan M. Ladd, Joshua A. Tucker and Sean Kates, 'The 2018 American Institutional Confidence Poll: The Health of Democracy in an Era of Hyper Polarization', A report by the John S. and James L. Knight Foundation and the Baker Center for Leadership & Governance at Georgetown University, 2018.

98 **The poll was repeated in 2021:** Sean Kates, Jonathan M. Ladd and Joshua A. Tucker, 'How Americans' Confidence in Technology Firms Has Dropped: Evidence from the Second Wave of the American Institutional Confidence Poll', A research report in the series on 'The Economics and Regulation of Artificial Intelligence

and Emerging Technologies' for the Center on Regulation and Markets, The Brookings Institution, 2023.

98 **Technology companies should be regulated:** Aaron Smith, 'Public Attitudes Toward Technology Companies', Pew Research Center, 28 June 2018: https://www.pewresearch.org/internet/2018/06/28/public-attitudes-toward-technology-companies/.

99 **People want tighter regulation:** For further details of our survey experiment, see Pepper D. Culpepper, Taeku Lee and Ryan Shandler, 'In the Metaverse, Politicians Can Hear You Scream: Corporate Scandals and the Microfoundations of Focusing Events', Working Paper, Blavatnik School of Government, University of Oxford, 2025.

100 **Arney's words:** Confessore, 2018.

100 **All Californians:** Alastair Mactaggart, 'My Turn: What I'll Tell Congress about CA's New Privacy Law', *CalMatters*, 4 October 2018: https://calmatters.org/economy/2018/10/my-turn-what-ill-tell-congress-about-cas-new-privacy-law/.

102 **Didn't catch that one:** Gilad Edelman, 'The Fight over California's Privacy Future', *WIRED*, 21 September 2020: https://www.wired.com/story/california-prop-24-fight-over-privacy-future/.

103 **CPRA:** The law also tripled fines for misuse of data of children under the age of 16.

103 **Could only be strengthened:** Sara Morrison, 'California Just Strengthened its Digital Privacy Protections Even More', *Vox*, 4 November 2020: https://www.vox.com/2020/11/4/21534746/california-proposition-24-digital-privacy-results.

103 **GDPR:** Bradford, 2023, p. 336. Unlike the GDPR, the California law concentrated not on whether companies could have access to your data, but what they could do with that access. Mactaggart summarizes the California law this way:

> The line I drew in the sand was [information you give to companies] shouldn't leave your corporate halls or walls. I should be able to stop that. I should be able to say, 'Don't sell my information, don't share it, don't do anything with it.' Because it's one thing for me to share my personal information with my doctor, but I don't expect my doctor to be then going and posting it on the internet. And at some level, a lot of the stuff that we share with these Big Tech companies is very personal. So that was how

I arrived at 'Do Not Sell, Do Not Share'. That's where I drew the line. Other people could have drawn it other places.

103 **Collapse of public confidence:** Kates, Ladd and Tucker, 2021.

104 **Model for other states:** Brendan Bordelon and Alfred Ng, 'Tech Lobbyists are Running the Table on State Privacy Laws', *Politico*, 16 August 2023: https://www.politico.com/news/2023/08/16/tech-lobbyists-state-privacy-laws-00111363.

105 **Amazon drafted the Virginia bill:** Jeffrey Dastin, Chris Kirkham and Aditya Kalra, 'Amazon Wages Secret War on Americans' Privacy, Documents Show', Reuters, 19 November 2021: https://www.reuters.com/investigates/special-report/amazon-privacy-lobbying/.

105 **Industry-led effort:** Todd Feathers, 'Big Tech is Pushing States to Pass Privacy Laws, and Yes, You Should be Suspicious', *The Markup*, 15 April 2021: https://themarkup.org/privacy/2021/04/15/big-tech-is-pushing-states-to-pass-privacy-laws-and-yes-you-should-be-suspicious.

105 **Connecticut:** Feathers, 2021.

105 **Coordinated national push:** Todd Feathers and Alfred Ng, 'Tech Industry Groups are Watering Down Attempts at Privacy Regulation, One State at a Time', *The Markup*, 26 May 2022: https://themarkup.org/privacy/2022/05/26/tech-industry-groups-are-watering-down-attempts-at-privacy-regulation-one-state-at-a-time.

106 **Wolf in sheep's clothing:** Tom Kemp, 'Big Tech Wolf in Sheep's Clothing? Californians Unite in Opposition to the ADDPA "Trap"', *Medium*, 10 August 2022: https://medium.com/golden-data/big-tech-wolf-in-sheeps-clothing-californians-unite-in-opposition-to-the-adppa-trap-948a3a37a412.

107 **Executive order:** Rana Foroohar, 'The great US-Europe antitrust divide', *Financial Times*, 5 February 2024.

108 **Influential article:** Lina Khan, 'Amazon's Antitrust Paradox', *Yale Law Journal*, vol. 126, 2016, pp. 710–805.

108 **Culture change:** Callum Jones, '"She's Going to Prevail,"' *Guardian*, 9 March 2024.

108 **Billionaire Accountability Project:** David McCabe, 'The Trustbuster Who Has Apple and Google in His Sights', *New York Times*, 22 March 2024.

108 **DoJ won a second antitrust case:** Emma Roth and Lauren Feiner, 'Google Loses Ad Tech Monopoly Case', *The Verge*, 17 April 2025:

109   https://www.theverge.com/news/650665/google-loses-ad-tech-antitrust-monopoly-lawsuit.

109   **The current movement:** CNBC Interview with Jonathan Kanter and Lina Khan, 4 June 2024: https://www.cnbc.com/2024/06/04/cnbc-transcript-dojs-jonathan-kanter-and-ftcs-lina-khan-speak-with-cnbcs-andrew-ross-sorkin-from-cnbcs-ceo-council-summit-today-.html.

109   **End politically motivated investigations**: Elizabeth Nolan Brown, 'Trump is Coming for Tech Companies' *Reason*, 9 December 2024: https://reason.com/2024/12/09/trump-is-coming-for-tech-companies/.

109   **How democracies work:** Culpepper, 2011.

110   **Tech bros spent big:** Emily Birnbaum, 'Tech Giants Broke their Spending Records on Lobbying Last Year', *Seattle Times*, 2 February 2023.

CHAPTER 6   #EXXONKNEW

113   **Five to ten years:** Neela Banerjee, Lisa Song and David Hasemeyer, 'Top executives were warned of possible catastrophe from greenhouse effect, then led efforts to block solutions', *Inside Climate News*, 15 September 2015.

115   **Initiated the investigation:** 'Sen. Whitehouse Offers Terse Comment on Cianci's Death', Associated Press, 29 January 2016: https://eu.providencejournal.com/story/news/politics/2016/01/29/sen-whitehouse-offers-terse-comment-on-cianci-death/32596746007/.

116   **First wake-up calls:** Lisa Song, 'Sen. Whitehouse's Climate Crusade Aims to Awaken Congress "Sleepwalking through History"', *Inside Climate News*, 12 February 2013.

116   **Democratic colleagues intimidated:** Andrew Restuccia, 'Where's Al Gore?', *Politico*, 5 September 2012.

117   **In this place:** Coral Davenport and Lisa Friedman, 'Five Decades in the Making: Why it Took Congress So Long to Act on Climate', *New York Times*, 7 August 2022.

119   **The dirty secret:** Sheldon Whitehouse, 'Republicans Want to Fight Climate Change, but Fossil-Fuel Bullies Won't Let Them', *Washington Post*, 10 January 2017.

NOTES 249

120 **Sway over politicians:** Leah Cardamore Stokes, *Short Circuiting Policy: Interest groups and the battle over clean energy and climate policy in the American States*, Oxford University Press, 2020; Matto Mildenberger, *Carbon Captured: How Business and Labor Control Climate Policies*, MIT Press, 2020.

120 **Equally likely to believe:** Patrick J. Egan and Megan Mullin, 'Climate change: US public opinion', *Annual Review of Political Science,* 2017, pp. 209–27.

120 **Politicians have been sending:** Eric Merkley and Dominik A. Stecula, 'Party Cues in the News: Democratic elites, Republican backlash and the dynamics of climate scepticism', *British Journal of Political Science*, vol. 51, 2021, pp. 1439–56.

120 **Most polarized of issues:** American National Election Studies, 2016.

121 **Stamp out disagreement:** 'Prosecuting Climate Dissent', *Wall Street Journal*, 8 November 2015.

122 **Left-wing effort:** 'Marco Rubio Calls Exxon Scandal Nothing but a Left-Wing Effort to Demonize Industry', *EcoWatch*, 8 January 2016: https://www.ecowatch.com/marco-rubio-calls-exxon-scandal-nothing-but-a-left-wing-effort-to-demo-1882146126.html.

122 **Hillary Clinton:** Katherine Bagley, 'Hillary Clinton Joins Call for Justice Dept. to Investigate Exxon', *Inside Climate News*, 29 October 2015.

123 **Republicans bridled:** Alan Yuhas, 'Senators Demand US Halt Inquiries into Climate Denial by Oil Companies', *Guardian*, 26 May 2016.

124 **Block climate bills:** Climate bills can only avoid the use of the filibuster, and thus the threshold of 60 votes discussed in Chapter 3, when they have budgetary implications, meaning they are passed through a measure known as budget reconciliation.

124 **His final speech:** Edward Fitzpatrick, 'Senator Whitehouse Delivers 279th and Final "Time to Wake Up" Climate Change Speech', *Boston Globe*, 27 January 2021. See also: https://www.whitehouse.senate.gov/news/speeches/time-to-wake-up-279-finale/

124 **Emissions trading system:** Emissions trading, also known as 'cap and trade', refers to a system in which governments set a limit (cap) on the amount of emissions, and issue permits that line up with that cap. Those wanting to emit, say, carbon, have to buy offsetting carbon permits.

125 **Shape legislation they oppose:** Jacob M. Grumbach, 'Polluting Industries as Climate Protagonists: cap and trade and the problem of business preferences', *Business and Politics*, vol. 17, 2015, pp. 633–59.

125 **More political donations:** Anthony Zurcher, 'Joe Manchin and Kyrsten Sinema Blocking Biden's Climate Agenda', BBC News, 28 October 2021: https://www.bbc.co.uk/news/world-us-canada-59060739.

125 **More carrots than sticks:** Manchin and Sinema also received concessions on other issues of interest to them and the states they represented. Democrats assured Manchin that Congress would pass legislation to allow the operation of the Mountain Valley Pipeline in West Virginia, which environmental groups had blocked for years. Sinema got drought relief for her state of Arizona and the elimination of the crackdown on carried interest, which mainly benefits private equity and hedge funds. See Lisa Friedman, 'Manchin Won a Pledge from Democrats to Finish a Contested Pipeline', *New York Times*, 1 August 2022; Andrew Ross Sorkin et al., 'A Tax Loophole's Powerful Defender', *New York Times*, 5 August 2022.

125 **Significant climate legislation:** Patrick J. Egan and Megan Mullin, 'US Partisan Polarization on Climate Change: Can Stalemate Give Way to Opportunity?', *PS: Political Science & Politics*, 2024, pp. 30–5.

126 **Unimpeachable evidence:** Hiroko Tabuchi, 'Exxon Scientists Predicted Global Warming, Even as Company Cast Doubts, Study Finds', *New York Times*, 12 January 2023.

127 **Constructed similar articles:** Our UK article was mainly based on stories from the *Guardian* and the *Telegraph*; our German article was primarily from *Die Zeit* and the *Frankfurter Rundschau*; and our French article drew from the websites of *Les Echos*, *Le Monde* and *Libération*, as well as huffingtonpost.fr.

128 **Effect of wildfires:** Chad Hazlett and Matto Mildenberger, 'Wildfire Exposure Increases Pro-Environment Voting within Democratic but not Republican Areas', *American Political Science Review*, 2020, pp. 1359–65.

128 **Deeply partisan beliefs:** Studies in European countries have not found the same partisan political response to climate change events observed in the United States. See Leonardo Baccini and Lucas Leemann, 'Do natural disasters help the environment? How voters respond and what that means', *Political Science Research and*

Methods, 2021, pp. 468–84; and Tobias Rüttenauer, 'More talk, no action? The link between exposure to extreme weather events, climate change belief and pro-environmental behaviour', *European Societies*, 2023, pp. 1–25.

129 **His own fortune:** John Schwartz, 'Exxon Mobil Accuses the Rockefellers of a Climate Conspiracy', *New York Times*, 21 November 2016.

130 **Carson castigated:** Rachel Carson, *Silent Spring*, Houghton Mifflin, 1962, p. 13.

130 **Chemical companies fought back:** Eliza Griswold, 'How *Silent Spring* Ignited the Environmental Movement', *New York Times*, 21 September 2012; Robin McKie, 'Rachel Carson and the Legacy of *Silent Spring*', *Observer*, 27 May 2012.

130 **Carson's book:** Kirkpatrick Sale, *The Green Revolution: The American Environmental Movement 1962–1992*, Hill and Wang 1993, p. 4.

131 **First national poll:** John C. Whitaker, *Striking a Balance: Environment and Natural Resources Policy in the Nixon-Ford Years*, AEI-Hoover Institution Policy Studies, 1976, pp. 8–9.

131 **Two focusing events:** Robert Gottlieb, *Forcing the Spring: The Transformation of the American Environmental Movement*, Island Press, 2005, p. 176.

131 **Santa Barbara:** Robert O. Easton, *Black Tide: The Santa Barbara Oil Spill and Its Consequences*, Delacorte Press, 1972.

131 **People it mainly affected:** Teresa Sabol Spezio, *Slick Policy: Environmental and Science Policy in the Aftermath of the Santa Barbara Oil Spill*, University of Pittsburgh Press, 2018, p. 3.

131 **Time was ripe:** Some people think about Earth Day in April 1970, in which 20 million people demonstrated in cities and university campuses throughout the United States, as the seminal event in American environmental policy breakthrough. But that gets the timing wrong – Earth Day happened several months after President Richard Nixon had signed the National Environmental Protection Act on 1 January 1970. Senator Henry 'Scoop' Jackson in fact presented the bill to the Senate less than a month after the Santa Barbara oil spill. See Adam Rome, 'Give Earth a Chance: The Environmental Movement and Sixties', *Journal of American History*, 2003; Soumya Karlamangla, 'How a California Disaster Inspired the First Earth Day', *New York Times*, 22 April 2022.

132 **No visible signs of life:** 'America's Sewage System and the Price of Optimism', *Time*, 1 August 1969.
133 **Nixon signed the Act:** '"The 'Carbon Dioxide Problem"': Nixon's Inner Circle Debates the Climate Crisis', National Security Archive, George Washington University: https://nsarchive.gwu.edu/briefing-book/climate-change-transparency-project/2024-04-26/carbon-dioxide-problem-nixons-inner.
134 **Chafee was endorsed:** David Karol, *Red, Green, and Blue: The partisan divide on environmental issues*, Cambridge University Press, 2019, p. 49.
135 **Younger Republicans:** Lawrence C. Hamilton, Joel Hartter and Erin Bell, 'Generation gaps in US public opinion on renewable energy and climate change', *PLOS One*, 2019.
135 **Benefit of future generations:** Thomas Hale, *Long Problems: Climate Change and the Challenge of Governing Across Time*, Princeton University Press, 2024.

CHAPTER 7 FTX – RASHOMON FOR THE CRYPTO ERA

137 **Hallmark of crypto:** Erin Griffith, 'Why the Crypto Collapse Matters', *New York Times*, 17 November 2022.
137 **As old as original sin:** 'Sam Bankman-Fried's Crypto Crash', *Wall Street Journal*, 13 December 2022.
137 **Crypto token as voucher:** Technically, a token is a financial asset connected to a cryptocurrency, but that does not have its own blockchain. See https://crypto.com/university/crypto-tokens-vs-coins-difference.
138 **$35 million penthouse:** Bankman-Fried had moved FTX to the Bahamas specifically to avoid regulation. See Leo Schwartz, 'FTX broke ground on $60m Bahamas headquarters in April. Construction never started', *Fortune*, 17 November 2022.
138 **A secret backdoor:** David Yaffe-Bellany, J. Edward Moreno and Matthew Goldstein, 'Gary Wang, an FTX Founder, Says Sam Bankman-Fried Steered Misuse of Funds', *New York Times*, 6 October 2023.
140 **A simple knowledge question:** The question survey respondents had to answer was, 'Which of the following is true about cryptocurrencies, such as Bitcoin?' Potential answers included: 'Cryptocurrency is underpinned by blockchain technology'

(the correct answer); 'Cryptocurrency was invented by Shigeru Miyamoto'; 'Cryptocurrency is insecure because is it easily hacked'; and 'Cryptocurrency is backed by US dollars'. Respondents could also answer, 'I don't know'.

140 **Country of Poland**: https://www.polytechnique-insights.com/en/columns/energy/bitcoin-electricity-consumption-comparable-to-that-of-poland/.

141 **Interpret the world**: Spencer Goidel and Paul M. Kellstedt, 'Economic opinion', in Thomas J. Rudolph, ed., *Handbook on Politics and Public Opinion*, Edward Elgar Publishing, 2022, pp. 400–12. On the general problem of partisan learning, see Jennifer Jerit and Jason Barabas, 'Partisan Perceptual Bias and the Information Environment', *Journal of Politics*, vol. 74, 2012, pp. 672–84.

142 **So too can media outlets**: Pepper D. Culpepper, Ryan Shandler, Jae-Hee Jung and Taeku Lee, '"The Economy is Rigged": Inequality Narratives, Fairness, and Support for Redistribution in Six Countries', *Comparative Political Studies*, 2024.

142 **Played video games**: The most entertaining account of Sam Bankman-Fried and FTX, from which we take the anecdote of Bankman-Fried's video-game prowess, is Michael Lewis's *Going Infinite: The rise and fall of a new tycoon*, Allen Lane, 2023.

143 **Silicon Valley's super-rich:** Dylan Matthews, 'How Effective Altruism Went from Niche Movement to Billion Dollar Force', *Vox*, 8 August 2022, https://www.vox.com/future-perfect/2022/8/8/23150496/effective-altruism-sam-bankman-fried-dustin-moskovitz-billionaire-philanthropy-crytocurrency

143 **Bankman-Fried met MacAskill:** Alex Christian, 'FTX's Sam Bankman-Fried believed in "effective altruism". What is it?', BBC, 10 October 2023: https://www.bbc.com/worklife/article/20231009-ftxs-sam-bankman-fried-believed-in-effective-altruism-what-is-it.

144 **Except for Mark Zuckerberg:** Hank Tucker, '15 Under 40: The youngest billionaires on the 2021 Forbes 400', *Forbes*, 21 April 2022.

144 **Second-largest donor:** 'Oops. Sam Bankman-Fried's implosion took down Democrats' second biggest donor with it as the party gears up to regulate crypto', *Fortune*, 10 November 2022.

144 **Seventy-six per cent of those:** *Economist*/YouGov poll, 17–20 December 2022, available at https://docs.cdn.yougov.com/by8wjw1hur/econTabReport.pdf.

145 **Were affected in the same way:** The technical details of the research reported here are available in Pepper D. Culpepper, Taeku Lee and Ryan Shandler, 'Media Effects Revisited: Corporate Scandals, Partisan Narratives, and Attitudes Toward Cryptocurrency Regulation', working paper, Blavatnik School of Government, University of Oxford, 2025.

146 **Less regulation among Republicans:** We did not randomly assign knowledge of the scandal, as we have done in the experiments discussed in previous chapters. So we cannot say that knowledge causes an increase in the regulatory preference in Democrats and a decrease in regulatory preferences among Republicans. There are many other characteristics that determine awareness of the scandal that also influence regulatory preferences.

147 **Wild Wild West:** Matt Egan, 'FTX crash is eerily similar to the Bernie Madoff Scandal, ex-regulator Sheila Bair says', CNN, 15 November 2022, https://edition.cnn.com/2022/11/15/business/ftx-madoff-bankman-fried-bair/index.html.

147 **Regulation of these products:** Zeeshan Aleem, 'The stunning collapse of FTX, explained', MSNBC, 17 November 2022: https://www.msnbc.com/opinion/msnbc-opinion/ftx-collapse-sam-bankman-frieds-crypto-rcna57263.

147 **Crypto went mainstream:** Erin Griffith, 'Why the Crypto Collapse Matters', *New York Times*, 17 November 2022.

147 **Moral cover:** Tucker Carlson, 'Sam Bankman-Fried was considered a moral leader even as he was ripping off millions of people', FoxNews, 17 November 2022: https://www.foxnews.com/opinion/tucker-carlson-sam-bankman-fried-considered-moral-leader-ripping-off-millions-people.

147 **Moral vanity:** Daniel Henninger, 'The Moral Vanity of FTX', *Wall Street Journal*, 1 December 2022.

148 **Potential causes of the scandal:** The percentages do not add up to 100 because multiple answers were possible and some people selected 'I don't know'.

148 **Biases of American media:** https://www.allsides.com/media-bias.

148 **More moderate views:** Obviously, we do not know all the ways in which those on the right who get their news from the *New York Times* differ from those on the right who get their news from Fox News. It may only be more moderate Republicans who make that choice. But this remains speculative, given the limits of our data

to answer the question. However, research independent of ours shows that Republicans who generally watch Fox News moderate their views on policy questions when they consume news from a left-leaning network like CNN. See David Broockman and Joshua Kalla, 'Consuming Cross-Cutting Media Causes Learning and Moderates Attitudes: A Field Experiment with Fox News Viewers', *Journal of Politics*, 2024.

149 **From a right-wing source:** There were, however, very few people on the left who learned about the scandal from a right-wing source, at least in our survey. There were many more people on the right who learned about the scandal from a left-wing source.

150 **Rife with fraud:** Gary Gensler, 'Partners of Honest Business and Prosecutors of Dishonesty', remarks before the 2023 Securities Enforcement Forum: https://www.sec.gov/newsroom/speeches-statements/gensler-remarks-securities-enforcement-forum-102523#_ftn11.

150 **Binance and Coinbase:** Niamh Rowe, 'Hitting a Record High in 2023, SEC Enforcement Actions against Crypto Firms Have Nearly Doubled since 2021 – the Year Gensler Took Over', *Fortune*, 24 January 2024; Declan Harty, 'SEC's Gensler Turns Tide Against Crypto in Courts', *Politico*, 5 May 2024: https://www.politico.com/news/2024/05/05/gary-gensler-sec-crypto-00154769.

150 **Regulation through litigation:** Declan Harty, '"Shark Tank": Mark Cuban goes after the SEC's Gensler', *Politico*, 14 October 2024: https://www.politico.com/news/2024/10/11/mark-cuban-gary-gensler-fight-sec-future-harris-00183090.

150 **Single largest corporate donors:** The crypto industry, especially Coinbase and Ripple, accounted for almost half of corporate donations to the 2024 campaign. Since 2010, the crypto industry's contributions to US election exceeded that of every industry except fossil fuel. See https://www.bankrate.com/investing/where-trump-and-harris-stand-on-crypto/.

151 **Crypto capital of the planet:** Thomas B. Edsall, 'Why Trump Wants to Make America the "Crypto Capital of the World"', *New York Times*, 2 October 2024.

151 **The judge who sentenced Bankman-Fried:** Natalie Sherman, Kayla Epstein and Michelle Fleury, 'Fallen "Crypto King" Sam Bankman-Fried Gets 25 Years for Fraud', BBC News, 29 March 2024: https://www.bbc.co.uk/news/business-68677487.

151 **Intrusive future monitoring**: Tom Wilson, 'Who is Changpeng Zhao, Binance CEO Ousted for US Crimes?', Reuters, 22 November 2023: https://www.reuters.com/technology/changpeng-zhao-crypto-king-binance-chief-ousted-us-crimes-2023-11-21/ ; Liv McMahon, 'Binance Crypto Boss Changpeng Zhao Sentenced to 4 Months in Prison', BBC News, 30 April 2024: https://www.bbc.co.uk/news/technology-68930465; Henry Farrell, 'How the Feds Bounced Binance', 27 November 2023: https://www.programmablemutter.com/p/how-the-feds-bounced-binance.

CHAPTER 8   SASOL AND THE DEATH OF MOSSVILLE

153 **Jim Crow South:** Heather Rogers, 'Erasing Mossville: How Pollution Killed a Louisiana Town', *The Intercept*, 4 November 2015: https://theintercept.com/2015/11/04/erasing-mossville-how-pollution-killed-a-louisiana-town/.

154 **Toxins in Mossville:** Tim Murphy, 'A Massive Chemical Plant is Poised to Wipe This Louisiana Town Off the Map', *Mother Jones*, 27 March 2014: https://www.motherjones.com/environment/2014/03/sasol-mossville-louisiana/.

154 **CDC toxicologist:** Rogers, 2015.

154 **Mossville's 50 households:** Ava Kofman, 'The EPA Administrator Visited Cancer-Causing Air Pollution Hot Spots Highlighted by ProPublica and Promised Reforms', *ProPublica*, 24 November 2021: https://www.propublica.org/article/the-epa-administrator-visited-cancer-causing-air-pollution-hot-spots-highlighted-by-propublica-and-promised-reforms.

156 **Beliefs about race:** Taeku Lee, *Mobilizing Public Opinion: Black Insurgency and Racial Attitudes in the Civil Rights Era*, University of Chicago Press, 2002.

156 **Linked fate:** Michael Dawson, *Behind the Mule*, Princeton University Press, 1994.

156 **Antipathy as resentment:** Donald R. Kinder and Lynn M. Sanders, *Divided by Color: Racial Politics and Democratic Ideals*, University of Chicago Press, 1996.

157 **Hochschild's *Strangers in Their Own Land*:** Arlie Hochschild, *Strangers in Their Own Land*, The New Press, 2016. See also, in a similar vein, Katherine J. Cramer's *The Politics of Resentment*, University of Chicago Press, 2016.

157 **Empathy wall:** Hochschild, 2016, p. 5.

158 **Calcasieu Parish:** National Institute of Minority Health and Health Disparities database at https://hdpulse.nimhd.nih.gov/data-portal/home.

158 **Sasol had grown:** From the *Wall Street Journal* markets database: https://www.wsj.com/market-data/quotes/ZA/XJSE/SOL/financials/annual/income-statement.

159 **Largest emitters of carbon dioxide:** Liezl Human, 'Sasol Makes the World CO_2 Emissions Blacklist', *GroundUp*, 17 April 2024: https://groundup.org.za/article/sasol-makes-the-world-co2-emissions-blacklist/; 'Balancing People, Planet, Profit on our Pathway to Net Zero', Sasol stakeholder letter, 29 November 2023: https://www.sasol.com/ceo-stakeholder-letter; Anthony Sguazzin, 'The World's Biggest Emitter of Greenhouse Gases', *Bloomberg*, 17 March 2020: https://www.bloomberg.com/news/features/2020-03-17/south-africa-living-near-the-world-s-biggest-emitting-plant.

159 **Condea Vista was routing toxic chemicals:** James Ridgeway, 'Environmental Espionage: Inside a Chemical Company's Louisiana Spy Op', *Mother Jones*, 20 May 2008: https://www.motherjones.com/environment/2008/05/environmental-espionage-inside-chemical-companys-louisiana-spy-op/.

159 **Elevated rates of cancer:** Kathleen Navarro, et al, 'Health Alert: Disease Clusters Spotlight the Need to Protect People from Toxic Chemicals', Report from the National Resources Defense Council (10 May, 2011): https://www.nrdc.org/sites/default/files/disease-clusters_issuepaper.pdf.

159 **Premium market value:** *Daily World,* 17 March 1998. 'Company agrees to settle contamination case', Opelousas, Louisiana, 21 September 2024: https://www.newspapers.com/article/daily-world-03171998-vista-agrees-to/16394659/?locale=en-US.

159 **Homeowners who accepted this buy-out:** Murphy, 2014.

159 **Lake Charles area:** Clifford Krauss, 'South African Company to Build U.S. Plant to Convert Gas to Liquid Fuels', *New York Times*, 3 December 2012: https://www.nytimes.com/2012/12/04/business/energy-environment/sasol-plans-first-gas-to-liquids-plant-in-us.html.

159 **Largest single manufacturing project:** News release from Louisiana Economic Development, 12 November 2013: https://www.opportunitylouisiana.gov/news/sasol-s-louisiana-project-wins-foreign-direct-investment-deal-of-the-year; see

also news release from Louisiana Economic Development, 27 March 2015: https://www.opportunitylouisiana.gov/news/gov-jindal-highlights-groundbreaking-for-sasol-s-8-1-billion-ethane-cracker-complex-at-westlake.

160 **The state issued regulatory waivers:** Eleanor Bell and Talia Buford, 'Black History and Heritage Bulldozed by Gas Boom', report from the Center for Public Integrity, 6 February 2015. November 2024: https://publicintegrity.org/environment/black-history-and-heritage-bulldozed-by-gas-boom/.

160 **Seventh largest source of greenhouse gas emissions in the US:** Johannes Friedrich, Mengpin Ge and Alexander Tankou, '8 Charts to Understand US State Greenhouse Gas Emissions', World Resources Institute, 10 August 2017; updated August 2021: https://www.wri.org/insights/8-charts-understand-us-state-greenhouse-gas-emissions.

160 **7,000 construction jobs:** Clifford Krauss, 'South African Company to Build US Plant to Convert Gas to Liquid Fuels', *New York Times*, 2 December 2012: https://www.nytimes.com/2012/12/04/business/energy-environment/sasol-plans-first-gas-to-liquids-plant-in-us.html.

161 **In neighbouring Brentwood:** Joshua Petersen, Ruhan Nagra and Margot Lurie, 'They Didn't Pay Us for Our Memories: Environmental Racism, Forced Displacement and the Industrial Buyout of Mossville, Louisiana', report from the University Network for Human Rights, November 2021: https://www.humanrightsnetwork.org/publications/mossville-environmental-racism. See also Sara Sneath, 'A Chemical Firm Bought Out These Black and White US Homeowners – With a Significant Disparity', *Guardian*, 17 November 2021: https://www.theguardian.com/us-news/2021/nov/17/this-communitys-black-families-lost-their-ancestral-homes-their-white-neighbors-got-richer.

162 **Sasol's very public promise:** Mike Smith, '"Startling": EPA Head Pledges Action for Vanishing Black Community of Mossville', *The Advocate*, 18 November 2021: https://www.theadvocate.com/lake_charles/startling-epa-head-pledges-action-for-vanishing-black-community-of-mossville/article_880d5144-48b7-11ec-b879-ff1730140962.html.

162 **Ryan's family property:** Alexander Glustrom, *Mossville: When Great Trees Fall*, Fire River Film, 2019.

NOTES

- 163 **Holding up progress:** Rick Mullin, 'Mossville's End', 21 March 2016: https://cen.acs.org/articles/94/i12/Mossvilles-end.html.
- 163 **Flea on a dog:** Mullin, 2016.
- 163 **'I've caught Sasol people on my property':** Tom Valtin, 'Louisiana Man Takes a Stand Against a Petrochemical Giant', 21 July 2015: https://www.sierraclub.org/planet/2015/07/louisiana-man-takes-stand-against-petrochemical-giant.
- 163 **'Whoever's left here needs help':** Valtin, 2015.
- 164 **'The oil companies had bought democracy':** Valtin, 2015.
- 164 **He, too, ultimately capitulated:** Mullin, 2016.
- 164 **'Journey to Justice' tour:** US Environmental Protection Agency press release, 22 November 2021: https://www.epa.gov/newsreleases/icymi-his-journey-justice-epa-administrator-michael-s-regan-toured-historically.
- 164 **Regan's response was unsparing:** Ava Kofman, 'The EPA Administrator Visited Cancer-Causing Air Pollution Hot Spots Highlighted by ProPublica and Promised Reforms', *Pro Publica*, 24 November 2021: https://www.propublica.org/article/the-epa-administrator-visited-cancer-causing-air-pollution-hot-spots-highlighted-by-propublica-and-promised-reforms.
- 164 **50 households remained in Mossville:** Maryum Jordan, 'The World is Watching How a Petrochemical Giant Denies Its Neighbors Justice', *Earth Rights International*, 14 December 2023: https://earthrights.org/blog/the-world-is-watching-how-a-petrochemical-giant-denies-its-neighbors-justice/.
- 165 **'They're erasing everything':** Glustrom, 2020.
- 165 **27 per cent of the region's economic output:** From the American Manufacturing Communities Collaborative. Employment figures include both direct and indirect employment in the industry: https://americanmcc.org/louisianamc/.
- 165 **23 per cent poverty rate:** 'Economic Snapshot: Louisiana', from the Joint Economic Committee: https://www.jec.senate.gov/public/_cache/files/8676d21f-1a46-466b-bed6-34e0d09dbdde/louisiana.pdf. See also LeRoydna Brooks, Lam X. Cao and Ralph M. Rodriguez, 'Gross Domestic Product by State', from the Bureau of Economic Affairs, July 2013: https://apps.bea.gov/scb/pdf/2013/07%20July/0713_gdp_by_state.pdf.
- 166 **'Reminders of the racial divide were everywhere':** Hochschild, 2016, pp. 19–21.

166 **Deep Story:** Hochschild, 2016, pp. 182–4.
167 **Environmental racism:** The term 'environmental racism' is also credited to Robert Bullard, a legal scholar who is known as the 'Father of Environmental Justice', and who penned the foundational book, *Dumping in Dixie: Race, Class and Environmental Quality*, Westview Press, 1990.
168 **Central feature of American politics:** Zoltan Hajnal, Vincent Hutchings and Taeku Lee, *Race and Inequality in American Politics: An Imperfect Union*, Cambridge University Press, 2024.
169 **White resentment:** Taeku Lee and Pepper D. Culpepper, 'Two Worlds of Welfare Racism? Resentment and redistribution in comparative context', working paper.
169 **Significant financial investment:** Our story of Noel Stevens follows the account in Adele Ferguson, *Banking Bad: Whistleblowers. Corporate cover-ups. One journalist's fight for the truth*, HarperCollins Australia, 2019, pp. 111–15.
170 **Victims whose stories:** For more information on the sort of media stories generated by the Banking Royal Commission in Australia and the response of Australians to them, see Tom Nicholls and Pepper D. Culpepper, 'Computational Identification of Media Frames: Strengths, weaknesses and opportunities', *Political Communication* vol. 38, 2021, pp. 159–81, and Pepper D. Culpepper and Taeku Lee, 'Media Frames, Partisan Identification and the Australian Banking Scandal', *Australian Journal of Political Science*, vol. 56, 2021, pp. 73–98.
171 **Tracey Walsh:** Ferguson 2019, p. 248.
171 **Misrepresent its links with the Indigenous community:** Ben Butler and Lorena Allam, 'Youpla: how Aboriginal funeral fund evaded regulators despite 30 years of complaints', *Guardian*, 26 May 2022.
172 **If this was a mainstream insurer:** Butler and Allam, 2022.
172 **29th most toxic county:** 'The Most (And Least) Toxic Places in America', *Forbes*, 7 November 2017: https://www.forbes.com/sites/priceonomics/2017/11/07/the-most-and-least-toxic-places-in-america/.
173 **Single largest source:** Greg Hilburn, 'Is Ouachita Parish Toxic? Yes, says EPA', *Monroe News-Star*, 10 November 2017: https://thenewsstar.com/story/news/2017/11/10/ouachita-parish-toxic-yes-says-epa/851754001/.

173 **Killed eight workers:** Keith Schneider, 'Petrochemical Disasters Raise Alarm in Industry', *New York Times*, 19 June 1991. The plant was owned by Angus but operated by IMC Fertilizer.
173 **Twisted them like pretzels:** 'Federal Investigation into Plant Explosion will Take Three to Four Months', Associated Press, 4 May 1991.
173 **Killed six workers:** Schneider, 1991.
174 **Sleazy manoeuvre:** Karen Ball, 'OSHA Reaches $10 Million Settlement with LA. Plant', *Washington Post*, 31 October 1991.
174 **The Angus settlement:** The Angus Chemical Company changed its name in 2023 to the Advancion Corporation.
175 **'Do your damn job!':** Zoë Schlanger, 'Former Army General Lambasts Oil Industry for "Hijacking" Democracy', *Newsweek*, 9 September 2014: https://www.newsweek.com/former-army-general-lambasts-oil-industry-hijacking-democracy-269086.

CHAPTER 9 THE FALL OF A SAMSUNG PRINCE

179 **Wealthy *Yangban* family:** Yangban were Korean men belonging to the highest non-royal social class during the Joseon dynasty (from 1392 to 1910). Originally used to designate a scholar class of civil officials in the Koryo dynasty, the term was eventually used to describe Korea's landed aristocracy as well.
180 **Quote from Lee:** Geoffrey Cain, *Samsung Rising*, Crown, 2020.
181 **Gross national income in the 1950s:** World Bank: https://www.worldbank.org/en/country/korea/overview.
181 **Korea's nominal GDP:** Federal Reserve St Louis: https://fred.stlouisfed.org/series/MKTGDPKRA646NWDB.
182 **Park promised economic growth:** For an excellent synthesis on Park Chung-hee's presidency, see Carter J. Eckert, *Park Chung Hee and Modern Korea: The Roots of Militarism, 1866–1945*, Harvard University Press, 2016. See also B. K. Kim and Ezra F. Vogel, eds, *The Park Chung Hee Era: The Transformation of South Korea*, Harvard University Press, 2011.
183 **Highest-profile affiliate companies:** For a good overview on the rise of chaebol, see Sea-jin Chang, *Financial Crisis and Transformation of Korean Business Groups*, Cambridge University Press, 2010. On Samsung, see Cain, 2020.
183 **The Samsung group alone:** From Statista, using data from Citizens' Coalition for Economic Justice: https://www.statista.

184 **Korea Herald poll on chaebol:** https://www.koreaherald.com/view.php?ud=20230912000718.

184 **A career with Samsung:** Jaeyeon Woo, 'Samsung Puts New Hiring Plan on Hold', *Wall Street Journal*, 28 January 2014: https://www.wsj.com/articles/BL-KRTB-4923.

187 **The mother pleaded with him:** From the BBC News story, 'Park Geun-hye and the friendship behind South Korea's presidential crisis', 31 October 2016: https://www.bbc.com/news/world-asia-37820112.

187 **Diplomatic wire:** Ambassador Vershbow's communique was made public through WikiLeaks. From *Korea Herald*, 'Mystery of Park's Heavy Reliance on Choi', 30 October 2016: https://www.koreaherald.com/view.php?ud=20161030000180.

187 **Motive behind Park Chung-hee's assassination:** BBC News, 31 October 2016.

188 **Choi's 'boy toy':** Chung Hyun-chae, 'Scandal unveils Choi Soon-sil's "boy toy"', *Korea Times*, 30 October 2016: https://www.koreatimes.co.kr/www/nation/2025/02/113_217091.html.

188 **'She treated me like a slave':** 'Park Geun-hye impeached: Did a puppy bring down South Korea's president?' BBC News, 9 December 2016: https://www.bbc.com/news/world-asia-38259068.

189 **Incorruptible:** Katharine H. Moon and Duyeon Kim, 'Park Geun-hye Bad Chois', *Foreign Affairs*, 9 November 2016: https://www.foreignaffairs.com/articles/south-korea/2016-11-09/park-geun-hyes-bad-chois.

191 **He's sort of like a god':** Cain, 2020.

192 **Highest levels of government:** Jin-kyung Yi, 'The Flow of the Masses and the Candlelight Demonstrations in South Korea', *Korea Journal*, 60(3), 2020, pp. 218–72. See also Woo-jin Kang, 'Determinants of Unaffiliated Citizen Protest: The Korean Candlelight Protests of 2016–17', *Korea Journal*, vol. 59, 2019, pp. 46–78.

192 **President Park's approval:** Jun Ji-hye, 'Park's Approval Rating Falls to Record Low', *Korea Times*, 7 November 2016: https://www.koreatimes.co.kr/www/nation/2024/05/113_215614.html.

193 **Park's approval ratings plunged:** 'South Korea's presidential approval remains at all-time low', Reuters, 11 November 2016:

https://www.reuters.com/article/world/south-korea-presidents-approval-rating-remains-at-all-time-low-gallup-idUSKBN13603J/.

193 **National Assembly voted to impeach:** Ju-min Park and Jack Kim, 'South Korean Parliament Votes Overwhelmingly to Impeach President Park', Reuters, 9 December 2016: https://www.reuters.com/article/world/south-korean-parliament-votes-overwhelmingly-to-impeach-president-park-idUSKBN13X2JT/.

193 **Constitutional Court unanimously upheld:** Choe Sang-hun, 'South Korea Removes President Park Geun-hye', *New York Times*, 9 March 2017: https://www.nytimes.com/2017/03/09/world/asia/park-geun-hye-impeached-south-korea.html.

193 **Park then faced criminal proceedings:** Choe Sang-hun, 'Park Geun-hye, South Korea's Ousted President, Gets 24 Years in Prison', *New York Times*, 6 April 2018: https://www.nytimes.com/2018/04/06/world/asia/park-geun-hye-south-korea.html.

194 **Lee received five years in prison:** Choe Sang-Hun, Jeyup Kwaak and Paul Mozur, 'Samsung Verdict Sends a Tough New Message to South Korea, Inc.', *New York Times*, 25 August 2017: https://www.nytimes.com/2017/08/25/business/samsung-bribery-embezzlement-conviction-jay-lee-south-korea.html.

194 **Kept failing before Samsung:** Choe, Kwaak and Mozur, 2017.

195 **'Mad cow disease':** For excellent overviews of South Korea's tradition of dissent and its roots in its prior authoritarian era, see Paul Chang, *Protest Dialectics: State Repression and South Korea's Democracy Movement, 1970–1979*, Stanford University Press, 2015; Joan E. Cho, *Seeds of Mobilization: The Authoritarian Roots of South Korea's Democracy*, University of Michigan Press, 2024; Namhee Lee, *Making of Minjung: Democracy and the Politics of Representation in South Korea*, Cornell University Press, 2007.

195 **Celebration of Democracy:** Alexis Dudden, 'Revolution by Candlelight: How South Koreans Toppled a Government', *Dissent*, Fall 2017.

195 **Highest suicide rate:** OECD: https://www.oecd.org/en/data/indicators/suicide-rates.html.

195 **Lowest fertility rate:** OECD: https://www.oecd.org/en/data/indicators/fertility-rates.html?oecdcontrol-00b22b2429-var3=2020.

197 **'Chaebol sniper':** See the Center for Strategic and International Studies' brief biography by Matthew Ha, 'Impact Player: Kim

Sang-jo', 22 June 2017: https://www.csis.org/analysis/impact-player-kim-sang-jo.

197 **'I will lead the reform of the chaebol:** Kim Jaewon, 'Moon vows to cut government ties with conglomerates', *Nikkei Asia*, 10 May 2017: https://asia.nikkei.com/Politics/Moon-vows-to-cut-government-ties-with-conglomerates.

197 **Antitrust czar:** 'South Korea's antitrust tsar has a good shot at taming the chaebol', *Economist*, 6 January 2018; 'South Korea taps chaebol reform activist as antitrust chief', Reuters, 17 May 2017: https://www.reuters.com/article/world/south-korea-taps-chaebol-reform-activist-as-antitrust-chief-idUSKCN18D0U4/.

197 **A slew of changes:** Kim Jaewon, 'Moon's party passes bill to limit power of South Korea's chaebol', *Nikkei Asia*, 9 December 2020: https://asia.nikkei.com/Politics/Moon-s-party-passes-bill-to-limit-power-of-South-Korea-s-chaebol.

198 **Scandalize public opinion:** This section is based on multiple sources, including the following: Choe Sang-hun, '"My Last Stand": In South Korea, a Protester's Lone Fight Against Samsung', *New York Times*, 19 April 2020: https://www.nytimes.com/2020/04/19/world/asia/samsung-tower-protest.html; Jungmin Choi, 'The South Korean Samsung protester living in the sky', *BBC Korea*, 25 May 2020: https://www.bbc.co.uk/news/av/world-asia-52792953; Kelly Jarman, 'A People's History of Samsung's Rise: Korean Workers Make a Last Stand for Justice', International Strategy Center Report, 20 April 2020: https://www.goisc.org/englishblog/2020/4/20/a-peoples-history-of-samsungs-rise-korean-workers-fight-for-justice.

198 **Kim's father went missing:** Choe Sang-hun, 19 April 2020. This *New York Times* article also mentions an uncorroborated newspaper story speculating that Kim Yong-hee's wife had been sexually assaulted by a perpetrator with ties to Samsung.

200 **Samsung's tradition of passing the reins to one's children:** Choe Sang-hun, 'Samsung Heir Apologizes for Corruption and Union-Busting Scandals', *New York Times*, 6 May 2020: https://www.nytimes.com/2020/05/06/business/samsung-lee-apology.html.

200 **A new management-labour relationship:** Choe Sang-hun, 'South Korean ends year-long tower protest after Samsung apologizes', *New York Times*, 29 May 2020: https://www.nytimes.com/2020/05/29/world /asia/south-korea-protest-tower-samsung.html.

NOTES

200 **Winning only 108 out of the 300 seats:** Hannah Kim, 'South Korean elections cast a shadow over Yoon's presidency', *East Asia Forum*, 27 April 2024: https://eastasiaforum.org/2024/04/27/south-korean-elections-cast-a-shadow-over-yoons-presidency/.

200 **Gallup approval ratings for Yoon:** 'Yoon's approval rating sinks to lowest point since taking office', *Korea Times*, 31 May 2024: https://www.koreatimes.co.kr/www/nation/2024/11/113_375749.html.

201 **$2,200 Dior handbag:** Martin Fletcher, 'How a Dior handbag brought down South Korea's president', *Telegraph*, 16 December 2024: https://www.telegraph.co.uk/news/2024/12/16/how-a-dior-handbag-brought-down-south-koreas-president/. See also Lee Hyo-jin, 'How scandals surrounding first lady contributed to Yoon's downfall', *Korea Times*, 16 December 2024: https://www.koreatimes.co.kr/www/nation/2025/02/113_388567.html.

CHAPTER 10   GOOD POPULISM

205 **Every governing party:** John Burn-Murdoch, 'Democrats join 2024's graveyard of incumbents', *Financial Times,* 7 November 2024.

209 **Responsive and responsible:** Peter Mair, 'Representative versus Responsible Government', working paper of the Max Planck Institute for the Study of Societies, 2009: https://edoc.vifapol.de/opus/volltexte/2010/2121/pdf/wp09_8.pdf; see also Jonas Linde and Yvette Peter, 'Responsiveness, Support and Responsibility: How democratic responsiveness facilitates responsible government', *Party Politics,* vol. 26, 2020, pp. 291–304; Johannes Karremans, *Between Voters and Eurocrats: How do governments justify their budgets?* Oxford University Press, 2024.

211 **Corporations are people:** Ashley Parker, '"Corporations are People", Romney Tells Angry Hecklers over his Tax Policy', 11 August 2011.

212 **Tendency with authoritarian populist leaders:** Steven Levitsky and Lucan A. Way, *Competitive Authoritarianism: Hybrid regimes after the Cold War*, Cambridge University Press, 2010; Kurt Weyland, *Democracy's Resilience to Populism's Threats: Countering global alarmism*, Cambridge University Press, 2024.

212 **Evil twin of pluralism:** See, for instance, Jan-Werner Müller, *'What is Populism?'* University of Pennsylvania Press, 2016.
213 **Wide discretion and autonomy:** See, for instance, Daniel Carpenter, *The Forging of Bureaucratic Autonomy*, Princeton University Press, 2001; John Huber and Charles Shipan, *Deliberate Discretion? The Institutional Foundations of Bureaucratic Autonomy*, Cambridge University Press, 2002; Edward Page, *Policy Without Politicians: Bureaucratic Influence in Comparative Perspective*, Oxford University Press, 2012; Carl Dahlstrom and Victor Lapuente, *Organizing Leviathan: Politicians, Bureaucrats, and the Making of Good Government*, Cambridge University Press, 2017; Susan Rose-Ackerman, *Democracy and Executive Power*, Yale University Press, 2021.
213 **Highest level of convenience:** Culpepper and Thelen, 2020.
215 **Point of the spear**: 'Crafting Better Privacy Laws, Based on the California Model with Alastair Mactaggart', *Wirewheel*, 20 July 2021: https://wirewheel.io/blog/ccpa-state-privacy-laws/.
217 **Increasing the transparency of private companies:** In the context of technology companies in particular, Marietje Schaake has an excellent discussion of transparency reforms that could be democracy-enhancing. We differ on the details but agree on the importance of transparency for bringing democratic control to Big Tech. See Marietje Schaake, *The Tech Coup: How to save democracy from Silicon Valley*, Princeton University Press, 2024, especially pp. 225–32.
217 **SpaceX owns Starlink:** Lewis Page, 'Elon Musk is Changing the Course of Human History', *Telegraph*, 24 November 2024.
217 **Submarine drone attack:** Walter Isaacson, *Elon Musk*, Simon and Schuster, 2023; see also https://www.yahoo.com/news/elon-musk-power-space-x-starlink-satellite-ukraine-russia-191847719.html.
217 **Billionaire Palmer Luckey:** Jeremy Bogaisky, 'Facebook Made this 29-Year-Old Rich; war made him a billionaire', *Forbes*, 3 June 2022.
218 **Three of those vessels exploded**: Kenneth Chang, 'Twin Test Flight Explosions Show SpaceX is No Longer Defying Gravity', *New York Times*, 8 March 2025.
218 **Financially opaque**: Even the market-friendly *Wall Street Journal* has criticized the degree of opacity at SpaceX: Corrie Driebusch, Becky Peterson and Susan Pulliam, 'A Side Hustle for Friends of Musk: Selling Access to Stakes in His Private Companies', *Wall Street Journal*, 25 April 2025.

218 **Public scrutiny:** Scholars of corporate law would add that the disclosure required of public companies also makes capital allocation in the economy more efficient. Merritt B. Fox, Randall Morck, Bernard Yeung and Artyom Durnev, 'Law, Share Price Accuracy and Economic Performance: the new evidence', *Michigan Law Review*, vol. 102, 2003, pp. 331–86. Some legal scholars have moved beyond the mere pricing advantage of disclosure to emphasize that disclosure could allow investors to more effectively price in climate risk, and thus make companies bear those costs in the market. See John Armour, Luca Enriques and Thom Wetzer, 'Mandatory Corporate Climate Disclosures: now, but how?', *Columbia Business Law Review*, vol. 3, 2021, pp. 1085–146.

219 **Altered the algorithm:** Media reports suggested Musk had already had his engineers change the algorithm to favour his posts in February 2023, when he was disgruntled that a post during the American Super Bowl by then President Joe Biden received more impressions than one by Musk. See Kari Paul, 'Elon Musk Reportedly Forced Twitter Algorithm to Boost His Tweets After Super Bowl Flop', *Guardian*, 15 February 2023. On the post-endorsement change, see Timothy Graham and Mark Andrejevic, 'A Computational Analysis of Potential Algorithmic Bias on Platform X during the 2024 US Election', working paper, Queensland University of Technology, 2024: https://eprints.qut.edu.au/253211/1/A_computational_analysis_of_potential_algorithmic_bias_on_platform_X_during_the_2024_US_election-4.pdf.

219 **Repeatedly posted disinformation:** Kate Conger, Aaron Krolik, Santul Nerkar and Dylan Freedman, 'How Elon Musk's Own Account Dominates X', *New York Times*, 3 November 2024; Joe Miller, Hannah Murphy, Lucy Fisher, Peter Andringa, Sam Joiner and Anna Gross, 'How A Handful of X Accounts Took Elon Musk "Down the Rabbit Hole" on UK Politics', *Financial Times*, 8 January 2025; Mathieu Polet, 'Europe's Press Goes After Musk's X', *Politico*, 15 November 2024: https://www.politico.eu/article/donald-trump-elon-musk-european-press-x-twitter-disinformation-fake-news-big-tech/.

219 **Bezos personally overruled:** 'Jeff Bezos Defends Decision to End *Washington Post* Endorsements', *Guardian*, 29 October 2024.

220 **$3.4 billion contract:** Claire O'Shea, 'NASA Selects Blue Origin as Second Artemis Lunar Lander Providers', NASA press release, 19 May 2023: https://www.nasa.gov/news-release/nasa-selects-blue-origin-as-second-artemis-lunar-lander-provider/.

220 **Rich democracies:** For the US, see https://www.fool.com/investing/stock-market/market-sectors/communication/media-stocks/big-6/ and James B. Stewart, 'When Media Mergers Limit More than Competition', *New York Times*, 25 July 2014. For the UK see 'Who Owns the UK Media? 2023 Report', Media Reform Coalition report, 3 October 2023: https://www.mediareform.org.uk/blog/new-report-who-owns-the-uk-media. The trend in the US is particularly noteworthy, given that it has typically had the lowest ownership concentration of the media industry in international comparison. See Eli M. Noam, ed., *Who Owns the World's Media? Media concentration and ownership around the world*, Oxford University Press, 2016, p. 1024.

220 **Competing with influencers:** On the increasing importance of online influencers in the American news ecosystem, see Galen Stocking et al., 'America's News Influencers', Pew Research Center, 18 November 2024: https://www.pewresearch.org/journalism/2024/11/18/americas-news-influencers/.

220 **Increasing media fragmentation:** Jon Allsop, 'Our Fragmented Media Age, and What Might Come Next', *Columbia Journalism Review*, 22 November 2024.

221 **Lost 10 per cent:** Elahe Izadi, 'After Non-Endorsement, 250,000 Subscribers Cancel the *Washington Post*', *Washington Post*, 29 October 2024.

221 **Public sector broadcasters:** Victor Pickard, *Democracy without Journalism? Confronting the misinformation society*, Oxford University Press, 2020.

222 **Systematic bias:** The data on left- and right-wing views of bias are from Patrick Barwise: https://blogs.lse.ac.uk/medialse/2024/06/04/ge24-and-bbc-bias-what-does-the-real-silent-majority-think/.

222 **Philanthropic intervention:** We do not mean to imply that public regulation and public spending have no role in responding to the crisis of news. For a discussion of some of the innovative solutions underway to reinvigorate local news, see for example https://www.rebuildlocalnews.org/.

222 **Classification scheme:** A self-governance distinction between opinion and factual journalism. See 'The Awareness Doctrine', *Harvard Law Review*, vol. 135, 2022, pp. 1907–28.

222 **NewsGuard:** A study of different sites that rated news reliability, including NewsGuard, found that they were highly correlated with each other. This suggests that it is possible to produce reliable estimates of news reliability; reliability ratings are not simply a matter of partisan opinion. See Hause Lin, Jana Lasser, Stephan Lewandowsky, Rocky Cole, Andrew Gully, David G. Rand and Gordon Pennycook, 'High Level of Correspondence across Different News Domain Rating Sets', *PNAS Nexus*, vol. 2, 2023, pp. 1–8.

223 **News consumers:** One recent study of social media found that priming people not to share misinformation – which is a light-touch intervention, like our distortion report cards – was among the most effective ways to reduce sharing of misinformation while not limiting the sharing of true information. See Sergei Guriev, Emeric Henry, Théo Marquis and Ekaterina Zhuravskaya, 'Curtailing False News, Amplifying Truth', SSRN working paper, 29 October 2023: https://papers.ssrn.com/sol3/papers.cfm?abstract_id=4616553. On the effectiveness and scalability of rating the reliability of news sites, see also Tatiana Celadin, Valerio Capraro, Gordon Pennycook and David G. Rand, 'Displaying News Source Trustworthiness Ratings Reduces Sharing Intentions for False News Posts', *Journal of Online Trust and Safety*, vol. 1, 2023, pp. 1–20.

A study of NewsGuard, published in 2022, found that the system boosted the quality of news consumed by those who consumed the lowest quality news, though the study did not find an effect on the population as a whole; see Kevin Aslett, Andrew M. Guess, Richard Bonneau, Jonathan Nagler and Joshua A. Tucker, 'News Credibility Labels Have Limited Average Effects and News Diet Quality and Fail to Reduce Misperceptions', *Science Advances*, vol. 8, pp. 1–10.

223 **Local news sources endangered:** See Edmund L. Andrews, 'Media Consolidation Means Less Local News, More Right-Wing Slant', *Insights by Stanford Business*, 30 July 2019: https://www.gsb.stanford.edu/insights/media-consolidation-means-less-local-news-more-right-wing-slant. See also Katerina Eva Matsa, 'Buying

spree brings more local TV stations to fewer big companies', Pew Research Center, 11 May 2017: https://www.pewresearch.org/short-reads/2017/05/11/buying-spree-brings-more-local-tv-stations-to-fewer-big-companies/ and https://localnewsinitiative.northwestern.edu/projects/state-of-local-news/2024/report/.

225 **That Buddhist thing:** from an interview reported in Confessore, 2018.

Picture credits and permissions

The Bosses of the Senate. @ Library of Congress Prints and Photographs Division Washington, D.C. 20540 USA. https://www.loc.gov/pictures/item/2002718861/

Picture from the *Inside Climate News* story on the Exxon strategy of challenging climate science. Source: Paul Horn, https://insideclimatenews.org/news/22102015/exxon-sowed-doubt-about-climate-science-for-decades-by-stressing-uncertainty/

Senator Sheldon Whitehouse making one of his 'Time to Wake Up' Speeches in the Senate. Source: https://thebulletin.org/2021/03/senator-its-time-to-wake-up-whitehouse-drops-his-climate-change-mic/. Image used with the permission of the Office of U.S. Senator Sheldon Whitehouse

Protestors in front of the New York Supreme Court in 2019. The court ruled in favour of Exxon. Source: https://edition.cnn.com/2023/01/12/business/exxon-climate-models-global-warming/index.html. © Angela Weiss/AFP/Getty Images.

The Cuyahoga burning. Source: https://time.com/3921976/cuyahoga-fire/. © Bettmann/Getty Images

Sam Bankman-Fried with supermodel Gisele Bündchen at a 2022 crypto conference © Joe Schildhorn/BFA.com/Shutterstock

Stacey Ryan next to his fence. Alexander Glustrom (2020). Source: https://www.collectiveeye.org/products/mossville-when-great-trees-fall

Stacey Ryan's property. Alexander Glustrom (2020). Source: https://www.earthisland.org/journal/index.php/articles/entry/last-man-standing/

Samsung man: Photograph by Park Gee-Young in *The Korea Herald*, 'The Samsung man' (6 March 2015). At https://www.koreaherald.com/view.php?ud=20150306000299.

Candlelight rally at Gwanghwamun Square, Seoul. Source: AP from https://www.japantimes.co.jp/news/2018/07/10/asia-pacific/politics-diplomacy-asia-pacific/south-korea-probe-alleged-plan-military-quell-park-geun-hye-protests/. © sinsy/Getty Images

Kim Yong-hee gesturing to supporters from his CCTV tower. Source: https://www.dw.com/en/fired-samsung-worker-climbs-down-seoul-tower-after-year-long-protest/a-53623723; © picture-alliance/AP/Yonhap/Yun Dong-jin. © YONHAP/EPA-EFE/Shutterstock

Index

Abacus, 43–4, 47
Aboriginal Community Benefit Fund (ACBF), 170–2
abortion, 49
Agent Orange, 130
Alameda Research, 138, 144, 149
Albrecht, Jan Philipp, 77
Allan, Richard, 71
Amazon, 19, 76, 84, 87, 92, 98, 105, 108–9, 213
American Chamber of Commerce in Europe (AmCham), 76, 79
American Civil Liberties Union, 105
American Institutional Confidence Poll, 98
Anduril, 217
Angus petrochemical plant, 173–4
apartheid, 158, 165
Apple, 65–6, 70, 72–3, 82, 84, 108, 213
ARM, 108
Arney, Rick, 91, 99–100
Arthur Andersen, 6
artificial intelligence (AI), 6, 21
Atkins, Paul, 150
Atlantic magazine, 97
Australian Securities and Investment Commission, 171

Banking Royal Commission, 170–1
Bankman-Fried, Sam, 137–40, 142–4, 146–9, 151–2, 221
Barclays, 61–2, 64
BBC, 222
Beef Trusts, 1, 203, 220
Beijing Olympics, 11
Bezos, Jeff, 219–21
Biden, Joe, 85, 107–8, 124–5, 144, 164
Bild, 71
Billionaire Accountability Project, 108
Binance, 139, 150–1
Bitcoin, 139–40, 144
Black Lives Matter, 16
Blankfein, Lloyd, 45, 48, 54, 60
Blue Origin, 220
Boeing, 217–18
Bogost, Ian, 97
Bohr, Niels, 201
Booz Allen Hamilton, 65
'Bosses of the Senate, The', 21
BP, 175
Brentwood, Louisiana, 157–9, 161, 166
Brown, James, 153
Brown, Michael, 16
Browner, Carol, 133
Bush, George W., 113

Cain, Geoffrey, 180, 191
Calcasieu Parish, 158, 163, 166, 172–4
California
  climate policy, 123
  oil spill, 131, 133
  privacy regulation, 89–92, 95, 100–7, 110, 214–16, 225
  wildfires, 128
California Air Resources Board (CARB), 23–5
California Consumer Privacy Act (CCPA), 101–3, 215
California Privacy Protection Agency (CPPA), 103, 105, 215–16
California Privacy Rights Act (CPRA), 103
Cambridge Analytica, 7, 96–100, 103, 107, 110, 126, 144, 155
Cameron, David, 61
'Cancer Alley', 154
carbon black, 173
carbon pricing, 125
Carlson, Tucker, 147
Carson, Rachel, 130
chaebol, 183–6, 190, 192, 194–5, 197–8, 200–1
Chafee, Lincoln, 134
ChatGPT, 6
Chávez, Hugo, 212
Chavis, Benjamin, 167
Chernobyl, 78
China, baby formula scandal, 11–16, 192, 208
Choi Soon-sil, 186–95, 197, 200–1
Choi Tae-min, 186–7
Chun Doo-hwan, 201
Church of Eternal Life, 187
Churchill, Winston, 207
Cianci, Vincent 'Buddy', 114, 120
Citibank, 52
Clean Air Act, 133
Clean Water Act, 133
Clegg, Nick, 85

Cleveland, Ohio, 131–2
Clinton, Bill, 31–2, 34–6, 149
Clinton, Hillary, 122
CNN, 25, 89, 146
Coburn, Tom, 46
Coinbase, 150
CoinDesk, 139
Cold War, 31
collateralized debt obligations (CDOs), 46–7
'collective action problem', 3–4
Collins, Susan, 53–4
Colorado, 106
Committee to Protect California Jobs, 92
Commonwealth Bank of Australia (CBA), 169–70, 172
Computer Weekly, 18
Condea Vista, 159, 161
confirmation bias, 141
Connecticut, 105
Consumer Financial Protection Bureau (CFPB), 205
Corporate Europe Observatory, 84
Couper, Teghan, 169–70
COVID-19 pandemic, 29, 198
Cow Clicker app, 97
Crown Prosecution Service, 18
Cruz, Ted, 123
cryptocurrencies, 137–52
  see also FTX
Cuban, Mark, 150
Cuyahoga River, 131–3

DDT, 130, 133
De Blasio, Bill, 93
Deepwater Horizon oil spill, 175
'democracy, pulse of', 17
Der Spiegel, 38
derivatives, 43–4, 60
Detroit, 165
Deutsche Bank, 61
Deutsche Welle, 25
Diess, Herbert, 38

INDEX

Digital Markets Act (DMA), 84–5, 87
Digital Services Act (DSA), 84–5, 87
dioxin, 154
Dodd-Frank Act, 53–5, 59–61, 205
Dowd, Anthony, 55
drug trials, 57–8, 99, 126–7
Durkheim, Émile, 37

Earth Day, 131
Economist, 144
effective altruism, 137, 143–4, 146–7
electrification, 62–3
Ellison, Caroline, 138
empathy walls, 157–8, 168–9, 174
Endangered Species Act, 133
Enron, 5–7, 139
Entergy, 163
environmental racism, 167–8
Europe v Facebook (EVF), 70–1, 79
European Commission, 38, 64, 74–5, 77, 81–3, 87
European Council, 74–6, 79, 85
European Court of Justice (ECJ), 80–2
European Parliament, 74–9, 85, 88
European Union (EU), 33, 64, 207
    American lobbying, 84–5
    privacy regulation, 68, 74–88, 221
ExxonMobil, 113–15, 121–4, 126–30, 135

Facebook, 3, 65–6, 68–73, 75–6, 79, 81–2, 84, 86–8, 90, 92, 94, 96–9, 101–3, 110, 143, 155, 204, 212
FaceMash, 72
facial recognition, 69–70
Farrell, Henry, 81
Faulkner, William, 197
Ferguson, Adele, 170
Ferguson, Andrew, 109
filibusters, 53–5, 57–8
Finance Watch, 64
financial crisis (2008), 4–5, 15–16, 43, 45–6, 52, 56–60, 63–4, 140, 149, 151, 224

Finnish Central Bank, 64
Florida, 105, 134
Flowers, Gennifer, 34
Floyd, George, 16
Four Corners, 170
Fox News, 142, 147–8
France, baby formula scandal, 13–15, 208
Francis, Pope, 78
Frank, Barney, 55
Franklin, Aretha, 153
FTT, 138–9, 150
FTX, 35, 137–42, 144–6, 148–52, 221

Gallup, 57, 200
Garner, Eric, 16
Gates, Bill, 76
GCHQ, 66, 77
General Data Protection Regulation (GDPR), 75–9, 81, 84–9
General Motors (GM), 19
Gensler, Gary, 149–50
German, John, 23–4, 25, 28, 30, 39, 214
Glancy, Dorothy, 68
Glustrom, Alexander, 161, 164
Goldman Sachs, 15, 43–9, 51–6, 58–9, 64, 67, 117, 155, 204, 224
Google, 65–6, 73, 75–8, 81–6, 90, 92, 98, 101–3, 108, 110
government, responsive vs responsible, 209
Greenwald, Glenn, 66
Greyball programme, 93
Guardian, 65–6
Guillemain, Quentin, 13–14
Gulf of Mexico, 175

Hallyu, 196
Harris, Kamala, 124, 219, 221
Hawkes, Billy, 80
Hayes, Denis, 131
Hayne, Kenneth, 170–1
Hazlett, Chad, 128
Hertzberg, Bob, 100, 102

Hochschild, Arlie, 157, 166–8
Honoré, Russel, 163–4, 175
HSBC, 62
Hudson Mezzanine, 47, 51
Hurricane Katrina, 163
hurricanes, 129, 134–5
Hyundai, 183, 190, 197

Independent Commission on Banking (ICB), 62
Indigenous Australians, 170–2
Inflation Reduction Act (IRA), 125–6, 133
Inside Climate News (ICN), 113, 114
Instagram, 72, 82
Irish Data Protection Commission (DPC), 69–70 74, 79–81, 86
Irish High Court, 80, 82
Isaacson, Walter, 217

Jane Street Capital, 143
Jindal, Bobby, 159–60
Johnson, Boris, 29
Johnson, Hiram, 90
JTBC, 188–9

Kanter, Jonathan, 108–9
KDI School of Public Policy and Management, 194
Keeler, Christine, 30–1
Key, Valdimer Orlando, 17
Khan, Lina, 108–9, 224
Kidney Stone Babies, 12
Kim Sang-jo, 197–8, 224
Kim Yong-hee, 198–200, 225
Kingdon, John, 67
Ko Young-tae, 188–9
Kodak, 165
Kogan, Aleksandr, 96–7
Korea Herald, 184
Korean Central Intelligence Agency, 186
Korean Fair Trade Commission, 197
K-pop, 196

Kurosawa, Akira, 137
Kyoto Protocol, 113

Lactalis, 13–15, 208
Lake Charles, 153–4, 157, 159, 164, 166–8
Lake Erie, 132
latent opinion, 15, 17–18, 56, 81, 91, 129, 131, 166, 200, 202–4, 206, 209–10, 220, 226
Le Monde, 77
Le Point, 85
League of Conservation Voters, 134
Lee Byung-chul, 179–80, 182–6, 195, 196
Lee Jae-yong, 186, 190–1, 194–5, 196, 199–200, 202
Lee, Jennifer, 105
Lee Kun-hee, 186, 191
Lehman Brothers, 4
Letterman, David, 46
Levin, Carl, 43–9, 51–60, 63–4, 67, 117, 119, 205, 224
Lewinsky, Monica, 32, 34–6, 149
LG, 183, 190
LIBOR scandal, 60–3
Liikanen group, 64
Lloyds, 63
Lo, Andrew, 61
lobbying, 3, 5, 150, 211, 215
  banks, 55, 60, 63–4
  Big Oil, 113, 116, 129
  Big Tech, 75–8, 84–5, 89, 92–4, 96, 101–3, 107, 109–10
Lockheed Martin, 217
Los Angeles Times, 113
Lotte Group, 183, 190, 200
Louisiana Green Army, 163, 175
Lucas, George, 104
Luckey, Palmer, 217
Lynch, Loretta, 122–3

MacAskill, Ewen, 66
MacAskill, William, 143

INDEX

McLean, Bethany, 6
Macmillan, Harold, 30
MacTaggart, Alastair, 89–92, 95, 99–107, 110, 214–16, 225
majoritarianism, 206, 211–12, 215
Manchin, Joe, 125
Mandela, Nelson, 168
Marsden, David, 105
Massachusetts, 123
Melbourne, Consumer Action, Law Centre, 172
Merkel, Angela, 66
Merkley, Jeff, 54
Meta, 82, 84, 87, 94, 108–9
Microsoft, 65–6, 76, 81, 92, 105
Mildenberger, Matto, 128
Mississippi River, 154
Mitsubishi, 180
mobile phone roaming charges, 74
Monsanto, 130
Moon Jae-in, 197–8
Morgan, J. P., 2
Moskovitz, Dustin, 143
Moss, Jack, 153, 161
Mossville, Louisiana, 153–5, 157–66, 174
Mossville Environmental Action Now, 154, 163
Mr Bates vs the Post Office, 18
MSNBC, 142, 147–8
Murdoch, Rupert, 147
Musk, Elon, 2, 205–7, 216–19, 221

Nader, Ralph, 4
Napoleon Bonaparte, 115
Narragansett Bay flounder fishery, 116, 134
NASA, 217, 220
National Environmental Protection Act, 133
New Deal for Consumers, 38
New South Wales, 171
New York state, 123
New York Stock Exchange, 217

New York Times, 55, 71, 96, 99, 130, 137, 146–7, 148, 222
New Yorker, 66
Newman, Abraham, 81
NewsGuard, 222, 223
Nix, Alexander, 97
Nixon, Richard, 28–9, 131, 133, 219
North Dakota, 105
NOYB, 86–7
Nvidia, 108

Obama, Barack, 45, 52, 95–6, 122
Obamacare, 56
Observer/Guardian, 96, 99, 142
Occupy Wall Street, 5
Octopus, 90
Oculus virtual reality, 217
Office Depot, 99, 127
Oil, Chemical and Atomic Workers Union, 174
Oliver, Jamie, 4
OpenAI, 6
Opinion Research Corporation, 131
Orwell, George, 77, 80
Ouachita Parish, 172–4
Ouimette, Gerard, 115
Oxley, Michael, 7

Packer, George, 66
Palmieri, Ed, 68
Parasite, 196
Paris climate agreement, 124
Park Chung-hee, 182–3, 184–7, 194
Park Geun-hye, 186–91, 192–5, 197
Parliamentary Commission on Banking Standards (PCBS), 61
Partygate, 29, 32
Pattenden, Ron, 170–1
Paulson & Co., 43–4, 47
Pelosi, Nancy, 106
'people, the' (definition), 210–11
pet food, 11
Phillips, David Graham, 2, 5
Pichai, Sundar, 85

Pittsburgh steel industry, 165
platform power, 94
pluralism, 212
Pohang Iron and Steel Company, 182
Poitras, Laura, 66
policy entrepreneurs, 4–5, 14, 67–8, 82, 87–8, 95, 121, 197
Politico, 45
Post Office scandal, 18
PRISM, 65, 77–80, 86, 88, 95, 144, 204, 221
Pritzker, Penny, 95–6
Privacy Shield, 81–2, 88
Private Eye, 18
Profumo Affair, 30–2
proprietary trading, 54–5
Prudential Regulation Authority (PRA), 62
public service broadcasting, 221–2
'Puppygate', 188

Rashomon, 137, 152
Ray, John, 139
Redding, Otis, 153
Reding, Viviane, 74–6, 79, 88
Regan, Michael, 164
reproductive rights, 49
Rhee, Syngman, 182
Rhode Island, 115, 116, 124, 134
RICO law, 120–1
Rockefeller, John D., 2–3, 129
Rogan, Joe, 220
Rolling Stone, 45
Romney, Mitt, 211
Royal Bank of Scotland (RBS), 61–3
Rubio, Marco, 122
Rudolph, Samantha, 172
Rumsfeld, Donald, 18
Ryan, Stacey, 160–4, 166–7, 172

Sacks, David, 150
Safari web browser, 108
Safe Harbour Framework, 80–2, 88

Sale, Kirkpatrick, 130
Salmonella Contaminated Victims' Families Association, 13
Samsung, 179–81, 183–6, 190–1, 194–5, 197–8, 199, 200, 202, 225
Sanlu, 11–16, 192, 208
Santa Barbara oil spill, 131, 133
Sarbanes, Paul, 7
Sasol, 158–67
Save our Future Act, 125
'Scandals in the Wild' project, 145–6
Schmidt, Eric, 81
Schneiderman, Eric, 121
Schrems, Max, 68–71, 73–5, 78–80, 81–2, 86–8, 225
Schwab, Andreas, 85
Science, 126–7
sea levels, rising, 134
Securities and Exchange Commission (SEC), 44, 47, 51, 147–50
Shell, 127
Sherman Antitrust Act, 21
Shin Dong-bin, 190, 200
Sierra Club, 134, 163
Silicon Valley, 66, 68, 72, 77, 82–3, 95, 104, 109, 143, 205
Silva, Margarida, 84
Sinclair, Upton, 1–2, 203–6, 220
Sinema, Kyrsten, 125
Skilling, Jeffrey, 6
Slater, Gail, 109
Snowden, Edward, 65–6, 77–9, 81, 88, 95, 204, 220
Social Network, The, 72, 77
Society of Environmental Journalists, 175
Solidarity for Economic Reform, 197
Soltani, Ashkan, 105, 215
South Korea, 179–202
    Candlelight Protests, 192–5, 198
    Celebration of Democracy, 195
    civil society, 195–7
    economic 'miracle', 181–2, 196–7
    Gwangju Uprising, 201

INDEX

independence, 181–2
suicide rate, 195–6
Yoon's downfall, 200–1
Southern Pacific Railroad, 90
SpaceX, 216–18
Squid Game, 196
Stadler, Rupert, 37
Standard Oil, 2, 129, 214
Stanford, Leland, 2, 90
Star Wars, 104, 107
Starbucks, 138
Starlink, 217
Starmer, Keir, 21
Sterlington, Louisiana, 173–4
Stevens, Noel, 169–70, 172
Stewart, Jon, 59–60
Supran, Geoffrey, 126
Sydney Morning Herald, 170
'systemic greed', 147

Tarbell, Ida, 2
taxation, 55, 70, 141, 216
 carbon taxes, 124–5
 sugar tax, 4
Tempora, 66
Tesla, 38, 216
theft, understanding of, 141–2
Thelen, Kathleen, 93
This is Your Digital Life, 96
Thompson, John, 30
TikTok, 87, 220
Tillerson, Rex, 124
Timberlake, Justin, 138
Timberwolf, 48–9, 51
Time magazine, 132–3
tobacco companies, 121
Total, 127
Tourre, Fabrice, 43–4, 47
'Treason of the Senate, The', 2, 5
Treasury Select Committee, 61
Trump, Donald, 21, 60, 97, 109, 124, 144, 150–1, 205–6, 219–20
Tuna, Cari, 143

Turner, Tina, 153
TV Chosun, 188
Twitter/X, 73, 115, 139, 219, 224
Tyrie, Andrew, 61–3

Uber, 93–4
UBS, 61
Ukraine, 217
United States
 climate policy, 117–30, 134–5
 cryptocurrency regulation, 146–52
 environmental legislation, 133–4
 financial reform, 53–6, 63–4, 67, 224
 food regulation, 1–2
 media ownership, 219–22
 presidential election (2024), 219–20
 privacy regulation, 94–6, 105–7
 Progressive Era, 2–3, 21, 90, 134, 205–6
 racial considerations, 156–7, 167–9
 robber barons, 2, 20–1
US Centers for Disease Control and Prevention (CDC), 154
US Commerce Department, 96
US Department of Government Efficiency (DOGE), 205–7, 216
US Department of Justice (DoJ), 107–9, 122
US Department of Labor, 173
US Environmental Protection Agency (EPA), 24–5, 38, 133, 154, 162, 164, 214
US Federal Aviation Administration, 216
US Federal Reserve, 54
US Federal Trade Commission (FTC), 95–6, 107–9, 215
US Food and Drug Administration, 2
US National Labor Relations Board, 216
US National Security Agency (NSA), 65–6, 77, 79, 95
US Occupational Safety and Health Administration (OSHA), 173

US Senate Judiciary Subcommittee on Constitutional Rights, 68
US Senate Permanent Sub-Committee on Investigations (PSI), 43–8, 56
US Steel, 214

Vanderbilt, Cornelius, 2
Venezuela, 212
Vershbow, Alexander, 187
very large online platforms (VLOPs), 84
Vestager, Margrethe, 82–4, 87–8, 224
Vickers, John, 62
Vietnam War, 130
Viniar, David, 48
Virginia, 104–5
Viscusi, Kip, 174
Volcker rule, 54–5, 59–60, 62, 67
VW Dieselgate scandal, 7, 23–8, 30, 32–9, 144, 214

Wages, Robert, 174
Wall Street Journal, 121, 137, 146–7, 149, 222
Walsh, Tracey, 171
Wang, Gary, 138
Warren County, North Carolina, 167
Washington Post, 65, 70, 119–20, 219–21

Washington state, 105
Watergate, 28–9, 31–2, 68, 219
weight-loss drugs, 97
Weldon, Chris, 26
Wells Fargo, 100, 146
Westlake, Louisiana, 153–4, 158, 166
WhatsApp, 72
Whitehouse, Sheldon, 115, 116–17, 119–26, 134–5
Wilde, Oscar, 28
wildfires, 128–9, 135
Williams, Damian, 151
Winterkorn, Martin, 37
Woods, Tiger, 138
WorldCom, 7

Xerox, 165

Yahoo, 66
Yoon Suk-yeol, 200–1
You Jong-il, 194
Youpla, 170–2
YouTube, 84, 220

zaibatsu, 180, 183
Zhao Changpeng, 139, 151
Zhao Lianhai, 12, 14
Zuckerberg, Mark, 3, 72–3, 77, 109, 144